Politics and the News

POLITICS AND THE NEWS

The Political Functions of the Mass Media

Edwin R. Black

BUTTERWORTHS
Toronto

Politics and the News: The Political Functions of the Mass Media
© 1982 – Edwin R. Black.

Printed and bound in Canada
5 4 3 2 1   2 3 4 5 6 7 8 9/8

Canadian Cataloguing in Publication Data

Black, Edwin R., 1929–
  Politics and the news

Bibliography: p.
Includes index.
ISBN 0–409–81525–X

1. Mass media – Political aspects. 2. Communication in politics. I. Title.

P95.8.B62   302.2'34   C82–094239–1

C,2

Ho, 071

The Butterworth Group of Companies
Canada:
Butterworth & Co (Canada) Ltd., Toronto and Vancouver
United Kingdom:
Butterworth & Co. (Publishers) Ltd., London
Australia:
Butterworth Pty. Ltd., Sydney
New Zealand:
Butterworths of New Zealand, Wellington
South Africa:
Butterworth & Co. (South Africa) Ltd., Durban
United States:
Butterworth (Publishers) Inc., Boston
Butterworth (Legal Publishers) Inc., Seattle
Mason Publishing Company, St. Paul

Contents

Preface

An apprentice journalist needs to work in a newsroom for only a very short time before being exposed to the wisdom of his elders concerning the power of the press. The usual approach is to minimise its real influence but the way many journalists rejoice in trying to exploit that power demonstrates where their real beliefs lie. Few newsmen ever agree that 'you can't fight city hall,' and, indeed, many see it as their duty to do just that. Our myths about the power of the press are many and highly varied, depending on whether it is journalists, politicians, or academics who are spreading and adding to them. It was this lack of agreement on the mythology that initially led the writer into the inquiries represented in these pages.

A journalist for ten years, the author is now an academic who begins almost every university year with a group of politics students seeking answers to burning questions about the press and public affairs. Despite great interest, imagination, and sometimes even hard work, my students have not yet managed to answer all the questions that keep popping up. In like manner, this book cannot answer every question. If this discussion is successful, it will give some of you a different perspective on what you know about the mass media and inspire further questioning. While not burdening you with surveys of all the latest academic research, the book does look at enough to suggest the extent to which the mass media play important political roles and to explore the reasons why they are not the political institutions our ideals lead us to expect. This is offered the reader free of the confusions which would attend any effort to marry it with development and presentation of an integrated theory of the political influence of the mass media. Possible directions are pointed out in the book, but much difficult thinking remains to be done on such a theory, whether one seeks answers through a rigorous structural-functionalism, a dynamic political economy approach, or by way of the semimysticism of McLuhanist insights.

Important contributions to my learning and work have been made by many former students and assistants like Frederick J. Fletcher and Michael Bolton. Special gratitude for their work in the agenda-setting section is owed to Peter Snow, Gail Wood, Mary Louise McAllister, and Nick Sidor. Suggestions made by the publisher's readers of the manuscript were valuable, particularly those of Professor William Melody of Simon Fraser University and Professor G. S. Adam of Carleton University. I wish my present competence extended to being able to write the book we would all like to see. For now, I can only recognise the validity of their critiques. Queen's University and its Advisory Research Committee helped substantially in the work with a sabbatical leave and research assistance. That my time in Britain proved as fruitful and enjoyable as it was is due in no small measure to friends like Maurice Vile and Colin Seymour-Ure of the University of Kent at Canterbury and to the Leicester University Centre for Mass Communications Research. Thanks are also due to my publishers for indulging my wish to reproduce the book in this form. How grateful I should be to Bob Stevens and his associates at BERRN Research for getting me deep into the mysteries of word-processing is a question I have not resolved.

Only spouses know how much a book has cost them and what they have contributed to it. The author can only appreciate it, acknowledge it, and dedicate the work, as I do, to Anne.

Edwin R. Black
Kingston, Canada

Decisions in a Hurry

The real power of the modern mass media is that it is changing the whole of our political life while we, the chief actors or victims, remain largely unaware of the nature of the transforming force. Can anything be done about it? Probably not a great deal—unless we plan a revolution of some sort and few of us seem ready for that.

What we can and should do is start trying to sort out some of the facts from the fictions that surround politics and the news. One problem, though, is that there are very few 'facts' about our society that we know with any degree of certainty and we are always trying to tackle our problems with inadequate concepts or patterns of understanding. It's much like eating vegetable soup with a fork. We might pick up some scraps but we are guaranteed to miss most of the broth and real flavour. Because they are geared to the communications methods and cultures of other times and places, our usual way of looking at things tends to lead us badly astray. The result? Our impressions of 'reality' are not much more accurate than those of the man from Mars.

Even without taking television into account, the cultural status of the mass media has also changed significantly from what it was a century ago. While modern journalists dealing with government sometimes picture themselves in images akin to the persecuted Christians of ancient Rome, their position is more like that of the established church in imperial Spain or Puritan New England. There are, however, many more misleading conceptions of our mass media culture than that. First among them is the general misunderstanding of the nature of the news and public affairs product of our mass media institutions. Roy Thomson provided one of the clues here when he exclaimed that a British television franchise was like a licence to print money. News and public affairs content in the mass media are primarily commercial products —whatever the different notions are that might be suggested by the ideals of nineteenth century liberalism. That was never plainer than when Roy Thomson's son put The Times and The Sunday Times on the market. There have been no more prestigious newspapers in the English-speaking world but when they started losing too much money they were sold to another media imperialist, Rupert Murdoch of Australia.

The Power of the Press

The supposed ability of newspaper editors to sway the world of politics is legendary. "Great is journalism," proclaimed Carlyle, for "is not every able editor a ruler of the world, being a persuader of it?" Oscar Wilde observed that while the American president reigned for four years journalism governed "for ever and ever". Even the redoubtable Emperor Napoleon claimed that three hostile newspapers were more to be feared than a thousand bayonets.

Hearst's New York Journal and its competitors have been blamed freely for heating American politics into such a fever over Cuba that no president could have refrained from the Spanish-American War which brought the United States an overseas empire. American newspapers have been blamed for a

lot more than involving the United States in wars. They were
given all the discredit possible for corrupting a whole
generation of American youth by glamourising Scarface Al
Capone and the hoodlum era, for squelching a host of liberal
reforms, for maintaining the Republicans in the presidency
(whenever they happened to hold it), and for effecting all
the other reactionary political schemes which conservative
publishers were thought to favour. Social democrats have
long argued that capitalist control of newspapers has
seriously inhibited working class attempts to win real
social justice. In New York State, California, British
Columbia, Ontario, and in many other places, daily newspaper
partisanship has been given sole credit or blame for the
election to office of particular governments. The marvel of
the Roosevelt period for many was that F.D.R. managed to win
and retain office despite the opposition of 90 per cent of
the supposedly all-powerful American press.

So influential did nineteenth-century politicians believe
the press to be that heroic efforts were made everywhere to
buy, establish, and maintain a party viewpoint in the daily
journals. In this century, the British Labour party poured
millions into the **Daily Herald** to subsidise a continuing
expression of reliable pro-labour opinion in the national
daily press. What it ever received for these huge
subsidies-- besides psychic satisfaction--does not seem to
have been investigated. Neither this nor any other example
serves to dissuade dozens of groups in North America from
similar efforts. Other people's often-misinformed attempts
to capitalise on what they believe to be the power of the
press should not mislead us into thinking that such activity
demonstrates anything about political influence. Just
because political parties, governments, and others pour
millions into mass media campaigns does not provide
conclusive evidence of their effectiveness. Scholars have
been examining the uses that governments and other groups
make of advertising and mass communications. Such studies
are important but chiefly for what they tell us about the

people and organisations involved. They do not enlighten us about effects like voter persuasion or issue-conversion.

Political Communications

Before going further into the influence of the news media on voters, we can probably get a better picture by pausing for a moment to think of politics as a series of inter-connected message circuits—as a communications network. This approach leads us to see a great variety of government-related acts as communications activity. Significant political data, such particular occurrences of public injustice, are communicated to a number of points in the circuit (citizens), dissatisfaction grows, and the system is unbalanced. Demands for change are generated and conveyed to a central accumulator or legislature. If the charge is great enough, it stimulates appropriate reactions and information flows until the system is balanced once again.

It is not necessary to push analogies like that very far to appreciate that the effectiveness of all governments depends on their ability to handle and act on information. It is clear that before governments take action, they must have a wide and continuing flow of information about situations to be dealt with. Suppose a poverty-stricken region is to be given an economic boost. Policy-makers and administrators alike will need a vast array of data about the people, the area, and its resources. They will need information about social and economic projects elsewhere and how well certain methods turned out in similar circumstances. They need the ability to relate experience and general knowledge to particular cases. Regional development programs do not always work. When that happens, failure is often blamed on incompetence or a lack of good faith. There is another, often more common cause of program failures: people not having the right information, or enough of it, or not even knowing that it was needed.

More than technical or program-oriented information is

required. To maintain their legitimacy or moral standing with the public, political leaders need mechanisms to help them discover, assess, and act on the opinions people hold on public affairs. It is very seldom, if ever, that they even try to put all public opinions into effect, but governments must be able to judge which they have to pay attention to. The survival at the polls of many political parties and their leaders is closely related to their information about the political environment and their ability and willingness to act on it. Many changes in partisan control of government can be explained by politicians' refusal or inability to interpret the various storm signals. Some politicians are so poorly organised they don't even receive the storm warnings.

While a little different from others, this discussion —like most of those taking a communications approach to politics—is essentially macroscopic; it looks at the whole system of government in terms of information flows. Before this kind of approach can take us very far, we need to know much more than we do about how the bits and pieces work. In short, we need a more microscopic attack on the problem. One difficulty is that we do not really know a great deal about the modern mass media. They have not been given the extensive and systematic attention you might expect. Many people have worried about the social or cultural effects of the mass media. Others have had a great deal to say about particular aspects: advertising, ownership, broadcast technology, press libel laws, freedom of information, etc. In these areas, the research groundwork has been laid, but it has not been in most other areas of direct political relevance. Because, among other things, there has been little apparent attempt to do it so far, one of the central purposes of this study is to stimulate thinking about the mass media in their character as political institutions. In this respect, they are certainly different from our formal political institutions. Where others have public and governmental concerns as their major reason for being, the so-called Fourth Estate is more concerned about profit, entertainment, and audience-building. These concerns affect mass media performance of political functions and their behaviour as political actors. These effects and some of their implications for different groups in society are among the major questions raised in this study.

Secondhand Experience

Our society is not simply a golden age gone wrong, one in which the colour tuning knob on the TV simply needs radical readjustment. People have pictured our times simply as our great-grandparents' rural society put on motorised wheels, fantastically multiplied, urbanised, and begrimed with industrial exhausts. That is misleading in a number of ways. We have a very different culture. Among other things, it includes millions of people, many of whom may never know the truly individual life, nor have any yearning for it. Their social attitudes seem influenced more by their connections with larger groups and the world at large than by personal connection to the soil, the fisheries, or even families. And many of those ties are mediated through mass communications.

The life experiences of our friends and neighbours mark them off from their grandparents in a number of important ways. At one time, the common view of life was shaped and directed rather closely by our real, personal experiences. That is not the case today. Now, rather than depending on personal experience, many of our perceptions of society find inspiration in common communications experience. That means we depend on that view of life and love, of liberty and licence, which we get through increasing exposure to other people's versions of reality conveyed to us by television, radio, newspapers, and other forms of mass media.

Ours is a vicarious age, a characteristic that profoundly affects the nature of the news product. Of course, our life is not wholly vicarious or secondhand, but it is becoming increasingly so. One of the reasons for this

is that our ability to participate in the lives of notable
people (almost by definition more glamorous than our own) is
made ever more possible by developments in the technology of
mass communications. Our lives and politics have been
electrified. Now, in the hour of its happening, we can join
those inside the cathedral for a fairy-tale royal wedding,
whirl in space with a cosmonaut, cry bravo with the audience
at an opera house, or join thousands of soccer fans in
cheering or jeering the referee's decision in a far-off
World Cup match. Electronics have immensely expanded the
horizons of our lives and in doing it they have considerably
increased the weight that secondhand or vicarious experience
exerts in shaping the way we see the world. Personal or
firsthand experience has not disappeared, but it is playing
a smaller role in the lives of many urbanised people.

Political life is changing in several ways. Just as more
of us are 'seeing' more of the world via television and
satellite so, too, more and more of us are being brought
within the reach of the decision-making process.
Unfortunately, while communications technology may be
widening our vicarious experiences, more democracy does not
necessarily come hand in hand with it. The new technology
may mean no more than a change in which elite groups get
preferential access to the political communication network.
Without debating what governments do, and whether they
should, we can agree they are doing more of it and to more
people. They are also doing it in different ways. The
processes of both our politics and administration are
changing rapidly. Whether that will improve the the quality
of our democracy is more debatable. The famous democracy of
Periclean Athens is not much of a guide. It worked only for
the small group of people who had citizenship. The society
had to be small enough to allow each citizen to acquire, by
actual and personal experience, knowledge about his city
that would let him contribute to making informed judgements
at public meetings. It also required a considerable degree
of continuous personal involvement of all the citizens in

decision-making. The classic model of democracy has seldom, if ever, been realised anywhere other than in rhetoric.

Western society has grown so big that not many people can get very much knowledge that is relevant to state-wide political decision-making. That is one reason the common form of government in our history has been rule by the few. In some cases, political power can be usefully defined as the effective monopoly of all relevant public information. Developments in inventing and collecting statistics have been married to new technologies, with consequences that are neither all good nor all bad. They have, for example, made it possible for large groups of people to work together to give themselves fairly rapid increases in certain kinds of joint benefits. At the same time it must be recognised that as new ways of controlling people have been developed, they have almost invariably fallen into the hands of the few rather than the many. Expanding the range of government activity meant more and more people gained personal experience in the consequences of public decisionmaking. Sometimes the public just got more frustrated as a result, but occasionally the public won a little more power. How? People everywhere dislike uncertainty and try to reduce it by securing control over whatever causes it. One means of reducing political uncertainty is making rulers answerable to some standard other than their own whims. The answer devised and put in place by a few lucky peoples during the nineteenth century was representative government which is certainly imperfect but may still be the best found so far.

Until a century ago, most government remained the private business of a rather small elite. That elite might be 'enlightened' by Christianity, liberalism, or responsible conservatism. It might even submit itself to the (rather small) electorate to have its actions approved—at least retroactively. But it was still an elite acting almost entirely on its own initiative. It kept that initiative because of its near-monopoly over information relevant to public decisions.

The apostles of liberal democracy based their theories almost to a man on the notion of the informed individual citizen. Unfortunately, most of them forgot to provide for an adequate information process. Presumably, they thought that the society was small enough for personal experience and that the primitive newssheets of the time were good enough to fill in the gaps. Their usually sound thought processes seem to have short-circuited somewhere. The crude newspapers of the mid-nineteenth century were weak instruments for performing the role liberal theory required.

The basic problem lies with the theory. Despite the preaching of propagandists as famous as John Stuart Mill, the theory never became the working policy of governments. Instead of accepting that citizens have a wide-ranging 'right to know' what is going on, governments have nearly always operated on the premise of general secrecy—unless it suited the administration to let us know something in particular. Even to discover the normal operations of government, journalists have taken some extreme steps. Relying on opposition politicians became standard working procedure (no matter that they were violently partisan and given to exaggeration or downright lying). Courting and cajoling civil servants was another standard procedure.

Newspapers in the early days did not strive mightily to be the objective instrument of political communication that an ideal liberal democracy needed. The owners of newspapers published them for three main private reasons:

1 to spread party propaganda,
2 to publicise their own pet projects or ideas, and,
3 To provide more work for the parent printing business.

The philosophers of democracy, in short, counted on citizens being able to make rational decisions on public affairs based on personal objective assessment of all relevant data. The infant democracies were utterly lacking in the communication instrument that the masses of voters required.

These primitive newspapers of the infant democracies had their beginnings with the book and the invention of moveable, repeatable type. The Gutenberg printing process gave western man his first means of social communication that could be received and studied in private rather than as part of a group gathered around a priest or similar teacher. The spread of literacy and development of a plentiful supply of cheap newspapers and books were interdependent. Improvements in the technology of printed mass communications were accompanied by the growth of representative government on a large scale. The development of electrified mass communication was followed by modern totalitarianism. How closely are those things linked? We don't know. About all we can be certain of is that totalitarian governments rely very heavily on controlling all mass communications for use as a major weapon to control their own populations.

Whether politics has ever really escaped the clutches of the elite classes is questionable. As the English-speaking peoples underwent radical changes in population and social composition, their governments became more representative. A few adjustments usually allowed the traditional elites to stay in political control. They were helped in this by the paternalist obligations toward society which their own class, cultural, and educational institutions led them to accept. In some places, incorporating new classes of voters into the system was made easier by transferring elements of the aristocratic idea of noblesse oblige into government policies and programs. The argument is also made that these societies became more democratic because at least a few members of the lower classes could work their way upward into some of the elite groups. Whatever the case, access to political information was still limited to a few people, chiefly those who held power. The belief in knowledge as a form of power helped to maintain the liberal philosophers' continuing interest in the means of mass communication, and an obligation to be 'informed' about public affairs has been inculcated into the civic culture of most western countries.

Instant Politics

Our politics differ markedly from those of other cu.
in several ways. Most noteworthy for our purposes are tnose
aspects related to the invention of instantaneous communications and associated changes in our social institutions. For
centuries, getting messages from one place to another
depended on animal or mechanical power—such as runners,
horses, and steam engines. Problems considered 'public' were
relatively few in number and were decently separated from
each other in time and space. Rulers could deal with them at
their leisure. Giving the vote to the general population,
which expanded rapidly during the nineteenth century,
transformed many of their difficulties into public problems,
a process that to the present increase in the activity and
complexity of government.

The development of steam power and railways brought great
changes in the means of physical transport and in message
transmittal. The politics of the day were still marked by
long delays in political reaction time. During the
nineteenth century, a prime minister would often receive new
information about some distant situation and have time to
think about it and discuss it with colleagues, before
eventually arriving at a decision, and ordering official
action. Before the public heard of the original situation, a
great deal of time had gone by, and the situation might
already have changed—perhaps as a result of the moves the
government had ordered. Long reaction times gave
decisionmakers time to react emotionally, cool off, seek
advice, and take their decisions with little if any
immediate public pressure to worry about.

Today our situation is different. A crisis in Africa,
Central America, or the Middle East causes immediate crisis
in Washington, London, and sometimes even Ottawa. But the
politician no longer has a monopoly on such information. He
may not even have a head start. Sometimes, everybody,
whether prime minister or fish-packer, learns of the crisis

at the same time--through the mass media. What is more, normal journalistic activity generates demands for action NOW! Common sense tells leaders to move slowly. They know that acting sensibly requires far more data than the mass media carries. The problem is with the phenomenon of 'news'. While the public may treat news as though it were a fair and complete digest of all the relevant facts, it is not. What is relevant depends on whose need or interest we are talking about and the mass media audience has so far demonstrated little interest in the dull details that public officials need to make balanced appraisals.

Relatively little public decisionmaking is concerned exclusively with reacting to foreign events. Much of it is concerned with routine domestic business, with running programs-in-being, with trying to deal with known trouble spots in the society, and with trying to anticipate the development of other needs and desires before they reach the public and turn into political demands. Even in cases like these, political action may be stimulated by developments or happenings that were wholly unexpected and certainly outside the control of the decisionmakers.

Some of the most critical of all public decisions are those made in response to events quite outside the normal control of domestic politicians. Examples are natural disasters, crop failures, threatening actions by multinational corporations, impending countrywide strikes in essential services, and so on. It is not the mere occurrence of these events that makes them politically significant. It is their translation into political communication--into data circulated in the political system--that gives them importance. Look at the way politicians like to try out certain ideas without running any risk that might come from being connected with unpopular notions. They 'leak' these ideas to the press anonymously to see how the 'trial balloon' flies. The device is a fairly safe one for politicians who can wait to see what the general reaction is before deciding whether to adopt the idea publicly or forget it.

Occasionally, they get fooled. A trial balloon may escape and run of control. Public reaction can come so swiftly and decisively that the politician has no choice: regardless of his original plan, public sentiment may force his hand.

The reaction time available to liberal politicians is much shorter than it once was. The major reason lies in the invention of electric circuits, the extraordinary spread of mass communications, and the way in which the press institution developed functions that were political in character and not simply entertainment or commercial. The mass media's political functions are anything but fixed. They change steadily and in line with new communications technologies and the institutions that exploit them.

Assessments of the Media

Mass communications have forever been the subject of moralising by students of the social system. Even Plato was concerned with the social effects produced by popular poets and playwrights. The judgement of the mass media generally reflected the ways in which commentators have analysed society. Where they saw its central facts as property, production, and distribution, they have deplored the conversion of the communication systems into mere vehicles of advertising to promote commercial profit. Where the essence of social relations was thought to be power and decision making, the critics bewailed the media's immorality and told of the perils facing any society which allowed the powerhungry to use communications as propaganda media. Other people see society primarily as a form of communications through which experience is described, shared, modified, and preserved. Critics of this disposition would have us develop the mass media deliberately so as to encourage the expansion of men's powers to learn and exchange ideas and experiences.

Two contradictory inclinations underpin popular concern about the political effects of the media. According to one school of thought, the newspapers, radio, and television should be engaged in creating that kind of informed public opinion which was thought to have characterised Periclean Athens or the New England town meeting. Citizens might once again have complete and equal access to a detailed account of those public affairs requiring their attention and judgement. The mass media, such people argue, should help to recreate some of the conditions of the village, in which the main instruments of social control are gossip and public opinion. Communications 'rightly' used are thought capable of educating a public to break out of its parochial confines and enter into a new discourse with people in ever-widening circles until a new democratic world has emerged.

In distinction to this New Democracy approach is the nasty-minded manipulative approach, which was much discussed by Vance Packard and others during the fifties. In this light, the mass media appear as agents of evil likely to set back democracy by a full millenium. The argument pointed out that freedom in the western world grew in direct relation to the success of liberalism. By that they meant the forces that tended to liberate and insulate one's private affairs from those of the government and other corporate institutions like state churches. It has been through dividing up such public power, and parcelling it out into different institutions and social sectors of society, that liberals have tried to preserve and expand our freedoms. Packard and those like him thought that the growth of advertising and the other 'persuasive arts' would pose threats to the liberal society just as great as any it had ever faced before. The question remains unresolved.

At times, there seems to be a widespread reaction against privacy and individualism. Eric Fromm made popular the idea of 'escapes from freedom', instances in which people turn from the problem of having to cope entirely for themselves with their own inadequate personal resources and put their faith and trust in a new leader. While freedom of speech (which is the only basis of freedom of the press) has undoubtedly aided in increasing the rights of citizens, it may have brought with it the right and even the obligation to be persuaded. At first, the mass circulation newspaper, and then radio and television broadcasting were feared as powerful weapons which could be used to stamp ideas upon the minds of helpless readers, listeners, and viewers. During the nineteen-twenties, it was widely held in the U.S.A. that newspaper propaganda launched the country into the first world war. During the thirties, Roosevelt's unexpected successes at the polls illustrated for many the dangers of control possible to a man with a golden voice. Developments in Nazi Germany--exaggerated as they were by Anglo-Saxon counter-propaganda--did nothing to reduce popular fears of manipulation by mass communications. Many argue that mass persuasion is the great modern threat to individual freedom. "I wanna hold your hand," the Beatles wailed during the sixties, and hundreds of thousands responded by thrusting out their hands seeking comfort and identification with a larger whole that seemed so much more satisfying than their own inadequate selves. Readers will decide for themselves whether phenomena like advertising, pop singers, and rock group mania demonstrate that television and other mass media have such a grip on our thought patterns that they menace our freedom.

In one respect, the new democracy and the manipulative concepts of the media are similar. They employ the same image of the actual process of mass communications. They envision a vast, completely atomised society in which millions of individuals wait with receptive minds for whatever is poured into them by the controllers of the media. Every image from the unseen controllers is seen as a direct and powerful stimulus to action which brings immediate responses of the type desired. This is the image of the mass media that George Orwell and Aldous Huxley gave us in their morbid literary warnings about the future.

In short, the mass media are pictured time after time as a unifying force touching everybody. All are characterised as living in a society of wholly alienated individuals. This atomised society is apparently a conglomerate of millions of sand grains, a vast disarray of beaches and sand dunes, waiting to be shaped and reshaped by the whims and waves of the mass media. Nothing holds these individuals together in this horrid new world, neither tradition nor family, neither economic interest nor religious belief; all are at the virtual mercy of the mass media.

The viewpoints have been exaggerated and ridiculed but the fears remain real. What is important for our purposes is to realise that opinions about what the mass media might become and opinions about what they ought to be are not the same thing as knowledge about what the press is or does in reality. Cataloguing one's fears and preferences about social institutions is not the same as knowing what functions these institutions perform and what their effects are. It is not even a reasonable substitute for knowledge. Only when we have verifiable data in these areas can we hope for realistic assessments about the performance and potential for good or ill of these forces in our lives.

Changing communications technology and its institutions have significantly affected the evolution of our culture. The effects on its political aspects seem to be the most obvious and the least explained. Understanding those influences means finding answers to a whole variety of questions about the significance of television, radio, and general newspapers in influencing political decisions and events. What the most important questions are will be determined by the way in which we conceive the political system. Here, philosophers and scholars through the centuries have offered not one best way but many different ones. Most of those discussed in the next chapter seem to provide clues to important questions. While the selection itself implies a certain perspective, the task of overt criticism of these approaches has been left to the reader.

All writing slants the way a writer leans, and no man is born perpendicular although many men are born upright. While E. B. White was speaking of journalism and literature when he made that remark, it is as true in social studies as anywhere else. Living up to the spirit of the statement is where all writers have trouble at some time. Not long ago Science ruled supreme both in objectivity and public regard. Many people thought it reasonable for a truly scientific observer to see and analyse natural objects and social happenings completely and accurately. The observer's personal experiences or biases didn't have to get in the way. Today, much as they might wish for it, few social scientists share that old faith. For a time the study of politics and the mass media was marked by a period of 'scientizing'. Some academics tried to focus their research on projects which would yield results in terms like numbers, which could be manipulated by computers in scientific patterns of analysis, and which could be reproduced (in theory at least) by other observers. Unfortunately, scientific truth which none could dispute has continued to elude students of man and society.

There are no objective grounds dictating the next piece of social relations to be studied or how to do it. Individuals have to choose their subjects of study, and their methods, and location, and time frames, and so on. Survey questions have to be asked this way--or that way. Numerical values are arbitrarily assigned to the answers tabulated. Someone has to decide whether a difference of two on this scale--or .13 on another scale--is really twice as relevant as a difference of four on the first scale, or .026 on the other. Unfortunately, bite-sized chunks of politics cannot be broken off the lump of social reality and isolated for analysis in the way that a mineral sample can be chopped out of an ore body and examined in a metals laboratory.

The Bias of Making Choices

Choices run through and infect all social research. The choices arise from sets of personal preferences and values. Arrange these values and preferred ways of seeing things into repeatable patterns and we have a framework of personal values that help us to organise and make sense of our world. If these frameworks are relatively free of internal contradictions and are consistent and comprehensive enough, they may be dignified with the title of personal philosophy. Whether they are or not, it makes some sense to call them ideologies, even though for most of us ideologies are like accents, something the other person might have but never us.

Most discussion of the political role of the mass media is heavily value-oriented, or biased in some direction or other. It always has been. The bulk of the considerable literature that has grown up is concerned with judging the performance of the press in terms of the commentators' philosophical convictions. Some of this comment deals with the presumed effects of the mass media on the society's ethical, religious, social or cultural values, an inclination that is increasing. Most of it, however, is oriented toward politics and government. Too little of it is conscious of the value framework that the critics are using.

Journalists trying to answer the critics operate in the same fashion; they make a few basic assumptions about what things are important and which are not, and their comments fall wide of the point made by the original critic.

The result of many disputes about the role of the press is what the French call a 'dialogue of the deaf'. Nobody hears the other side's argument at all. In Canada, for example, there is a continuing argument about how much prime time should be devoted to broadcasting television programs that are of Canadian origin (and thus expensive to make in comparison to the cost of showing American imports). The fierce argument revolves around how much, if any, should be the required minimum Canadian content shown, what should be counted as 'Canadian', and how the rules should be enforced. The parties to the so-called debate are arguing on the basis of quite different conceptions of the political functions of the mass media. Many private broadcasters, for example, seem to assume that the broadcasting of cultural and entertainment programs has no real effects on people beyond passing amusement. Others seem to think there are effects but they are solely economic and concerned with commercial advertising. Still other private broadcasters might agree that there could be effects but the audience should be entitled to decide the question with their dialing fingers without government 'interference'. Other mass media commentators argue vociferously that continued political independence from the United States depends crucially on the survival of a distinctive Canadian culture developed and fostered all across the land by the broadcast media. Still other ideological approaches can be discerned in the debate. Some relate to the role of private enterprise, to dislike of multinational capitalism, to anti-americanism, and to state responsibility toward the artistic community. Comparable debates centred on different topics go on in most western countries. At heart, the disputes revolve around differing concepts of the political role of the mass media and are justified by a variety of ideologies.

More than ideology conditions what goes into the content
of our mass media. Technology also has an important effect.
Although invisible to the audience, the technical means of
using any medium of mass communication add up to a unique
set of limitations and possibilities for those working in
it. Mass media journalists, in particular, must remain
acutely aware of those possibilities and limitations every
day of their working lives.

This technical conditioning enters into each stage of the
process, recording, reproduction, distribution, and
reception and interpretation. Even before the age of the
masses, the material methods used for communications
influenced what could be put into the system, what could be
taken out of it, and who could use it. So long as recording
was limited to soft stone and what could be chiselled into
it, the contents were brief, very important, and accessible
only to people living in that one place. The invention of
paper-and-ink systems greatly magnified the range of
possible contents and physical locations where it might be
read. Without horses and physically light message forms Rome
would have been unable to build and defend its huge, ancient
empire. The conquest and maintenance of the huge empire of
the American plains many centuries later was similarly
dependent on horse communications in the initial stages.

So much influence have the various technologies exerted
on mass communications content that one critic has insisted
that it is the technology of the communications medium that
conveys the real message--not its apparent content.

Greek Theatre as Mass Medium

Mass communications technology also affects ideas about
the political functions of mass media, what we have called
the ideologies of mass media. Whether most people can play
any real part as citizens (rather than as subjects) in a
political system depends entirely on the communication
system. In classical times, public oratory in a forum or

amphitheatre was the only medium of mass communication. Where the people were many, the range of possible citizen roles was very limited. Contrast that with a society in which every home could be linked by interactive or 'talk-back' TV with other homes and public institutions. Different kinds of communication technology are needed to make some types of political ideology physically possible; the technology first has to exist just to make those ideologies conceivable. It is the more remarkable, then, that the work of thinkers such as Plato and John Stuart Mill is relevant today to students of political communications.

Plato's influence can be traced throughout traditional western comment on the mass media and their role in politics. For Plato,[1] the truth could be discovered once and for all. It was not something ever-changing with shifts in the winds of popular preferences or the current leader's will. In the ideal society, all institutions would be directed at discovering and spreading scientific knowledge of the good and the true. Anything that did not lead in that direction was wrong and would be brought into line or eliminated. Plato recognised that some men might lack the intellectual capacity to discover and appreciate the good life, but his ideal society would provide people with examples and guides, which need only to be followed in order to attain the good life. Censorship of the dominant media of public communication (for the Greeks, poetry and drama) would obviously be needed to protect people from experiences and ideas that might get in the way of developing virtuous habits and the eventual attainment of the good life.

Since Plato thought a verifiable and unchanging truth could be discovered through a rigorous science such as philosophy, he thought nobody could argue about the directions in which dramatists and poets should work. Not Not everyone could understand truth scientifically. For those people he provided the famous 'noble lie'--a deliberately inspired legend that would give the masses an adequate 'explanation' of their universe. Plato's appraisal

of the influence of popular channels of communication and
his faith in education have been echoed and amplified
throughout western civilization. His work has contributed to
the ideologies of the far right, far left, and 'extreme'
centre. In particular, Plato's approach to the masses has
been echoed by all those who have seen the mass media only
as instruments of great disruptive potential if controlled
by somebody else. 'Noble lies' for the people are a
recurring feature of many mass media ideologies.

Liberal Ideologies

Western liberals have had even greater faith than Plato
in education and in the boundless limits of man's rationality. They have not universally agreed that the same truth
could be discovered through systematic inquiry. The 'noble
lie' of liberalism is that everyone who wishes can find his
own version of truth and the good life. Commentators of this
ideological persuasion have insisted that the press in a
liberal democracy should act as though everyone was not only
capable but likely to make independent judgements about
public affairs according to his individual appraisal of
social worth and truth. 'The libertarian theory of the
press' is the name given to one of the dominant versions of
liberal communications ideology.

The libertarian approach to the political functions of
the press involves a number of necessary and almost self-
fulfilling conditions. If these conditions are met, as the
doctrine insists they **ought** to be in any democratic society,
then the notion itself becomes a realistic explanation and
description of the press' role in government. As it developed from the thought of Milton, Locke, Jefferson, and
Stuart Mill, the libertarian theory required a society with
a free marketplace of ideas in which men might develop to
the full their gifts of reason and desire for the truth. In
ideas as in economics, a free marketplace was understood to
be possible only when government intervened as little as
possible. The self-righting principle, the 'invisible

guiding hand', was every man's wish for truth. That need could be served only by giving everybody access to the market. None must be denied the chance to contribute his ideas to the common channels of discourse and none must be denied the opportunity to hear what he wished. All ideas should be given equal chances of being expressed, heard, and debated. Above all, the state must refrain from suppressing any communications unless it could be indisputably agreed that particular communications threatened the very continuance of the free society itself.

Apparently essential to the practice of a libertarian press system are privately-owned communications media competing freely on the open market. Capital investment demands must be minimal so that all viewpoints can be communicated on approximately equal terms. The continued publication of particular opinions would depend not on government but on the desire of enough people to listen to them to make the publishing business economically viable. The marketplace activities of the private consumer of opinions and information would be the sole judge of the social utility of particular communications.

With such a libertarian state of affairs, society depends upon reason rather than authority for the discernment of truth. The reason relied upon is that of individuals rather than groups. In such a society it is morally right for every citizen to report his view of the world as he sees it personally. It matters not whether such views consist of 'facts' that others could easily check if they wished, or whether they were nothing more than outrageous interpretations of a situation which obviously favoured the speaker to the other people's disadvantage. The free market of ideas and opinion is especially important in matters of religion and politics--the two areas of ultimate importance to the individual as a private person and as a citizen. Consequently, no man should be forced to accept another's religious views and all men should have full information about government. Only by stimulating discussion, attack,

and defence could all citizens be stirred to rational
judgement and action that would keep government as servant
rather than master. The libertarian theory embodied great
confidence in the ability of rational men to distinguish
truth from falsehood, no matter how great the number of lies
or how cunning their distortions. Consequently, publications
were expected to reflect the world about them in precisely
the terms their owners and contributors wished it painted.
Theodore Peterson has summed up the theory in this way:

> Only if all men spoke freely what was on their minds, the
> ridiculous as well as the sublime, could they hope to
> discover truth. Given freedom to speak and to publish,
> men would express themselves. They would do so
> temperately and without capriciousness. There was no need
> to remind publishers of their public responsibilities;
> they would assume them without exhortation because of the
> moral sense which gave them their dignity. Nor need one
> worry about the occasional publisher who, because of
> human frailty, lied or distorted. Other publishers would
> find it profitable to expose him. His lies and
> distortions would be recognised, for the public would put
> his utterances to the powerful test of reason.[2]

How far from the idealism of the scholar the liberal practice might vary was suggested years ago by W. P. Hamilton of
the Wall Street Journal. As a publisher, he put his position
in this way:

> A newspaper is a private enterprise owing nothing
> whatever to the public which grants it no franchise. It
> is therefore affected with no public interest. It is
> emphatically the property of the owner, who is selling a
> manufactured product at his own risk....

The Press as Civic Institution

The ultimate purpose of politics and the state turns on
questions of morality and it has been on this point that
most students of politics have concentrated their attention

during the past few centuries. Only recently was there a general revival of interest in discovering how political systems operated in fact. Detailed information about the actual behaviour of societies and individuals and a systematic understanding of ultimate values and their social implications are both necessary to the student of politics. Unfortunately, questions of what is and what ought to be are frequently confused at the expense of both branches of inquiry. Particularly has this been the case during the growth of representative democracy and mass communication systems. Society was often presumed to operate more or less as it **ought** to, that is, in accordance with the prevailing ideology of democratic liberalism. Wherever anyone looked and found it was not really that way, the particular situation was presumed an aberration.

The English-speaking countries, such as Britain, Canada, the United States, Australia, have been popularly presumed to be 'democratic' for at least this century. Liberalism taught that all right-thinking societies believed in the common man, that they organised representative mechanisms through which individual citizens controlled their governments, and that the political information such citizens needed was furnished by individual experience, by personal communication networks, and, above all, by a free and vigilant press. John Dewey identified the very height of democracy as the time in which 'free social inquiry is indissolubly wedded to the art of free and moving communication'. Similar statements abound in writings on the press and politics. Precisely what role did the media of mass communication play in the nascent Anglo-Saxon democracies? We cannot readily tell. Social scientists were largely reformers at heart. They earnestly desired the continuance and expansion of liberal individualism and their biases, laudable though they might have been, pervaded their

observations on politics. If we were to judge solely by
their work we would be left to conclude that because
nineteenth century government should have operated in this
or that manner, that it therefore did so with only a few
temporary aberrations.

Before the second world war, social scientists appear to
have regarded the press primarily as a political
institution. That it happened to perform other functions,
and particularly that it was both privately owned and
operated was perhaps curious but inevitable under the
circumstances. As a political institution its chief
significance seemed to lie in its influence on public
opinion. As sophisticated an observer as E.M. Sait probably
typified the interwar period in holding that "since
democracy is government by public opinion, it is necessary
that the mass be educated through varied information sources
such as newspapers, radio, magazines, and movies."
Newspapers he thought were 'indispensable' to the formation
and development of public opinion. How did this happen?
Charles W. Smith, Jr., in his **Public Opinion in a Democracy**,
saw newspapers exercising their influences as a result of:

1 their virtual monopoly on the distribution of
   information on which readers largely based their
   opinions,
2 cleverly-written editorials,
3 the reflection of public attitudes, and,
4 the authority and prestige which most people associated
   with the printed page.

Many of the same notes were struck by Professor Sait in his
analysis. More perceptively, Harold Lasswell pointed to the
results of 'news focussing.' Across the country people would
never pay much attention to political events if their
newspapers differed so widely in their assessment of news
that everybody's attention was drawn in different directions
at any one time. But, by acting in concert to focus public
attention on particular happenings rather than on others,

newspapers might change the content and direction of public opinion. Lasswell's observations were analytically far ahead of the times.

The part the mass media is thought to play in politics is sometimes better revealed by the criticisms of the media than by positive assertions. In 1927, for example, Professor Sait held that the commercialisation of the press had led to distortion of the news, to business-oriented editorial policies, and a general debasement of the public mind through irrational appeals to the instincts and emotions of the readership. He went on to claim that public opinion could be "influenced, vitiated, and poisoned at the caprice of a few men", and quoted all the standard authorities of his day to demonstrate the widely-held conviction that the average citizen was unable to tell truth from falsehood or fact from opinion in the way that classical liberalism required. Nor did radio seem to offer a reliable alternative. "Radio is coming to assume more and more of the functions of mass direction hitherto associated with the newspaper," Professor Bauer declared in 1934. In the early twenties some had argued that radio would eliminate demagoguery. Disillusioned political scientists of the thirties had only to point to figures like Huey Long and Father Coughlin to suggest that in the United States, as in Germany, radio appeared to provide little more than an efficient means of multiplying the audience for demagogues. Their dire warnings were twentieth-century echoes of earlier times, of Plato and Wordsworth (who had warned about the corrupting effect of popular novels). Those same echoes were heard again a quarter-century later with the coming of mass television. Technology might change but fears do not.

Social Responsibility and the Common Carrier

The ideal of the press as civic institution made its way from the inter-war critiques of liberal democracy into the midcentury dogmas of the liberal elites. As an adequate normative theory of the press, the pure libertarian ideas fell into disrepute among 'thinking people'. No longer could one be sure that the free marketplace of ideas, and biases, prejudices, and blind self-seeking, would be self-righting. The collapse of liberalism in Europe and the success of demagogues in depression-struck North America called into question just how much passion for truth-seeking was to be expected in the average citizen.

The idea developed after the war that the citizen should be given some help in his truth-seeking.[3] Social and political leaders set out to incorporate conservative versions of of the libertarian theory of the press into the brave new peace. What they sought to provide was a public warehouse of facts that would supplement, even if not replace, the retail marketplace of ideas. The regulatory experience of the American New Deal suggested a new analogy. The major means of mass communication should become 'common carriers', rather like telephone and telegraph or railway and highway systems, all of which carried whatever traffic they picked up without bias toward anyone. Under the influence of positivist philosophy, this revised approach to the press began by taking at their word the various occupational codes of conduct and canons of journalism that press and radio people had developed in their drives to improve their occupational status and rewards. Editorials and opinion columns were to be labelled as such and the 'news' reported with the greatest objectivity. Objective reporting meant presenting information as impersonally and completely as possible. Everything was to be done to enable the reader as citizen to build his own picture of reality for himself on the basis of 'the facts and nothing but the facts'. This common carrier model of the mass media was quickly and widely incorporated into the working norms of the accomplished journalist. Even Hollywood movies attested to its generality in the English-speaking world.

A variant of the common carrier model has been termed the 'social responsibility theory' by Peterson and Siebert. The term aptly describes the model evident in recommendations made by groups such as the U.K. Royal Commission on the Press (1949), the unofficial but prestigious American Commission on Freedom of the Press (1947-49), and similar groups in those and other English-speaking countries. The inquiry chaired by Robert M. Hutchins, then president of the University of Chicago, concluded that the mass media could fairly be asked to meet a number of social obligations. They should provide a truthful, comprehensive, and intelligent account of the day's events. They should project the diverse views and opinions of society's different groups to each other and provide a general forum of comment and opinion. Besides communicating news and information clearly and widely to every citizen, the Hutchins group thought the press should assist in the always necessary task of clarifying the values and goals of a liberal society. Not only did the press have an obligation to service the economic system and stand watchdog against government, but it must see that it has enough financial self-sufficiency to safeguard its complete independence. The premises on which the British royal commission framed their reports were very similar. They differed, however, from the Hutchins and later U.S. groups in one significant way. American commentators usually disliked but assumed that daily newspaper monopolies were inevitable in all but a few cities. Faced with a rather different industry structure, the British elites centred their concerns much more directly on the several systems of national newspapers which serve the British Isles. Despite extensive catalogues of criticisms and complaints, the U.K. approach employed substantially the same normative model.

The social responsibility doctrine adds to the common carrier and libertarian notions a major premise: freedom of the press brings with it the obligation to be socially responsible. In exchange for its privileges, the press must not be so selfish as to promote only its own opinions. It must act in the public interest, promote wide discussion and knowledge of all viewpoints, and consciously prod the public to seek truth and responsible public conduct. While the social responsibility doctrine is widely found among Australian and Canadian elites as well, there it has one more significant component: protection and promotion of the distinctive national culture.

The rather general labelling of the libertarian and social responsibility doctrines as 'theories' does not mean that they are in any way explanatory of the way the mass media acted. While they might describe the lines along which some elites thought, the liberal theories were wholly normative in character and simply prescribed codes of pre-ferred moral conduct for the mass media.

Political Power and the Press

Far more objective, at least in their explanatory aspirations, have been those academics who centred their studies on the phenomenon of political power. Their work began appearing during the thirties and flowered following the second world war. Among its most noted exponents were C.E. Merriam, Harold Lasswell, George Catlin, Carl Friedrich, and Robert Dahl. For most, political power consists in the demonstration of superior ability in some individuals to bring about a preferred state of public affairs which would not otherwise have happened. Membership in the political elite or groups of elites may or may not be relatively open to newcomers—the essential difference between 'democratic' and 'autocratic' policies. Elites control the major concentrations of political resources which derive from possession of society's most prized values --material goods, safety, deference, and the services of other people. The powerful defend and expand their dominance by manipulating public symbols, controlling the distribution of supplies and rewards, and ultimately deciding on the selective application of physical coercion.

Elites assert themselves in the name of treasured symbols and values. When the symbols relate to majority benefit and are given some real substance, powerful people are able to elicit blood, work, taxes, and applause from the masses, and the political system may operate relatively undisturbed without the necessity of much overt propaganda. If the ranks of the influential are too hard to enter, new elites may use violence to gain office. But if they are to consolidate their position without wasteful expenditures of physical resources--force, after all, is the most inefficient method of governing--then they must legitimate their authority. This the elites achieve by reinterpreting the old ideology to account for changes or by substituting a new set of symbols of order, hopes, and ambitions in the public's mind.

Current dogmas and political symbols receive their major exposition and chief circulation through the mass media. That emphasises the public significance of both the content and carrier of communications. Popular writers and broadcasters prefer to explain the complexities of public issues in terms of personality clashes, fuzzy abstractions, and vague generalisations. While such simplification may make messages easier to follow, the practice also assists in diverting citizen attention away from the government's unpopular actions including the occasional use of force against minority groups. While newspapers do print some peripheral criticisms of government, Lasswell and many contemporary observers suggested that editorial preferences for reporting events in terms of individuals without mentioning more important causative circumstances serves chiefly to smother a great many sources of potentially serious trouble for the regime. Thus, the housewife was injured, the report says, because she failed to read the instructions carefully--not because government inefficiency or favouritism permitted the sale of a dangerous device. A murderer is said to have slain his wife because he suspected she was running around, according to the newspaper. In another version of 'reality', though, unemployment and the lack of medical attention had undoubtedly driven the man desperately and even irresponsibly insane. The occupational biases favouring 'newsworthiness' and 'personalised' reporting in the mass media all tend to assimilate, reflect, and reinforce society's major values. Very seldom do these journalistic criteria lead audiences to question those values. In such cases little or no direction of communications content is needed to ensure that the mass media have the ultimate effect of giving the existing order widespread and continuous psychological support.

Robert Dahl has directed our attention away from the notion of a single homogeneous elite toward a plurality of elite groups. As he describes it, most elite group members are limited to one area of political life in terms of the weight they can bring to bear on important decisions. Only a few exert much influence in more than one area. So apathetic is the general public that it is content to leave decisionmaking entirely in the hands of the politically interested, that is, the elites. To keep the public content all the elites need worry about is seeing that their policies are not wildly inconsistent with the immediate interests and value frameworks of the general public.

The relative specialisation of their political interests averts routine conflict between elite groups. When interests do overlap, the decision-makers strive mightily, and privately, to reach compromises. When these imperatives fail and conflict becomes irreconcilable, the elites in English-speaking states find themselves reluctantly but of necessity appealing to the masses for support. The previously uninvolved and often uncaring public finds itself suddenly asked to decide matters ordinarily settled by the authorities--the very persons to whom the citizen normally looks for guidance in public affairs beyond his personal experience. But his authorities are caught in open conflict, virtually in flagrante delicto. The citizen's only remaining touchstone is the mass media and particularly the daily newspapers, which, in North America at least, seek to enhance their public authority through espousing the values of objectivity and non-partisanship.

At such times control of the channels of public appeal may become a considerable political resource. What was once an inter-elite dispute assumes a different guise in public where the terms of battle may well depend on the kind and degree of access to the mass media. The elite group that manages to augment its existing political resources with general public support (as expressed in demonstrations of various sorts, plebiscites, or election returns) wins the decision. The elites recognise this potentially critical role of the mass media. If their efforts to win the communications personnel to their own banner fall on deaf ears, they try instead to set up and maintain a social ethos and even legal atmosphere which will prevent their competitors from winning monopoly control over the media.

The Development Approach

In studies of modernisation using the concepts developed by Gabriel Almond, James S. Coleman, and others the state is viewed neither as a legal-ethical association nor as an organisation of competing or monopoly centres of public power. Rather, the state is seen as a society manifesting a set of 'legitimate, order-maintaining and transforming' processes. These processes comprise a political system that strives to attain its goals through the performance of seven functions, (a) the input group: political socialisation and recruitment, interest articulation, interest aggregation, political communication and, (b) the output group: rule-making, rule-application, and rule-adjudication. The degree to which a society has developed specialised organisations to carry out the seven political functions is a measure of the predominance of modernity over traditionalism, according to this approach to political analysis.

One should take care not to confuse the institution found performing a particular function with the function itself. Even in the most modern western states we find particular institutions performing more than their obviously intended functions. Thus, American superior court judges were not

only deciding civil rights cases but seeing to the execution
of some of their judgements in detail. Civil servants in
Great Britain, Canada, Australia, and other countries not
only administer but often make policy and sit in judgement
over cases as well. So too is it with the media of mass
communication.

"All of the functions performed in the political system
...are performed by means of communication," Professor
Almond observes, and the **modern** ethic of communication
specifies that "the dissemination of information ought to be
separated from the other political functions." The
imperative element of this statement indicates the extent to
which modernity was seen as the right goal for the
struggling, non-industrialised societies. Allied to the
concepts of rationality and secularism as indicators of
modernity is that of objectivity. Indeed, the desirability
of a neutral system of communications, manned by specialists
devoted to impartiality and the ideals of democratic
liberalism, underlies much of the work undertaken in the
pioneering studies of lesser-developed states. A 'neutral'
system of communications seeks to bring about a wide variety
of goals. They may be summarised as:

1 Regulation and control of covert communications in the
  bureaucracy, interest groups and political parties.
2 Free flow of information from society to political
  system.
3 Open feedback from output to input so that governmental
  activities are met by responses in the demand sector.
4 Articulation of latent interests independently of
  organised groups focussing on immediate or material
  concerns.
5 General limitation of functions performed independently
  by political parties, the legislature, executive, and
  bureaucracy.

In short, mass communications are expected to develop into
a system that 'regulates the regulators', and thus helps to

guard the "autonomies and freedoms of the democratic party." (The model is also thought to be applicable to dictatorial societies.) According to Professor Almond an autonomous, neutral, and thoroughly penetrative media of mass communications determines the extent to which a society enjoys "an active and effective electorate and citizenship." The electorate's ability to choose good candidates for office depends upon "an open and multi-directional flow of communications reporting on the performance of the other functions by the incumbents of the authoritative offices." Only if a wide variety of neutral information is accessible to all can there be enlightened discussion of public affairs "more or less independently of the influences of interest groups, political parties, politicians and bureaucrats."

According to Lucian Pye, in all societies there are direct relationships (a) between the structure and organisation of communications, (b) the accessibility of these media to would-be communicators, and (c) the character and content of political life. Pye has remarked that "the politician's role both as articulator of the collective identity and as champion of specific interests is invariably conditioned and limited by the media of communications available to him." No leader can either rise above the restrictions of the communications system he uses or escape the consequences of involvement in that system. The level of communications technology and the openness of the mass media are seen as two of the qualitative determinants of a political culture. Pye and his colleagues have sought with some success to show that the way in which the communications function is carried out is clearly related to the performance of two other political functions, interest articulation and interest aggregation.

Three fairly distinct models of communication systems underlie Pye's work in this area—those relating to traditional, transitional, and modern societies. While it is reasonable to seek approximations of the first two models in reality, the third model—that of the fully 'modern' communications system--does not exist anywhere, even in the United States on which the model is based. In the traditional society, the mass communications system is neither specialised nor differentiated from other social processes. People are communicators because of their social standing in the community and they pass information either downward along hierarchial lines or in patterns corresponding to kinship or other community relationships.

Since the communications process was generally so intimately related to the basic structure of the traditional society, the acts of evaluating, interpreting, and responding to all communications were usually strongly colored by considerations directly related to the status relationships between communicator and recipient.[4]

In a traditional system the reliability of a communication depends not on its content so much as on the relationship between the 'sender' and the 'receiver' of the message.

A modern communications system is defined as one in which the technical development of the mass media is high, control over the channel is independent of both political and social processes, and standards relating to content are distinctive, universalist, and based on the assumption that objective reporting of events and developments is both possible and desirable. Mass media of this type represent the first of at least two levels within a modern system. The second level involves series of interrelationships between 'general and specialised informal opinion leaders, and between attentive and more passive publics." The existence of a regular and orderly relationship between these two levels so that there is a 'two-step flow of information' is a critical feature. This interaction between levels produces two-way information flows between all active parts of the political system. These feedback mechanisms are themselves strengthened by the continual efforts of political leaders, the media controllers, and informal opinion leaders to suit their actions to each others' actions and reactions.

The transitional communications system model is a synthesis of the other two. A variant of the modern system based on urban centres operates alongside of--but not necessarily in any intimate connection with--a traditional system serving the rural parts of the transitional society. Pye says this lack of integration between traditional and modern communication systems within the state causes many of the political development problems such states experience.

Understanding McLuhan's Media

Perhaps the most controversial of the academic approaches to the mass media is that of Marshall McLuhan, a professor of English at the University of Toronto who brought tribal concepts to the study of technological cultures. Reading him as a prophet of perception rather than as a behavioural scientist is more rewarding for students of the mass media.

For McLuhan the critical technical difference between today's world and all previous worlds is our ability to transmit information almost instantaneously between any two points on earth. Where once communication between separated individuals depended on mechanical means such as the wheel, today electric circuitry makes it possible to eliminate the time separation. The communication methods we have developed also make radically different demands on human senses. Such changes in communications technology are bringing about equally radical changes in the quality of social culture and in the character of politics.

According to McLuhan, our method of thinking and acting, indeed, our whole culture, depends upon the exterior means by which we express ourselves and receive communications. Until the fourteenth century, European life was perceptually much like that of tribal people: knowledge was the preserve of the wise and was passed on through oral communication to people in social groups. Life was lived in depth by virtue of an undistorted development of the senses as a whole. The norm was living in groups and not as individuals. This mode

of living existentially and in 'total sense involvement' was
shattered by the development of phonetic alphabets and
movable type set in Gutenberg fashion (words fixed in
limited line after line and in left to right order).
Repeatable print ended the priesthood's near-monopoly of
knowledge. It made it possible to compare once-isolated data
bits and to integrate them into information wholes.

The communication of knowledge was transformed. What had
been an oral process conducted in groups became an
individual experience depending on eyes rather than ears.
The Gutenberg press created the book and newspaper--the
first social messages that individuals could receive in
private and free of group pressures. McLuhan's 'Gutenberg
culture' had four important features:

1 individualism,
2 social fragmentation,
3 distortion of the natural balance of man's senses in
  favour of the visual, and,
4 the spread of a logical, sequential mode of thinking
  and personal detachment.

This last stood in important contrast to the subjectivism of
total and simultaneous involvement of all the senses in
perceiving experience. While not made explicit, McLuhan's
approach implies direct links between the Gutenberg press,
books, large scale labour specialisation, privacy,
individualism, egalitarian movements, and mass participation
in decisionmaking.

Was the emergence of nationalism one of the many
unforeseen consequences of typography? McLuhan thinks so.
While not impossible before the invention of printing, it
was certainly difficult to unify populations politically
along language groupings. It could be done, and was, but it
took a lot of expensive military force. With a printing
press unification of territory on the basis of common ideas,
common aspirations, common appeals, and, above all, a common
language became much easier. McLuhan summarises the process

in his colourful language as: "the tribe, an extended form
of blood relatives, is exploded by print, and is replaced by
an association of men homogeneously trained to be
individuals." Nationalism required the rapid and almost
simultaneous transfer of similar data to many geographical
areas. The printing press was only part of it. Mechanical
means of physical communication such as the railway also
speeded up centralisation and the growth of nationalism.

Electrical communication is wreaking a second revolution
which has implications for both our natural senses and our
politics. Television is a particularly potent agent of this
new revolution but the telegraph and radio were important
precursors. As people turn away from excessive reliance on
vision and the print media, the natural balance of their
senses reapproaches normal and the old individualistic,
sequential society begins to give way. Where print media
were fragmenting in social effect, the electric media are
essentially unifying. McLuhan argues that electronic
cultures are in process of becoming less individualist and
more oriented toward the social or corporate whole.
Boundaries between private and public sectors are shifting
ever so surely toward the public side, and, as the
electronic world expands, we can expect to see new kinds of
tribalism. McLuhan calls this the 'global village'. Everyone
in it will be concerned about all others because of
television's ability to involve millions in the problems and
emotions of people both near and far.

"Involvement that goes with our instant technologies
transforms the most 'socially-conscious' people into
conservatives," according to this view. Presumably we become
conservative because we are no longer rebelling against
society as a whole, no longer fighting the battle of the
beleaguered individual, but are identifying ourselves more
with the corporate whole. He goes on to say:

The immediate prospect for literate, fragmented Western
man encountering the electric implosion within his own

culture is his steady and rapid transformation into a complex and depth-structured person emotionally aware of his total interdependence with the rest of human society. Representatives of the older Western individualism are even now assuming the appearance, for good or ill, of Al Capp's General Bullmoose or of the John Birchers, tribally dedicated to opposing the tribal.[5]

McLuhan argues that the speed of modern communication systems knits together private and public awareness into an integrated whole. "We are compelled to react to the world as a whole...because electric media instantly create a total field of interacting events in which all men participate."

McLuhan's is an ideology of technology. It is notably trusting in its confidence that television in cooperation with its real or potential audience will be able to prevail over the regulatory powers of modern states. It is also trusting that the political corporatism that he sees going along with the radical 'reintegration' of society will necessarily be beneficial in his terms. In McLuhan's work and prophecies, the mass media are much more a creator and reformer of politics than it is an agent or institution.

The Psychic Fluidum

The operation of the mass media within political systems involves much more than the simple communication of data and opinion. It contributes in large measure to the total psychological environment of a society. While the concept of 'psychic fluidum' was developed by Carl Friedrich and Z. K. Brzezinski for their study, **Totalitarian Dictatorship and Autocracy**, it suggests intriguing lines of inquiry into other political communication systems. These authors have isolated six characteristics, which, because of their essentiality, unique combination, and mutually reinforcing nature, are identified as the syndrome of totalitarianism. In the modern form, we find an official ideology, a single mass party oligarchically organised, the scientific application of public terror, and extensive police tactics. All are combined with centralised monopoly control of mass communication, economic production, and the means of armed resistance. State or party direction of the mass communications system is deliberately integrated with the selective application of terror and in the name of the official ideology. Together they create a psychological atmosphere conducive to achieving the regime's objectives. The official ideology is so pervasive that it both enhances and is enhanced by the system of public rewards, incentives, and punishments. Integrated monopolies of physical coercion, economic force, the mode of popular expression, and all means of mass communication provide one of the most potent forms of social control ever conceived.

With minor modification, the Friedrich-Brzezinski model may be more applicable to the English-speaking countries than it appears at first blush. Western democracies may be seen as directed by political elites and infused with a fairly uniform and almost official ideology--one of the versions of modern liberalism taught to the young and which dominates the mass media and other social institutions. The political tension level is low rather than high but small groups do hold close control over political, military, and economic affairs in countries such as Britain. There and elsewhere the organisation of rewards and punishments of all types is approved by the official ideology and the general conformity of one with all is promoted by the major channels of public communications. Everything and everybody 'who matters' may be said to contribute to the overall psychological environment of the society.

One might easily object. Our picture includes no general system of terror, and dissent abounds. We should remember, though, that efficient autocracies themselves provide outlets for dissent. Indeed they harness it to serve what they call socially useful purposes. As analysts, we must ask whether the dissent reaching western mass media audiences has not similarly been institutionalised. How often does it

challenge the prevailing order fundamentally? For the
totalitarians' regime of terror we may substitute in the
model those degrees of economic deprivation which confront
many western nonconformists, a substitution that could
account for the difference in tension levels between the two
types of states. Few models ever approximate reality, nor
are they generally meant to do so, but that of the 'psychic
fluidum' does suggest investigating our systems of mass
communication and their connections with other methods of
social control, which together make up the social-
psychological environment.

Historical Materialism

Just as deterministic though not initially as optimistic
as McLuhan's ideology of communications technology is
another current ideology, that of Marxism and its variants.
Surprisingly for so powerful a mode of social analysis, once
its initial statement has been made, Marxism suggests very
little about the ways in which mass communications perform
their political functions. The link from grand theory to
operational code is difficult to find. Marxism tells us that
ideologies reflect the interests and result from the life
experience of particular groups in society. When one group
displaces another as the ruling class, its continued rule
depends on an ability to transform its ideology into one
that seems meaningful for the whole society. As Marx put it:

> For each new class which puts itself in the place of the
> one ruling before it, is compelled simply in order to
> achieve its aims, to represent its interest as the common
> interest of all members of society, i.e., employing an
> ideal formula, to give its ideas the form of universality
> and to represent them as the only rational and
> universally valid ones.

More than a century after that was written, Charles Wilson,
an American industrialist, resigned his job to become a
cabinet secretary. He did not agree with the suggestion of

possible conflicts of interest. "What's good for General Motors is good for the United States," he said. Marx could not wish for a better example.

The basic task of the mass media, according to Marxist analysis, is to help the ruling class maintain its dominance of the intellectual products of the society, to see that the ideas of the ruling class are everybody's ideas. The world is presented in terms that fit the long-term interests of the rulers. The masses in capitalist societies are blinded to their own group interests and to social forces of consequence. Everything is portrayed in individualist, personality, or other entertainment and consumption-oriented terms. However unknowingly, it is the press that manufactures and maintains the false consciousness of the masses by continually reinterpreting the world in terms appropriate to the interests of the elites. Neither hypocrisy nor even cynical manipulation is necessary to the process. The training and system of career advancement for all journalists sees to it that only those sharing the same basic view of the status quo win responsible positions.

Modern writers like Gramsci and Althusser have analysed the production of dominant ideology and laid out the role performed generally in society by members of the intellectual classes, including journalists. They do not, however, devote their attention to members of the mass media in particular. Althusser, for example, tells us only that mass communicators spend their time, more or less unconsciously, "cramming every 'citizen' with daily doses of nationalism, chauvinism, liberalism, moralism, etc." We are not told how the wool is so readily pulled over their eyes, why they behave the way they do, and how one accounts for the anticapitalist opinions that do find expression--even in governmental organisations such as the Australian, British, and Canadian broadcasting corporations.

Ralph Miliband tries hard to grapple with some of the difficult questions.[6] He concedes that critical ideas and opinions are freely expressed but argues they are mainly those that are "helpful to the prevailing system of power and privilege." Political differences that do show up within the media are more style than substance. Their occasional presence only helps to reinforce the illusions of freedom behind which the ruling classes work largely undisturbed. He argues that the press is basically committed to the status quo, and particularly to the norms and values of liberal 'consensual politics'. Their so-called independence is largely exercised at the expense of left-wing and other radical critics. Miliband points out the tendencies to chain journalism and cross-media ownership, something found readily throughout states like Britain, the United States and Canada. The mass media have become big business, and often very profitably so. Britain still has newspaper owners who boast of their political propaganda interests but elsewhere in the English-speaking world most publishers find vague expressions of devotion to public service more compatible with profit-making.

The picture Miliband paints is not one of the ruling class dictating the capitalist ideology in detail to editors and journalists. A good deal of dissent is published. But the right ideological ideas do seep downward to the newsrooms and provide a general ideological framework for the work done there. While some people working in the mass media do suffer political and other frustration, "there is little to suggest that they constitute more than a minority of the 'cultural workmen' employed by the mass media. The cultural and political hegemony of the dominant classes could not be so pronounced if this was not the case."

Analytical Summary

Political propaganda depends on ideology and the technology used to spread it. Propaganda is simply a deliberate attempt to change the way other people see the world and their place in it. As political communication, its major characteristic is one-sidedness.

The direction in which various kinds of information flow is the most important feature distinguishing the approaches outlined. Where political communication is viewed primarily as messages flowing in one direction, the direction is always from the top down, from rulers to the ruled. One-sided flow from the 'bottom' up is logically conceivable but is not part of our mainstream political thought. Multi-directional flows suggest something different about the degree to which political power is concentrated in society.

Allied to the question of direction of communication flow is that of public opinion. While the concept of public opinion takes on different forms depending on the approach under discussion, its nature and development show up only vaguely on the crude map of communications theory sketched this far. The idea will be explored more closely during our inquiry into the political 'effects' of the mass media.

The major political roles in which mass communications have been seen have varied considerably. They include:

1 Primary agent of moral instruction in citizen behaviour,
2 Agents producing political 'facts' and opinions,
3 A marketplace of political ideas,
4 Instruments to focus public attention on particular political issues,
5 Neutral channel of communication between political activists, and between them and attentive publics,
6 Agents to legitimate the status quo,
7 A means to help settle occasional inter-elite disputes.
8 Agents to facilitate performance of other political functions (socialisation, recruitment, interest articulation, etc.),
9 The major determinant, through its technology, of the conceptual modes of the entire polity,
10 An instrument to convey both orders and psychological tension to the general population, and,
11 A means of production and defence for the intellectual dominance of the ruling class.

This account of different approaches has not been critical. While each contributes to our understanding of the political role of the mass media, none even pretends to be a full theory of political communication, let alone satisfies the standard criteria. Elements of all of them appear in the analyses and reflections that follow. Unfortunately, many of the basic empirical questions still remain to be blocked out and answered--at least in rough. Not until a solid basis in some agreed 'facts' has been laid can we can hope for a synthesis of these approaches or a new one altogether that will have power as an explanatory theory. In the meantime, most work in the field--like that of this study--will go ahead in a number of directions drawing their hypotheses and research problems from a variety of sources. If we cannot demand scientific objectivity in that research we can hope, at the very least, for a degree of open-mindedness and uprightness in dealing with whatever findings result.

NOTES TO CHAPTER TWO

1. References to Plato are from **The Republic.** Unless other-wise noted, references to other writers' concepts have been drawn from the following: E. M. Sait, Harold Lasswell, Karl W. Deutsch, **Nationalism and Social Communication,** Cambridge and New York, MIT-Wiley, 1953. Richard R. Fagen, **politics and communication,** Boston and Toronto: Little, Brown, 1966.
2. Quoted in F. S. Siebert, Theodore Peterson, and Wilbur Schramm, **Four Theories of the Press,** Urbana: University of Illinois Press, 1956.
3. See, for example, reports and studies of the Commission on Freedom of the Press, chaired by Robert M. Hutchins.
4. Lucian W. Pye, **Aspects of Political Development,** Boston: Little, Brown, 1966, 167.
5. Marshall McLuhan, **Understanding Media.** Toronto: McGraw-Hill, 1964.
6. Ralph Miliband, **Marxism and Politics,** London: Oxford University Press, 1977.

The political activity and effectiveness of the mass media depend very much on how the people see their own influence over government If the citizens do not matter, neither will the press, for the political abilities of both are tied closely to popular attitudes and beliefs. These find expression in institutions such as parliaments and parties, courts of justice, cabinets and administrative boards, and so on. By political institution we mean an organisation of people who perform actions of political significance in regular and predictable patterns. The areas of life involved and the reasons for such regular actions flow from the expectations of the general population and its leaders.

Much the same is true of our press and broadcast organisations, and we can probably get a better grasp of their activities as political actors if we think of them collectively as an institution that performs a variety of roles in society. Some of those roles are economic. Others are cultural or entertainment in orientation. Still others, of course are political in nature and the performance of any one set of roles is unavoidably affected both by the other roles and by the other institutions in society. General agreement is lacking on just how the press should operate in the political world. Disputes about what that role is or should be are quite common but the competing job descriptions are reasonably compatible with each other and, taken together they constitute the dominant role expectations of the press. Whatever the different sets of expectations, how well the mass media carry out their political roles depends on a surprising variety of influences. Prominent among them are technological factors and the legal, cultural and economic environment within which the mass media operate

Technological Considerations

Countries like the United States Australia, Britain, and Canada are served by physical networks of television, radio broadcasting, and daily newspapers that blanket virtually the entire population. No voter is out of range of radio. Very few cannot receive television or current daily newspapers. The result is an extraordinary combination of speed simultaneity, diffusion, and range of expressiveness. The speed we now take for granted but in the past the lack of speedy delivery of news was responsible for many events changing the course of history. Outbreak of the war of 1812 (in which Americans sought to add Canada to their empire) might well have been prevented by speedier communications. To take that example even further, we might note that the biggest land battle of the whole war took place two weeks after the war had formally come to an end. The speed of news of John F. Kennedy's assassination is almost legendary but Franklin Roosevelt s death in 1945 was spread almost as quickly. News of events of certain types spreads almost simultaneously through society, regardless of whether the audience has much overt interest in some cases. Occasionally it is the very speed and 'channel swamping' of certain news items that creates the interest for much of the public.

Apparent near perfection in the physical efficiency of communications has both limits and limitations. They can only be suggested here. The development of television added the major dimension of the visual to the verbal with consequences that McLuhan discussed at great length in the cultural field. But beyond the notion of star' qualities demanded from contenders for public office the political consequences of this have been very little explored. Broadcasting the hearings of congressional inquiries into the Vietnam war and televising Question Period in the Canadian parliament were both thought to have increased the public respectability of the opposition forces. How or why we do not know. We can only speculate We might argue that real political news has very little visual dimension but that may only be a preference for definitions that emphasise issues and ideologies rather than physical circumstances and personal appearances. Other deficiencies are evident too. The incompleteness and relative expense of satellite and long-line communications in the early nineteen eighties deprived most political events of simultaneous visual reporting. Television covered very few events as they actually happened. Set pieces like conventions and counting election returns were notable exceptions. In general, TV executives devoted most of the broadcast time to political 'backgrounders' and the 'news behind the news'; these could be illustrated with 'timeless' pictures which were thought to make for better television.

The technology of broadcasting undoubtedly brings more overtly political news to more of the population than ever before. It also exposes them to more apparently authoritative opinions. What is not so clear is whether more people are better informed than before. Broadcast news deliberately sacrifices depth of understanding for breadth and variety. Do more people now know less and less about more and more? What they do know certainly covers a wider geographic spread. In older communication systems, the spread of information could be likened to the effects of dropping a stone in a pond. The individual citizen knew far more about the politics closest to him at the local level than about what went on in the far off capital. But not now. Where political news production for television and radio is highly centralised as in most English speaking countries, it takes a real effort of will for the average person to discover the substance of local politics. Meantime, images of national and international politics shower down on all sides of him. That shower probably provides literally all the political information available to people who take little or no interest in public affairs.

Except for personal affairs, the population's information patterns are generally the same as those dominating the mass media. When national issues become known with greater speed and detail than local issues- as is almost universally the case in England where the most important daily newspaper circulation is also national -then a remaking of the political community may be expected. In Canada, urban population concentrations are spread out over a vast and difficult terrain, which is expensive to bridge for both physical communications and mass audience television. Daily newspapers and many broadcasting firms are thus directed by technical and economic factors to build up local audiences and local advertising. This they do with local news and editorial content. Thus the mass media add their weight to the forces supporting regional rather than country-wide political interests. Mass media technology and economics lead to another result in the United States where there is a different mixture of population distributions and thus a unique mixture of centralising and decentralising forces.

Governments in the west have more to say about broadcasting and its operations than about newspapers. Democracy or the lack of it has little to do with it. Technical differences have much. Gutenberg printing and its successors could be exploited, and still is, by people with only a little capital and without particular need of favours from political authorities. The technology did not require public-owned space. Neither was it a 'natural monopoly. Broadcasting came on the scene long after the almost infinite expansion of the state into many areas of previously private affairs. In short it was born under governments widely expected, and expecting, to regulate any manner of things. Those hoping to exploit the new technology wanted a public favour the 'clear channel' in the electro magnetic spectrum that only government could guarantee. (Theoretically, private broadcasters could have continued to fight it out with each other in the domestic market place wars that characterised the early days of broadcasting. But even that process would not have dealt with international competition for the same air space.) Assuring 'clear channels' and the need to ration them out brought governments into full regulatory control.

Other technical considerations influence the roles the mass media play in public affairs. Although we are treating them collectively as a political institution, the media are anything but singular in technical terms. The multiplicity of communications channels permits catering to the interests and demands of a variety of special audiences. Not only do people pay attention to different things in the same medium (and take still different meanings even from the same content) but the messages of the various media are dissimilar both in kind and perceptual shape. Specialised audiences grow up paying particular attention and developing special understanding in select areas of government business. That is made possible in large part only because of the pluralist communications flow. The seeming permanence of print reports of early nineteenth century parliaments permitted -for the first time- making comparisons with things said and done in the past. Was that really 'progress'? Was not the potential flexibility of the parliamentary system considerably reduced as a result of that recording and comparing? We cannot say for sure but it seems highly probable. So long as reports had been second-hand (because of dependence on the journalist intermediary), politicians were able to manage reasonably well. The invention and use of sound, and then, of sound and sight tape recorders tends today to eliminate even that little bit of flexibility. Look how much harder it has become for a political leader to change his mind. The technology of the mass media has altered both the appearance and the substance of public behaviour by those who have been elected. One result is that politicians and press reporters alike now operate in never ending spiral sequences of adjustments to their behaviour designed to compensate for anticipated changes in the other party's reactions.

Some important influences on the political behaviour of the mass media stem from combinations of technical and socio economic factors. Despite the seeming flood of information, our news reports are not continuous. They are episodic and usually daily—largely because of the newspaper's economic cycle. Some events and developments can be chopped into even smaller bits as radio personnel strive desperately to wring the most out of their technical advantage in speed over newspapers and television While the mass media take their raw material in different sized chunks all three of them use a 'bite by bite' approach that chops all politics into jigsaw puzzles. Only keen players will try to fit the pieces together. Others will not bother trying. Whatever the ideological canvas, the audiences of most mass media will not see any larger picture. They settle for the impression that politics as a whole makes little sense. Conspiracy theorists will argue that it was all planned that way deliberately. Whatever the case, technology and economics have played a large role in it.

The most important audience for mass communications may not be those sitting in the darkened house at all. It may be the players, the leading political actors. An even more intensive rain of information bits hurtles down on their heads. For elected politicians whose very continuance in office depends on public attention, there can be no time for reflecting on the meaning of information bits. The cameras are waiting. The newspaper deadline is pressing. Radio reporters have their tape recorders running. The alternative to instant reaction may be instant oblivion. Rash, immature opinions based on incomplete data and inadequate contextual material pour forth in answer to the technological necessities of mass communications. In turn, instant opinions contribute to decisions of potentially great importance.

Today's politicians may be caught in the wrong generation. Most of them developed their political skills in communication cultures that prized reflection and mature judgements arrived at in some privacy. Increasingly we are developing societies in which elected representatives have lost their information superiority. Still those elected to office must work in the light of constant exposure to rival politicians and attentive publics that can muster equal or greater expertise on an issue by-issue basis. (The vulnerability of governments to superior private sector expertise on some matters is never more evident than when finance departments are forced to withdraw totally unworkable taxation proposals.) Even liberal politicians may soon see it as a case in which they either control the technology of instantaneous communication or surrender their future to those with a better grasp of it.

The Biases of our Environment

The main outlines of the cultural and economic environment within which the western press operates are wellknown. What is not so well understood is the value framework of that environment and the near-impossibility of any social organisation operating for long outside that set of values.

Even though great store is set by the potential benefits of private enterprise, in no country does private capital have an absolutely free hand. The public sector is larger in Britain and Canada than in the United States but all three societies employ a mixture of private enterprise and public regulations and corporations to perform economic and cultural functions. Commercial advertising directed at large or prosperous groups of consumers is viewed as a lubricant of the economy, if not its very engine. No wonder that it figures importantly in all the media of mass communications, although somewhat less so in radio in Britain. The ability to advertise through the mass media is sometimes seen as a concomitant of free speech. More often it will be argued that at least a degree of private ownership is all that stands in the way of complete public ownership and a consequent government monopoly of political mass communications. Complicating the picture for those opposed to the role of advertising is the demonstrated preference of many readers for newspapers that offer plenty of advertising as well as editorial and news matter.

Despite impressions to the contrary, the effective range of public debate is limited in even the freest of countries. Very seldom do arguments about public affairs involve even genuine socialist and genuine liberal views let alone those as conflicting as Marxism and multinational capitalism. Debates about government action or inaction nearly always take place within the framework of a society's dominant ideology. This is so even in Britain and Canada where the range of acceptable debate appears broader than in the United States. Fringe commentators like academics may try to inject more right- or left wing perspectives, but they reach few people. The issues are decided in the terms of those occupying the broad middle ground of the political spectrum. No communications medium trying to win and hold the attention of a majority of the people can do so by venturing very far or often outside the agreed set of general values. It is probably this consensus among political activists and the public, a consensus on what politics is 'really' all about, that makes it possible for the governing group to tolerate fierce criticism and even to accept the consequence of electoral defeat.

Awareness of their ideological environment and their place in it is rather low for most people, journalists included. Like many others they have absorbed an important belief of modern liberalism: this is that, in its realization in American society, liberalism means the 'end of ideology' and freeing men's minds from political dogma and other such quasi religious beliefs. But no more and no less than any other modern political faith liberalism fits the classic definition of an ideology. It presents a credible explanation of our historical development, it organises and justifies a set of principles and institutions for the present, and it gives us a set of goals for the future.

Variations of the liberal faith provide our societies with more than just a framework of values and analysis. In practice they also mark off the far limits of all political communication or discussion that is to be taken seriously. The boundary 'walls' are unobtrusive and few inside are aware that they exist. Anyone who wants to call attention to the presence of such limits can be dismissed as a crank or ideologue. We do tolerate expressions of anti-liberal sentiment. That doesn't prove the non existence of walls. What it does do is give evidence of their strength and effectiveness in marking off the serious from the foolish. In ancient China, the vain emperor was taken in by custom tailors who talked a much better line than they spun into his invisible new robes. In the modern West expert craftmen from the House of Liberalism have woven a good, serviceable suit of clothes indeed and then persuaded us that they don't exist. The suit can be seen by everybody except the wearers.

The values of this general environment penetrate and infuse the whole political communications system. For all of their professed cynicism, most journalists share as fully in the general set of social values as do their audiences and readers. Newsmen who do not cannot keep the public satisfied for very long.

None of this is what a journalist means by bias. The rules of his trade make him much more aware of bias than are most people and teach him constantly to guard against it. For media professionals, bias means allowing only one viewpoint to dominate a story. The prejudice against onesidedness runs deep in journalism. Sports reporters, for example, are often looked down on in the newsroom because their close association with the home team often biases their reporting. Curiously, the same scorn does not seem to be visited on police reporters whose stories consist largely of what the 'good guys' think and say. In this case, though, the biased reporting reflects more generally-held values, those of the law-and-order society.

Freedom of the Press

As an environmental condition, the freedom of the press is anything but well understood or widely appreciated. What is probably least understood of all by people claiming it as part of their working conditions is that its exercise must be qualified by all the other freedoms that men demand. None of the liberties of the citizen can be enjoyed to the full without some of them being limited. Even the most liberal society has to strike a balance, for example, between the right to free religious practice and the right to equal treatment regardless of inborn characteristics such as sex or race. Freedom of speech and of the press are forever clashing with people's right to a good reputation or to a fair trial. And all such rights give way, at times, to the primary right and duty of the state to defend the collective security against 'clear and present dangers'. Without such protection, the society that provides these rights might itself disappear. It is one of the paradoxes of liberalism.

Freedom of the press depends more on the balance of liberties that individuals actually enjoy than it does on constitutional documents. The principle in common law countries is that any citizen may do or say whatever he wishes unless the law specifically forbids it. So may the press. But as the reach of the mass media exceeds that of the individual so the range of legal prohibitions on press freedom appears to be effectively greater. The United States constitution forbids the passage of laws restricting the freedom of the press. Canada has some comparable statements in its various federal and provincial bills of rights but Canadian jurisprudence makes them weaker in force than the American, and Britain has none at all in statute form. These differences mirror many others in the three societies, differences in history, in perceived needs, and above all, in the balances struck among the various liberties enjoyed by individual citizens. To Americans, Englishmen must sometimes seem to have surrendered virtually all freedom of speech and of the press in their concern to safeguard the reputations of individuals and the sanctity of the legal process. In turn, English observers of the U.S. scene must think Americans have done just the opposite in their tolerance of press practices relating to libel, slander, and the trial of criminal cases. The peoples of both countries may be free but their mixture of liberties is almost as different as their societies.

The granting of a liberty carries with it no guarantee of the means to enjoy it to the full. Despite the arguments of liberal democrats, freedom of the press under the common law implies only the right to publish and not the right to know everything or anything in particular. Access to information about public affairs is constitutionally quite different from freedom of the press. While more solidly based in law, the latter right does not mean that you must publish your opinions or bits of news. You need not, and if you insist, then you publish at the same legal risk as you do anything. Arguments that the press or any other impersonal being should have rights not given ordinary citizens run into serious philosophical objections in a liberal society.

All legal restrictions on the right to publish may be seen as a series of things our rulers have decided the mass of the people is not to be told. That includes 'official' secrets, libels, and anything a trial judge thinks might interfere with holding a fair trial (contempt of court). While the laws of libel and slander are interpreted differently in the common law countries, the basic idea is that if someone says or writes something that tends to hold you up to hatred, ridicule, or contempt in public, he has committed a wrong against you and you are entitled to compensation and protection from the courts. Now that broadcast statements have been held to be libel rather than simple slander, the old distinction between the two offences (which rested on their relative degree of permanency) is irrelevant to our purpose here. The usual defences in libel cases are to plead that the statements constituted fair comment made in the public interest, that they were true, or or that they were protected by special privilege (such as a parliamentary debate report). U.S. courts give much more weight to these defences than do Canadian or British courts.

In Britain the libel laws are interpreted very strictly. Journalists complain they are often prevented altogether from publishing information that is essential to the public interest. What kind of a watchdog is it that can't even bark? The classic example is the Profumo Affair of the mid-sixties. Sections of the national press had evidence of a significant connection between John Profumo, the War Minister, and a prostitute called Christine Keeler. She was linked to the Soviet naval attache and was a key witness in an attempted murder trial. The situation made a very complicated jigsaw puzzle. While the mass media were able to present different little pictures, the public could not know that they were all bits of the same puzzle, let alone know how to fit them together. The journalists' fears of the laws of libel and the courts inhibited them from publishing the interconnecting bits that helped the puzzle make sense to those 'in the know'. For the complete picture, the general public had to await the results of an official inquiry many months later when its political significance had faded.

According to one prominent journalist, the British law of libel is an 'absolute nightmare'. Worst of all is not the reading of the law itself but the results of its practice: the legal and financial consequences of a possible libel are completely unpredictable. In advance of publication, there can be no certainty whatever whether legal proceedings are likely to be instituted and, if they are, whether courts would or would not find particular matter libellous. Coupled with this uncertainty is the growing scale of damages that British courts have awarded. They can be ruinous for any publishing enterprise that has been enjoying anything other than quite healthy profits. (And periodicals on the fringe of political acceptability are usually on the fringe of financial viability.) Newspaper lawyers are forever advising their clients against publication. There can be no doubt, as Colin Seymour-Ure said following a careful review of the British situation, that, rightly or wrongly, journalists do feel inhibited by the working of the libel laws. He went on:

> The important problem, then, is to assess the degree of their inhibition, and this is inevitably an impressionistic exercise. It could be that editors or proprietors rationalise their own shortcomings by blaming the libel laws. Some lawyers argue, too, that the Press is more frightened than it need be; but this could itself be regarded as evidence of the inhibiting effects.[1]

The question was investigated by a joint working party set up by British members of the International Commission of Jurists and the U.K. Committee of the International Press Institute under the chairmanship of Lord Shawcross. They were persuaded that in some respects the law of libel was too inhibiting. Recent cases had resulted in the scales of justice being "tilted somewhat against the Press" and their report in 1965 made a number of suggestions for redressing the balance. The beneficiaries of that imbalance have not been candidates for election to office. Ever since Harold Laski lost a famous libel case arising from the 1945 election, the balance between the press and elected

politicians has been fairly even with wins and losses on
both sides. The presumed sins of elected officials are still
ventilated in the British press without much apparent let or
restraint. The undue protection resulting from the imbalance
of the libel law has been to the considerable protection of
people active in public affairs without themselves in any
way being engaged in the electoral fray. That has seriously
inhibited exposures of inefficiency, bribery, and corruption
by those pursuing private profits behind the wide skirts of
the modern regulatory state. Any inquiry into their
activities that is marred by the slightest degree of
carelessness or incompleteness faces the journalist's
employer with the risk of bankruptcy. That is a risk that
owners will not often allow their reporters to expose them
to and the range of investigatory journalism is
correspondingly small in British politics.

The general American situation is in stark contrast with
the British. It can be illustrated with an important
decision in 1964, **New York v. Sullivan.** In it the United
States Supreme Court ruled that the Bill of Rights protected
a publisher despite the inaccuracy of a statement defaming
the public character of a government official. That official
could only have collected damages, the court said, had he
been able to demonstrate 'actual malice' on the publisher's
part. Erroneous statement was an inevitable part of the free
speech and debate which the constitution guaranteed, and so
the press was entitled to make an honest mistake without
suffering penalty. This and similar rulings have enabled
U.S. press lawyers to weld the doctrine of fair comment in
the public interest into a defence of formidable breadth and
depth. In very few American situations can the laws of libel
and slander be considered a significant determinant of what
goes into the public channels of political communication.

Even though the Canadian mass media are more like the
American in some ways than those of other countries, the
resemblance is weaker in political areas than in others. Two
libel judgements in the late seventies suggested a tendency

that would make libel law even more inhibiting for the political press than it is in Britain. In British Columbia, a provincial cabinet minister succeeded in a suit involving a daily newspaper cartoon attacking his conservatism in social welfare matters. It showed him picking the wings off flies. The judge rejected the defence of fair comment on public affairs. It went beyond the grounds of acceptability, he ruled. No finding of malice was necessary to the conviction and political observers across the country questioned the unacceptable limits which the decision seemed to place on public affairs comments. Potentially even more limiting was a judgement on a letter to the editor which the Saskatoon Star-Phoenix published. The daily newspaper disagreed with the letter-writer's opinion of a provincial politician, and said so editorially, but published the letter so that its readers could be exposed to a variety of conflicting political opinions. The substance was held to be libellous. The judge ruled that a defence of fair comment would have protected the newspaper had the views stated been its own. They were not, however, and the defence failed. A libel conviction was entered against the newspaper and editors everywhere faced the prospect of having to refuse newspaper space to almost every expression of opinion about public figures with which they disagreed. Some provincial legislatures moved to amend their local libel laws to extend the fair comment defence to letters to the editor but Canada entered the decade of the eighties with a set of libel laws even more politically restrictive in some cases than those in Britain. Much English law on the subject in this century has developed in reaction to popular newspapers chasing personalised gossip and sex sensations for their entertainment and circulation value with incidental spin-off effects on partisan politics. The Canadian press, in contrast, faced restrictive libel laws arising directly from criticising politicians' public actions and policies.

The press is allowed to publish one particular type of libel without legal threat. That is a libel found in a faithful report of a 'privileged communication.' In general, that means the proceedings of courts of law, parliaments, and similar supreme law-making assemblies. The protection for the press derives indirectly from that granted to elected Members in the Bill of Rights in 1689. It decreed that "the freedom of speech or debates or proceedings in Parliament ought not to be impeached or questioned in any court or place out of Parliament." Other countries with common law traditions have adopted this measure either through assimilation or reenactment of British provisions.

The circulation of politically relevant matter is also restricted, in all three countries, by the legal doctrines relating to contempt of court, by the power of judges to compel witnesses to testify, and, somewhat less importantly, by the granting of applications for injunctions against the mass media. Basically, a journalist--like any other person in the land--may be found in contempt of court if he under-mines the integrity of the court, comments on any case being tried or scheduled for trial, or publishes evidence which would be legally inadmissable in the trial such as hearsay evidence, some confessions, and so on.

The balance to be struck is that between the freedom of the press and the right of both individuals and the community to have trials conducted completely free of any prejudice or bias which might affect the decision. In contrast to many American situations, and they vary between states, the balance in Britain and Canada is weighted almost entirely on the side of fair trial. At one time, U.S. reporting was famous, or infamous, for journalistic investigation of crimes, shrill demands for particular prosecutions, and subsequent 'trial by newspaper' long before cases ever arrived in court. Even though their implied universality must be questioned, the images promoted by Hollywood and network television were based on many real situations. Until recently, many judges and legal officials depended on popular election and they were not often inclined to challenge newspaper 'crime-busting'. But times change. In the years since the Warren inquiry into the Kennedy assassination, more and more groups have been trying to tilt the scales to favour the process of law more and the freedom of the press less. In Louisiana, journalists were fined for contempt of court in 1971 for ignoring a judge's order not to publish testimony given in open court. Judges elsewhere followed suit. 'Gag orders' are becoming common with the press prohibited from publishing confessions, criminal records, interviews with witnesses, and testimony stricken from the legal record.

In the U.S.A. there is a continuing battle between the press and the courts. What happens in Britain and Canada cannot be called battle. The judges are the masters. They exercise an almost unfettered discretion to deny publication of anything they think might affect courtroom procedures. The power is near absolute, for generally there is no appeal from the trial judge's decision. A broadcasting company, Radio Forth Ltd., was convicted late in 1979 for 'gross contempt of court'. The offence? It had broadcast reports that four persons had been arrested in Scotland on drug charges (which was true), it had relayed material claimed liable to prejudice the administration of justice, and it had done so in an area in which potential jurors and witnesses must live. Rather than contest the charges, the broadcasters apologised abjectly to the court. They were convicted. The station was fined ten thousand pounds and the station manager another thousand pounds personally. Broadcasts of comparable and even more theoretically damaging material are made all the time in the United States without any judicial notice, let alone prosecution.

Closely related to contempt of court provisions is the legal ability of judges to compel the disclosure of information of any kind. If journalists report an incident on which the authorities want more data, the reporters can often be forced by a judge to provide the information in court. Refusal to testify results in conviction for contempt of court, fines, and often repeated jailing until the contempt is 'purged' by disclosure. The process applies not only to crimes but to the areas of inquiry of many public commissions and legislative committee investigations. Reporters have often argued that the democratic process is better served by allowing them to conceal the source of political information they have published. They have sought to escape a judge's compulsion by claiming the same immunity that courts often accord to the confessor/priest relationship. Courts have extended that immunity, in some places, to husband-wife and doctor-patient communications but not often to reporter-source relationships. A sizeable minority of the U.S. states have enacted 'shield' statutes giving journalists some of the protection they seek, but British and Canadian reporters lack such defences. They must answer all judges' questions just as any other citizen.

Many of us are concerned about the qualities of both our democracy and its justice. Is there any necessary conflict between them? Cannot we have those prohibitions on crime reporting that judges think 'reasonable' without unduly limiting our freedom of speech and press in political affairs? Reporters and defence counsel would give different answers, but both should recognise that accommodation is not possible. The impossibility stems from the nature of politics. It is all about justice. The two are inseparable, and justice and its administration are as changeable as politics. It is through the political process that we decide who may or must do things, and what a crime is, and what the fairest way of dealing with it is.

Elected politicians and civil servants, judges and policemen, all have different parts to play in the process, and in watching each other's performances. Their roles are separate but closely connected. The question is not simply who is to watch the watchers, although that is important. The question is whether any of them should be able to escape close watching from the public's perspective. In terms of the 'watching' they allow, the British and Canadian political systems are much more closed than the American is.

Legal restrictions in the two Commonwealth countries have the result of focussing the mass media's attention much more closely on the legislature and occasionally on the administration and scarcely at all on the judicial and similar parts of government. The result is a marked imbalance in the political information fed into the public communication system. Some areas of politics, and particularly the legal ones, have been effectively ruled out of bounds for the mass public.

Secrecy

Governments take directly opposite attitudes toward people knowing about their affairs, depending on whether they are asking questions about what governments have thought about doing or have actually accomplished. Information about real accomplishments is usually easy to get. Most public officials are eager to stuff the channels of political communication chock-full of data about the decisions and actions they have already taken. The so-called 'outputs' of government--like welfare programs, protective services, economic management and development, changes in rules and regulations--nearly all require public awareness to make them work well. And most of them allow politicians to present themselves as men and women of action who do get things done. No wonder, then, that journalists seldom get into legal difficulty publicising services. The major exception is in military areas.

The trouble arises when journalists try to put output decisions--the policies and programs--into the context of what went on beforehand. Which ideas and plans were considered and abandoned, how much and what kind of data and expertise were involved, who was listened to, and who was ignored? Information of this sort would allow citizens to judge the wisdom of their leaders' decisions and, perhaps, question them. It is when journalists try to dig out and explain these internal processes that they can find even so-called democratic governments snarling at them viciously.

All governments have secrets. Most people would concede
they were entitled to some. But how many and what type? That
is much disputed. The legal situation is covered by the
Official Secrets Act or equivalent legislation. How wide a
range of activities it touches, the penalties provided, and
the way the law is enforced says a good deal about the
relative 'openness' of a political system. And the openness
of a society is a crucial determinant of its character.

Constitutionally, countries with British-style regimes
begin with the premise that all pre-decision information is
confidential. Nothing may be disclosed unless the highest
authority makes a specific exception. That ban on insider
information covers virtually everything done by the hundreds
of thousands of civil servants, in many cases including even
their delivery of legally-authorised services to individual
citizens. After some discussion during the late seventies,
the short-lived Progressive Conservative government
introduced legislation to change the Canadian situation.
While a wide-open U.S. approach was not contemplated, a
considerable reform was. A government bill was started on
its way but it died with the Clark government in 1980. The
successor government promised to revive and improve it but
declined to give the concept constitutional status as part
of the package of radical change which preoccupied it
through its initial years. Apart from legislation permitting
disclosure of cabinet papers after 30 years in most cases
(50 and 90 years in others), British practice has remained
rigidly on the side of non-disclosure. Few elected officials
would dispute the desirability of greater public
understanding of government decisions. The practice, though,
could prove to be acutely embarrassing to a government. For
those in power the advantages of making decisions in the
greatest maximum secrecy far outweigh the dubious
satisfaction to be gained through implementing such an ideal
as a 'people's right to know'.

The people's right to know what their government is
doing, and how, and why, has a solid constitutional and

statutory base in the United States, one that stands in marked contrast to the British-Canadian situation. The secrecy of the war years ended for the Americans with a 1953 law that opened up a wide range of government documents and restricted the number of agencies that could hold material secret. Another law in 1961 opened things up further with a four-step 'declassification' system. Essentially it was embodied in an opinion of President J.F. Kennedy that:

Any official should have a clear and precise case involving the national interest before seeking to withhold from publication documents or papers fifteen or more years old.[2]

The U.S. Freedom of Information Act of 1966 finally gave Americans the absolute right to information about public affairs. A legal burden was put on the central government to justify any attempts to withhold information, a notable reversal of the onus of responsibility. Realising the potentialities of the American legislation has required not only further legislation but a number of court battles. Most of those decisions were resolved in the interests of public disclosure rather than of administrative secrecy. The working of the system is probably best illustrated by the eventual publication of the notorious Pentagon Papers --previously highly secret defence documents that revealed extraordinary government and military ineptitude in the conduct of the Vietnam war. With the failure of the U.S. federal government to prevent publication of these papers has come such a torrent of readily available government documents that no mass medium has been able to do anything other than take small samples from time to time. Individuals, however, have been able to see their personal files and even, in many cases, make corrections of factual errors. Several sets of amendments have been passed to the original statute in an effort to find an acceptable compromise between the people's desires to know and the ability of the American administration to devote at least some of its time to activities other than chasing and copying files for the press and public. The consequences of laying open nearly all the files of the most powerful government in the West have not yet been adequately assessed. Despite this, the impression may be ventured, that the impact has been much greater on the way in which American civil servants now go about their daily business than on the day-to-day content of the flow of political communications in the mass media.

Business Regulation

While not as basic as the quasi-constitutional elements, the legal environment features several other ranges of influence on broadcasting and press organisations. The first is the whole body of law affecting business in general. This takes in prohibitions of 'anti-social' activity, the laws of contract and legal enforcement procedures, as well as health, pensions, and social insurance requirements. Mass communications companies sometimes run afoul of these laws in particular ways. One common example is the frequent conflict between child labour laws and the tradition of using carrier boys in newspaper delivery systems.

Commercial advertising, on which so many mass media depend, faces a lot of regulation. Virtually all countries restrict the promotion of products such as tobacco, liquor, patent medicines, and dangerous drugs. Many states also prohibit advertising pornography, outright fraudulent schemes, and specified forms of violence. 'Fair employment' and other antidiscrimination legislation seriously affect advertising content. Legal attempts to control misleading advertising--of price, supply, and quality, for example--are increasing. Despite the temptation that election advertising offers, there are no reports of serious efforts to apply such controls to the political information content of the mass media, whether purchased or donated.

Mass media businessmen complain mightily about this range of legislative control. So far, however, almost all of it seems to affect the press and broadcasting in their character as commercial organisation rather than as political institution. Such is the case as well with respect to business concentration law. The liberal public philosophy places particular stress on the need for communications diversity. The increasing tendencies toward single press and broadcasting voices in many cities makes the mass media especially vulnerable to attention from governmental anti-monopoly authority. Despite the recent and recurring rash of afternoon newspaper closings, such as that of The Washington Star late in the summer of 1981, the effects of this body of law have been rather unremarkable so far in terms of mass media structure or content. That situation could still change. The royal commission that Canada set up in 1980 to investigate the practices of chain journalism, known as the Kent Commission, reported sourly on the increasing concentration of circulation control in the hands of Thomson Newspapers and the Southam group. Recommendations were made that the federal government stop the expansion of such communications groups and require them to give up some of their holdings. The Canadian government gave very little solid indication toward the end of 1981 (when the Commission reported) of placing much legislative priority on the recommendations. The report was typical, however, of the growing elite sentiment--in the United States and Britain, as well as in Canada--in favour of applying general anti-monopoly business laws to newspapers much more rigorously than has ever been the case in the past.

Required Performance

Of more immediate significance is the range of statutes, tax provisions, and semi-permanent sets of regulations that require the mass media to act in certain ways and to communicate specified messages. The U.K. legislation in 1945 was quite precise. It directed the British Broadcasting Corporation (then the only one) to "broadcast any announce-ment or other matter which a Department of His Majesty's

Government may require." The responsible minister (the Postmaster General) was authorised to prohibit the broadcast of particular matters and a daily account of the proceedings of the House of Commons was to be aired. The relative independence of British broadcasting in practice reflects the political culture not an absence of legal authority.

"Congress shall make no law...abridging the freedom of speech or of the press." That provision in the U.S. Constitution has had limited application to broadcasting. In 1934, the U.S. Congress replaced the previous hodge-podge of controls with the Federal Communications Act. Its provisions authorised a Federal Communications Commission charged with seeing that there was made "available, so far as possible, to all people of the United States a rapid, efficient, Nation-wide and world-wide wire and radio communication service with adequate facilities at reasonable charges." Section 326 added that "no regulation or condition shall be promulgated or fixed by the Commission which shall interfere with the right of free speech by means of radio communication." The act was later extended to television.

Despite these provisions, a doctrine based on 'the public interest, convenience and necessity' has been developed and elaborated, which led both the Congress and the Commission to issue a host of regulations for the broadcast media. Areas covered by these laws include obscenity, advertising matter, network and ownership combinations, local and regional production requirements, on-air expression of management opinions, election campaign advertising, and news and feature coverage of public events.

In vain have the broadcasters sought to claim freedom of the press privileges that might allow them to escape from the 'equal time' and 'fairness' laws. The U.S. Supreme Court squashed them firmly with a unanimous decision in 1969 (Red Lion Broadcasting, 395 U.S. 357). The court said: (1) that the First Amendment gave the public a right to be fully informed about controversial public matters, (2) that the public's right superseded any the broadcasters might claim, and, (3) that the fairness and equal opportunities provisions served to further the public's paramount constitutional rights.

Elections Equality

Elections are the area in which mass media activities are seen to be political by even the most uninterested citizen. It is not surprising, then, to find a great deal of regulatory legislation in western democracies that tries to influence, if not control, mass media handling of elections. While daily newspapers are not exempt from some such provision, it is the broadcasting media that are most closely controlled.

In their efforts to keep the airwaves relatively non-partisan during elections, the U.S. government has pursued quite a zig-zag course during the past quarter-century. Not surprisingly, its legislative efforts have often had a number of unintended consequences for the electoral role of the broadcast media. New legislation aimed at patching these up led to more unintended consequences, and so on to further patching up. American efforts begin with the candidate-oriented 'equal opportunities' doctrine. It is found in Section 315(a) of the Communications Act:

> If any licensee shall permit any person who is a legally qualified candidate for any public office to use a broadcasting station, he shall afford equal opportunities to all other such candidates for that office in the use of such broadcasting station: provided, that such licensee shall have no power of censorship over the material broadcast under the provisions of this section....

This provision was enforced literally. In 1959 the FCC ruled that it meant, as well, that all candidates had to have equal exposure even in regular newscasts. Such is the number of candidates and elections that this ruling would have meant almost no election news at all on television and radio. Congress tried to fix the situation by exempting four specified types of news programs from the equal opportunities clause. In what seems to have been intended as a one- time rule, it also allowed Richard Nixon and John F. Kennedy to meet in the so-called Great Debates (without the other dozen or more minor candidates for the presidency that year). The result was two-fold: a little more 'freedom of the press' elbow room for broadcasters to use news judgement, and creation of a distinct advantage for the two major parties because of the provisions for televising national conventions.

The governmental attempt to loosen but not cut the regulatory bonds simply added to the complexity of the rules. The news exemptions were seized upon by campaign managers who became ingenious inventors of 'news happenings'. What is more, the regulations left untouched those that prohibited face-to-face confrontations by the major party presidential candidates and discouraged live broadcasting of major news conferences by presidents and others who had legally qualified for election or reelection. Changes made late in 1975 eased some of the difficulties. The presidential 'great debates' resumed and that of 1980, for example, was given credit by some for the size of Ronald Reagan's presidential victory, but the FCC has continued to take a strong interest in the format and organisation of all broadcasting involving elections. During campaign periods, the FCC has been called on to give rulings on whether a president's attendance at the first baseball game could be televised (yes) or whether a huge nationwide charity appeal could be televised when the person launching it was also, incidentally, a candidate for election (no). By the eighties a vast thicket of FCC rules had grown up around all broadcasting and elections. One consequence of these rules has been the tiresome repetition of old, safe broadcasting formulas and the active discouragement of any innovation and often any coverage at all of local and state politics.

In contrast to the U.S.A., where regulators seem to have felt some inhibitions, the governments of Britain, Canada, and Australia have felt no compunction at all in limiting the freedom of the press in the interest of 'fairer' elections. British election laws insist on a rigid balance being maintained between candidates and parties. No station may broadcast anything portraying a candidate without that person's prior permission. That serves, among other things, to rule out the kind of commercials favoured in North American campaigns where one party uses videotapes of the other's candidates to demonstrate how unsuitable the other people are to hold elected office.

News and documentary broadcasts are also affected. In Canada, expenditure and timing restrictions have been imposed on both print and broadcast election advertising. On the last day or two of the campaign period, no political advocacy may be broadcast at all (except as part of regular news programs). The existence of five time zones in the country means that the polls close at different times and that some ballots have been counted before voting has finished in other parts of the country. Fearful of bandwagon effects, Canada has forbidden the publication in a province of any election returns until after its own polls have closed. (Even then, those in the west with access to American trans-border broadcasts have often heard the results of counting the eastern and central votes an hour or two before their own polls closed.) In Britain, Canada, and Australia alike, broadcasters are required to provide free prime time for recognised parties to air their views and appeals during a campaign. Similar time is often provided in non-electoral periods as well but is not always specified by law. More explicit controls on the contents of regular news broadcasts are not usually attempted. The question of appropriate 'balance' is left to the broadcasters' discretion. In this, the regulators can rest assured of good performance because they know that no broadcaster would want to face the wrath of a parliamentary post-election inquiry.

Issue-Oriented Controls

All broadcasting boards require fairness in dealing with public issues. Canadian legislation requires all broadcasters to "provide equitable opportunities for the expression of differing views on matters of public concern." British and Australian law have comparable provisions. In the United States, and following a somewhat different route, the FCC initiated the steps leading eventually to the 'fairness' doctrine, which was given statutory form in 1959.

American licensees are required "to operate in the public interest and to afford reasonable opportunity for the discussion of conflicting views on issues of public importance." (Sec. 315) This requirement, unlike the 'equal time' rule, applies to news as well as to non-news programs. Much is left to the discretion of the broadcaster--so long as he is able to demonstrate that he has exercised 'good faith' in trying to achieve a fair balance in issue presentation. Only occasionally have opponents succeeded in winning court approval for equal time to deal with what they feel is one-sided broadcasting on an issue of public importance. An associated American doctrine is the 'personal attack rule'. That can provide for an on-air response by an individual whose reputation has been injured through some non-news program. The 'fairness' doctrine in American broadcasting has been under constant criticism for years. It will remain so. So much personal judgement is involved that court arbitration is extraordinarily difficult. And for somebody on the losing side of a public issue argument, the strategy of shifting the attack to the messenger and his account of the controversy will often be an attractive one.

Difficulty in applying fairness doctrines does not make them irrelevant to the determination of content. Its significance for style of broadcasting may be illustrated by a Canadian case reported in 1972. It concerned a Halifax radio station whose news editor had broadcast a commentary that was highly critical of a fund-raising activity called

Miles for Millions. The news editor's dislike for the charity was matched by the displeasure his commentary brought the Canadian Radio-Television Commission. In the absence of a specific penalty for 'a breach of this nature'. the CRTC announced, it was issuing a public announcement "as a form of censure against the licensee, Maritime Broadcasting Co. Ltd. and for the information of all licensees." In addition to offering equal time for rebuttals, the commission said the station should have sent the charity a complete text of its critical comments in advance of the broadcast. From now on, such behaviour would be taken into account "in connection with any application by the licensee for renewal of its license." The threat of license denial was not an idle one. A few years earlier a radio station in Vancouver had lost its licence after an 'open line' broadcaster had repeatedly ignored the regulatory board's warnings against giving air time to bad taste and bad language. Broadcasters have run afoul of their authorities in a number of countries because lyrics in popular songs were thought to be too drug-oriented or 'anti-social' in other ways.

Even in the most liberal societies, there is no easy dividing line between good taste and social dissent. Does popular music constitute the only form of effective political protest left to young people today? Should we view the warnings of the FCCs and the CRTCs of this world as the mailed glove of the stuffy bourgeoisie? The answers vary considerably. Much of the music does originate on the social fringes. Complaints of repression and exploitation run all through many of the lyrics. For some people, so limited is their vocabulary that various forms of sacrilege and public bellowings of obscenities constitute the only way in which they can give their political sentiments 'truly free' expression. But there is another side. Whatever its origins, popular music is now the product of hard selling. Commercial broadcasters, invoking sacred visions of consumer sovereignty, have been pushing folk music, hard rock, and 'rockabilly' simply to build big audiences and big profits. They have cared not at all for the middle majority's standards of decency and good taste. Those with a taste for conspiracy theories will prefer to add another view: commercial music not only makes money but it adds to the creation of false consciousness and should be seen as a new and deliberately created form of opium for the exploited classes. Any governmental suppression or discouragement of political expression in any of the mass media must always be judged, at the very least, in terms of the standards of liberal freedom that those governments profess.

The Mass Media and Politico-Cultural Diversity

Many might argue about the extent to which popular opinion has any responsibility for, or even supports, the system of legal influences on mass media content. Although not all the opinions of national elites are embodied in legislation, few laws reach the statute books without their tacit support. Political elites have acted in several areas quite firmly--and sometimes in opposition to business interests--to compensate for the mass market's failure to appreciate and sustain certain 'higher values' like those of diversity. Strict ownership rules and domestic content quotas have been developed into yet another means of using law to direct the biases of mass communications.

Of all such policies those in the U.S.A. have probably been the least successful and possibly even counterproductive. The rhetoric of primitive American democracy glorifies localism in all its political forms and modern broadcasting law seems to embody those ideals with its apparently stringent requirement for local station ownership. The professed object was stated eloquently by two commissioners in a 1968 FCC case study in Oklahoma:

The greatest challenge before the American people today is the challenge of restoring and reinvigorating local democracy. That challenge cannot be met without a working system of local broadcast media actively serving the needs of each community for information about its affairs, serving the interests of all members of the community, and allowing all to confront the listening public with their problems and their proposals.[3]

The growth of the three major networks has combined with the marketplace and administrative practice to make a near mockery of such ideals. With only a few big city exceptions, all that has generally resulted has been a thin, low budget schedule of superficial local newscasts, a little high school sport, and some church services, nearly all of it broadcast outside prime time. The FCC has concurred in that judgement. The case study mentioned above observed:

As far as Oklahoma broadcasting is concerned, the concept of local service is largely a myth. With a few exceptions, Oklahoma stations provide almost literally no programming that can meaningfully be described as 'local expression.' They provide little that can be considered tailored to the specific needs of their individual communities.... It is unlikely that their performance differs greatly from the performance of broadcasters in other states.[4]

The big three television networks have been left virtually undisturbed in their oligopolistic position. Indeed some economists have asserted that the FCC local rule has actually bolstered the oligopoly's power and reduced the degree of meaningful choice even for mass audiences.

Paradoxically, it is the same economic 'fact of life' inhibiting the growth of local and regional television in the U.S.A that has bedevilled policy-makers in other countries. Taken as a whole, the American market is the world's richest. Many millions of potential consumers, more than anywhere else, are there to help spread the risks and pay all the initial costs of program production. On that foundation the major networks and their suppliers have built an unchallenged superiority in the world for production of mass entertainment television of impressive sophistication. Nothing even vaguely comparable can be made with both a distinctive regional or local perspective and anything like the same cost per thousand viewers. Oklahoma City just cannot compete with the financial, technical, and artistic resources of New York and the U.S. west coast. Neither can Melbourne, Toronto, Vancouver, Wellington, or even Birmingham. With only a few exceptions, the only light entertainment produced in Britain, Canada, or Australia that has been a mass audience success has been modelled on American techniques and with an eye to American sales. Day-long television consumes enormous amounts of material. Faced with that and with demands for large audiences, no programming director can ignore the ready availability of U.S. network material at half the cost or less of producing his own. Therein lies the peril to the national character of programming in most non-American countries.

In comparison to the U.S. regulators, the Australians and the Canadians have managed to find somewhat better legal instruments for tinkering with broadcast programming. But then, they had more political support. Coincidentally their efforts, like the American, have also been directed at building and maintaining domestic expressions of cultural diversity. Both Commonwealth countries have constructed extensive dikeworks of laws and tax provisions. All were designed to reduce the dangers of drowning in the floodtide of American media content sweeping the English-speaking world. While generally similar, the two policy sets have slightly different emphases with the Canadian being more explicit in its assumptions about a connection between cultural distinctiveness and political identity.

The initiative and sustaining impulse for national content regulations in Australia has come primarily from artistic groups, the union movement, and production companies. As W. H. N. Hull has pointed out, these quotas amounted a set of tariffs designed to protect an infant industry. The law spoke in 1932 of developing, establishing, and encouraging 'local talent' and musicians who through broadcasting would help stimulate growth in the Australian creative community. By the forties, commercial radio was required to devote at least 2.5 per cent of its time to broadcasting the works of native composers either from live performances or from Australian made records. Similar injunctions were laid on television when it arrived during the fifties. At first, Australian content ran about 40 per cent of the total. Then the proportions began to decline. Extreme reluctance was noted in broadcasting live drama and theatrical groups complained as their work was progressively squeezed out of the prime time schedules. The regulatory authority reported in the late fifties: "audience measurement surveys have shown that as a rule the public prefers imported programs to live productions." While the imports at first included substantial British material, foreign soon came to mean mostly American. During the sixties and seventies, the Australian government stipulated ever higher minimum quotas of national content that had to be shown and some of it in prime time. The regulatory board was caught in a constant whipsawing between the demands of theatrical, musical, creative, and production personnel on one side and popular tastes on the other. Audience surveys, advertisers, commercial broadcasting organisations, and sometimes populist politicians combined to argue the case for consumer sovereignty in opposition to the cultural diversity arguments put by the performers and the elites.

Australian content and prime time regulations have undergone constant re-examination and redefinition. Where the quota system had begun as fairly straightforward economic protectionism, during the seventies it took on an overlay of cultural nationalism as well. Throughout, little attention seems to have been paid to one of the major causes of trouble. That was the deliberate creation and proliferation of multiple systems of state and public broadcasting stations and networks. The demand for quality programming that supply of viewers and of advertising could also appeal to sizeable audiences far exceeded the required to finance it. Australia entered the eighties with yet another broadcasting inquiry to digest and all the old problems unsolved.

The Canadian problem has been political as well as cultural-economic. It has also been geographically unique. Unlike the Australians' Pacific barrier, the 49th parallel proved no obstacle at all to the torrent of American programming that so dominates the continental broadcasting spectrum. That environment makes it very difficult to build and hold a set of tiny rings within which Canadian performers might develop their talents in any way distinctive from the mass tastes of the giant market to the south. Ironically, this aspect of the problem is like that of U.S. local democracy alluded to earlier--only magnified several times over, and possibly even to the point where Canadian national survival comes into question.

The neighbours are a central and sometimes decisive factor in the daily operations of Canada's newspaper, radio, and television systems. The problem is in trying to serve 24 million people in two language groups who live in tempting, embarrassing, and almost smothering proximity to 230 million Americans who speak the language of Canada's majority. The neighbours are rich, friendly, and inventive. They also have the world's most penetrating and effective system for transmitting ideas en masse. "Canada, more than any other country, is naked to that force, exposed unceasingly to a vast network of communications which reaches to every corner of our land."[5]The country is caught in the dilemma of trying to survive politically and still live within the liberal traditions of the open society. That the doctrine of liberalism was a foreign creed born and nurtured in imperial societies to which it was better-suited than to small, former colonies only adds to the irony of the situation.

Although there was little thought of 'Canadianism' at the federation's founding more than a century ago, during the last thirty years there has emerged a strong and growing concern for the national identity. The torrential overspill of U.S. news and opinion has often drowned out even discussion of the issues in Canada. Even the country's premiers and prime ministers have had trouble gaining the attention of their fellow citizens. One result was the development of the mass media as a battle zone for the conflict between the values of Canadian nationalism and those of the antinationalist liberalism that dominates the intellectual climate outside the universities.

Almost from the beginning it was clear that broadcasting was no more likely in Canada than it was elsewhere to develop the role of fearless critic of political conduct. In any case, the public elites had another and, to them, more important role for the medium to play. From the beginnings of the nineteenth century railway boom, communications had always been expected to play a critical part in knitting Canadians together. Broadcasting was to be no different. "Properly employed, radio can be a most effective instrument in nation-building," the Conservative prime minister, R. B. Bennett, had declared in 1932. He and his contemporaries looked on radio as "a great agency for the communication of matters of national concern and for the diffusion of national thought and ideals,...the agency by which national consciousness may be fostered and sustained and national unity still further strengthened."[6]This thesis animated the pre-war discussions of radio, subsided briefly during the forties, then was revived and expanded to include other media as Canadians organised bands of diagnosticians charged with finding and probing the national psyche. The most important of these inquiries were those chaired by Messrs. Massey, Fowler, and O'Leary. The decade of the fifties was marked by an extraordinary discussion of the presumed close connection between the future integrity of the country and effective control over mass communications. Briefs to public inquiries, parliamentary debates, magazine articles, and royal commission reports shared very similar assumptions.

These posited a causal relationship between the quantity and quality of Canadian content in the mass media, the centrality of those media to the defence and expansion of a distinctive national culture, and continued political sovereignty in the face of the inevitable American challenge. The Fowler commission asserted in 1957 that

> as a nation we cannot accept, in these powerful and persuasive media, the natural and complete flow of another nation's culture without danger to our national identity. Can we resist the tidal wave of American cultural activity? Can we retain a Canadian identity, art and culture--Canadian nationhood?

This and similar inquiries concluded that domestically owned mass media must not be allowed to lose their audiences and advertisers, and then to founder just because mistaken free market notions had unfairly subjected them to vastly superior American competition. On that assertion rests much contemporary regulation in Canada.

"A society or community, deprived of searching criticism of its own, among its own, has within it seeds of decay." This theme from the O'Leary Report added a conservative philosophic justification to the economic-cultural one earlier noted. O'Leary not only echoed the feeling among leading Canadian politicians but sounds now like a harbinger of the American Federal Communications commissioners who, a decade later, were bemoaning the lack of local and regional broadcasting in Oklahoma and other nonmetropolitan centres. The order setting up the O'Leary inquiry into methods of protecting the magazine industry forcefully asserted an old Canadian theme in new dress:

> Communications are the thread which binds together the fibres of a nation. They can protect a nation's values and encourage their practice. They can make democratic government possible and better government probable.... In these functions it may be claimed--claimed without much

challenge--that the communications of a nation are as vital to its life as its defences, and should receive at least as great a measure of national protection.

In their report, the commissioners considered a recommendation that would have required magazines to devote a specified proportion of their editorial content to the Canadian scene. The idea was abandoned, partly because of enforcement difficulties, but chiefly out "of respect for the widest interpretation of press freedom." Despite the cabinet's earlier confident assertion, the commission's recommendations for protecting Canada's communications were challenged by many business spokesmen. It was largely to no avail. Moving slowly over a decade, the Canadian government acted to direct the flow of domestic advertising revenues and to regulate the ownership of daily newspapers and other print media. Basic to the provisions were taxation provisions that discouraged companies from buying advertising aimed at Canadians through any foreign-owned mass medium. Customs regulations were also used. Together they hit hard at American border television stations (who were using U.S. licences to 'poach' on Canadian territory) and U.S.-owned periodicals like **Time** and **Readers' Digest.** Special techniques like split-run editions had enabled the latter two to secure more than half of all Canadian advertising budgets with cut-rate prices. These they could afford because they could get editorial content from their head offices at 'dumping rates'--prices far below their original cost.

Where the nationalists thought the protective legislation failed to go far enough, the liberal free traders disliked it for opposite reasons. Most indignant was the U.S. federal department of commerce, spokesman of American business in general and broadcasters in particular. Late in the decade it was even protesting vehemently about conditions Ottawa imposed on Canadian cable systems distributing signals in Toronto. Some Canadian newspapers supported the protective legislation in general. Others attacked it. They claimed that what was at stake was freedom of the press--to choose its ownership. It was also a dangerous precedent for it might lead someone to think of reviving the old, iniquitous licencing laws of England in some modern form. Although unmentioned in the protesting editorials, the legislation did have one interesting effect. By ruling foreign bidders out of the marketplace, it marginally reduced the theoretical capital value of newspaper companies. Not for Canadian publications could there be a rescue operation by Atlantic-Richfield (of The Observer in London) or a major takeover by an Australian newspaper baron such as Rupert Murdoch (who has bought major papers in London and New York). The world's largest multi-national newspaper enterprise is, curiously, Canadian in both origin and control. But, then, Thomson Dailies had its mass media empire well launched before the mid-sixties.

Whatever the O'Leary commission might have thought about magazines, broadcasting has not benefited from similar concerns about press freedoms or difficulties in enforcing national content quotas. The Canadian regulatory commission put it bluntly in its 1970-71 annual report: "Broadcasting is not an end in itself. It is subject to higher and more general imperatives of national development and survival." For anyone still in doubt, the imperatives were spelled out in the Broadcasting Act of 1978. It said:

> the Canadian broadcasting system should be effectively owned and controlled by Canadians so as to safeguard, enrich, and strengthen the cultural, political, social and economic fabric of Canada.
>
>   .   .   .   .   .   .
>
> [T]he national broadcasting service should contribute to the development of national unity and provide for a continuing expression of Canadian identity.

Those obligations were laid on the private as well as the public broadcasters. That has ensured a quarter-century of wrangling over the definitions and applicability of Canadian content quotas. Penury and imminent bankruptcy were pleaded in requests for temporary relief from the requirements. Occasionally the pleas were accepted. But overall the quotas have been maintained, raised, and sharpened. Some successes resulted. One was the development of a significant popular music and recording industry. Others are much disputed.

In free societies, national content quotas work better as tariff and job protective devices than as agents of cultural change. Quotas have to be applied to the production end of broadcasting, not to consumption. Even single channel situations allow viewers to pick and choose what they will watch. Wherever frequency allocations result in broadcasting monopolies or oligopolies at the local level, program output may be regulated with reasonable hope of some success. That is seldom the case in Canada. Almost all the potential audiences can switch to programs from U.S. border stations.

Audience fragmentation is a rapidly-growing problem for station operators. Attracting large numbers of viewers is hardly less important for public than it is for private broadcasters. Any state system that wants to keep public funding at a decent level must show politicians that it appeals to a large proportion of the public that pays for it. Producing public service programs and catering to the many elite and other minority tastes is expensive. It strains the fattest public agency's budget. And still it must serve the majority. A mixed TV system drives public broadcasters almost as much as private systems to the 'solution' of buying more low-cost programming made in the U.S.A. The Canadian Broadcasting Corporation, for example, has paid premium prices for the privilege of showing American TV episodes a week before competing U.S. stations. Its justification is 'program drag' or schedule-building. Popular programs are used to attract audiences that might stay on the same station to watch Canadian-made productions. Such schedule-building is part of broadcast expertise everywhere. Its effectiveness depends, at least in part, on the variety and number of program choices available.

In all but one major city, Canadians have a wider program choice than audiences almost anywhere else in the west. The reason? Very early on, businessmen saw the possibility of good profits in snatching U.S. programs from the air and piping them into distant or difficult reception areas. They became world pioneers in long distance broadcast reception and signal distribution. With program choice approaching the technical maximum on the VHF spectrum, Canadian viewers developed into accomplished 'channel-jumpers'. A primary effect of the 'wired cities' is to let most viewers avoid Canadian quota programming any time they wish. Audience research indicates they do so--often.

Mass Media and their Environment

While the mass media are generally thought to exercise powerful influences on the political system, it is not so often recognised that the mass media are themselves subject to powerful influences from the political system within which they operate. Just how much does its environment condition the political content of the mass media? While it would not take much of an environmentalist to declare that most of the questions were already settled, it is not really all that easy. The very concepts of impact and consequence imply beginnings and ends. What is certain, if anything, is that there is a constant interplay of influences between the mass media institution and its environment.

Our picture of the environment is incomplete. Much more knowledge and analysis are needed. The British 'national press' has impressive journalistic resources. Relatively few of them are used effectively in 'watchdogging' the government. Why? The press is intimidated by the law and the courts. Conventional histories tell us that eliminating the licencing and stamp acts struck the shackles off the English press more than a century ago. If so, the prisoners were not left to dance their way in complete freedom outside the walls of law. Not at all. It is the legal environment that explains, at least in part, why British journalism does a

much better job of providing popular tittle-tattle and
"Tit-Bits" than it does of exposing political wrongdoing.

On the other side of the oceans, the premises underlying
the cultural nationalist controls of Australia and
especially Canada need unearthing. They should be
investigated in the light of both common sense and social
science. (The two standards should prove to be compatible.)
How necessary is a distinctive culture to maintenance of a
country's political integrity? A multiplicity of choices
among mass media messages is part of most Canadians'
environment. Political advantage or disadvantage? The highly
developed sense of regionalism and weak national feeling may
have their origin lie in the fault lines and incongruities
of the patterns of political communication. Other
explanations are also possible. The Canadian situation may,
for example, demonstrate just that sense and strength of
community feeling that is both missing and mourned elsewhere
in the west.

In the political and economic environment of the United
States, individual and consumer sovereignty has been
elevated to sacred dogma. The American mass media have
responded to those forces with behaviour quite unthinkable
in Britain, for example.

Historical materialists might be content to dismiss all
the materials of this chapter as mere epiphenomena totally
predictable from the underlying relations of production.
Even then, surely we should be interested to trace how the
connections are made and how the fundamental structures are
manifested and affected in the face of changing technologies
and cultural variations. A liberal might protest in turn
that too much attention was paid to the products of the
political system. What about the 'demand' side of things?
What of the struggles of various social groups to achieve
dominance or at least some of their short-term goals? A
short answer is that these matters are themselves inputs,

raw materials from which the mass media institution crafts its own outputs. These we see as news, opinion, documentary, live coverage, entertainment, and all the other components of the institutional share of the political communications of a society. What we need now is to see how the mass media turn inputs into outputs, how they change the raw materials of everyday life into 'news'.

NOTES TO CHAPTER THREE

1. Colin Seymour-Ure, The Press, Politics and the Public, London: Methuen, 1968, 135.
2. Quoted in D. C. Rowat, "How much administrative secrecy?" Canadian Journal of Economics and Political Science, v. 31 (1965) 486.
3. Quotations from Roger G. Noll, Merton J. Peck, and John J. McGowan, Economic Aspects of Television Regulation, Washington: Brookings, 1973.
4. Ibid.
5. Canada, Royal Commission on Publications, Report (Ottawa 1961), 5-6. Hereafter cited as O'Leary Report after the commission's chairman.
6. Canada, House of Commons Debates, 18 May 1932, 3035. For a more complete discussion of the period up to 1968, see, Edwin R. Black, "Canadian Public Policy and the Mass Media," Canadian Journal of Economics, v. 1 (1968) 368-379.

Content is what the mass media are all about. Reporters and editors would like to think that that was true but they know better. Tempting though the generalisation seems, it applies only in terms of the audience perspective. Industrial structure, personnel organisational forms, control systems, institutional policies, occupational routines, and the technologies of reproduction and distribution are responsible for bringing about hours of programming and columns of reporting. But they do more, much more, and that part is often missed.

The very presence and processes of the mass media contribute to the conduct of government. That sometimes happens even when no content at all results from a particular event. Examples may be seen in presidential and prime ministerial press conferences where the fact of these people being questioned is often more important than whatever answers they happen to give. So, we need to know

how the reporter got to the press conference, and why he or
she was not some place else reporting on some other person
or part of the social system. The answers lie in the
organisational character of the press institution.

Presidential press conferences provide undoubted grist
for the communications mill. So do parliamentary debates,
pressure group demands, foreign policy declarations, local
council decisions, party conventions, general elections, and
many other activities of the constitutionally recognised
institutions and processes. Few would dispute their being
labelled 'political'. Some social scientists would extend
such a list almost indefinitely, for everything in society
is within the potential reach of the state. Whatever their
individual stopping points, most political scientists would
include legal decisions, tax arrangements, the police, and
public opinion distributions on topics as diverse as the
basics of formal education, racial discrimination,
pornography, and military conscription. The general system
of private property and the social distribution of
privileges and rewards are outside the range of normal
partisan debate, and the mass media do not deal with these
matters as current issues. Despite this, and sometimes
because of it, these areas are highly significant in
political terms and their treatment in the mass media
deserves close attention. Those addicted to symbolism might
wish to consider the audience implications of dividing daily
newspaper content into sports, general news (including the
explicitly political), family/women's news, and financial.

As a political institution, the mass media might be
analysed very much as established churches has been.
Television replaces religion as the opiate of the masses.
Every day the mass media provide us with circuses and blind
us to the need of bread. The steady diet of escapism,
entertainment, and superficial enlightenment assures one and
all that their betters are looking after them and their
world. Meantime, the publishers and broadcasters combine
with the marketing system to keep the audience bound to the

Hierarchies and Structures

Press organisations remind one of modern military forces. To maintain one soldier on the front line or to put one pilot in the sky takes many, many others behind the scene. So it is with general audience newspapers and broadcast programming. To bring the work of one reporter, foreign correspondent, or documentary producer to the public requires a small army of people. They sell advertising, manage the finances, service the video machines, set up the presses, monitor the audiences, and sell and distribute the newspapers. The editorial and programming departments are often the smallest of the major divisions in a mass media company.

On a newspaper the chief executive is invariably called the Publisher. Broadcasting companies use a greater variety of titles for the same role: president, managing director, station manager, director-general, etc. Occasionally, publishers are the owners. More often they are the salaried appointee of the board of directors of the corporation or newspaper chain. At one time, publishers were active as journalists themselves and assumed the title of Editor as well. While some are former newspapermen, most have business backgrounds as accountants, advertising managers, and so on. The Editor is the senior journalist and is responsible to the publisher for all news, editorial, and feature content. As a department head, he is usually on a par with the Advertising Manager, the Circulation and Business Manager, and the Production Chief. Figure 4-1 (next page) illustrates the extensive organisation needed for these other functions. For a business that long resisted labour-saving changes, newspapers are now undergoing technical transformation at a surprising rate. The introduction of computer type-setting, photographic makeup processes, and various forms of offset printing (sometimes in distant locations) is considerably simplifying the overall system.

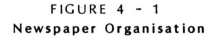

FIGURE 4 - 1
Newspaper Organisation

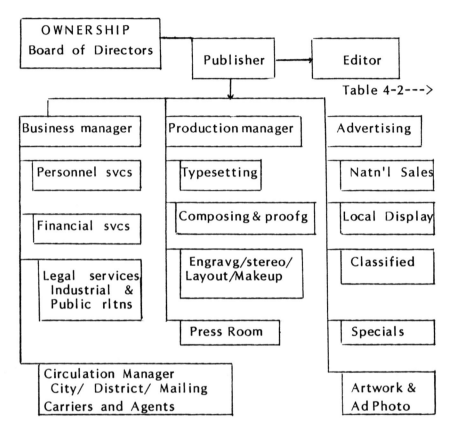

In contrast to their self-images as a relatively undisciplined, highly independent group of individualists, newspaper personnel are subject to very clear lines of authority. Figure 4-2 illustrates the editorial side of a medium size North American daily newspaper. Changing the titles of some roles and a few of the sub-command reporting lines will fit the chart to most comparable English-language newspapers. Dividing or telescoping the roles will suit it to larger or smaller cases. Journalists defend the complex structure of their work world as a common sense division of

FIGURE 4 - 2

Editorial Organisation: Newspapers

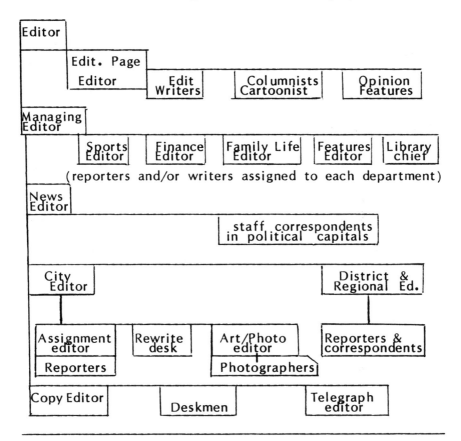

labours that are highly diverse, confusing, and pressured. Authority, exercised with a light touch, is seen as necessary for coordination and legitimate because those who have it have risen from the ranks of the craft/profession. A general egalitarianism is promoted by the frequent interchanging of roles which accompanies shift changes, days off, and high staff mobility. The resulting emphasis on function rather than status makes the hierarchy much less generally oppressive but all the more effective when it is consciously brought into play.

News Personnel

Who are these people who report and process the news for us? Their backgrounds are extraordinarily diverse. So varied are they that the usual sociological survey of family background, ethnic origin, religious affiliations, formal education, and the like gives us much less help than is usually the case. From its beginnings, journalism has had rather low social standing in England. Any higher status a journalist enjoyed was almost invariably due to claims other than his occupation. Its practitioners in North America have fared somewhat better, rising to about the midpoint on most scales of social status. Contemporary journalists in Britain generally go through secondary school and finish up with training in a vocational institute of some type but few beginning reporters and even fewer journalists with extensive experience have had a university education.

Newspapers used to pride themselves on being able to recruit the most talented young people available. That pride fed an old journalistic prejudice against formal education. Eventually It proved costly. As TV began its meteoric rise, it sucked in many of the most imaginative and experienced newsmen and attracted ever-larger numbers of those who used to hammer on newspaper doors for employment. With the aging of the wartime generation, serious problems developed in many newsrooms. Not until the seventies when the anti-university prejudice began to erode and labour prospects worsened for college graduates was the situation redressed. Some papers began to consider economics graduates to do financial reporting. Others even hired political science students to be trained for reporting politics. The point about specialist university education is that it gives the journalist standards and reference points to bodies of knowledge outside the lore of his occupation. Even then, the few surveys we have suggest that there remain substantially fewer well-educated people in journalism than are found in the social groups with which reporters must deal every day.

Except for sports, specialists are rarely recruited as experts by broadcasting organisations in North America although a few can be found in British television. Those hired for on-air work must meet show business standards. Sincerity, pleasing appearance, a look of authority, and a well-modulated voice are the major considerations. Popularity in audience surveys is valued highly. Good experience in print or radio journalism is helpful for those working off-camera, but imagination in the use of graphics and the literary skills to make still photos or stale, dated videotapes and films seem relevant are even more valuable. A North American study, The news people by J.W.C. Johnstone and his colleagues, reported in 1976 that in comparison to newspaper people broadcasting staff were more likely to be younger, mobile, trained in journalism schools, and planning to complete a career within the same medium.

Much time and ink is occasionally devoted to the question of journalism as a modern profession. The sociologist, John Porter, once disposed of the question in this way:

> There is ... nothing professional about the role of newspaper reporting. As a group, reporters have no disciplined academic training in any particular sphere, although they seem prepared to write about almost anything. They do not as an occupational group license themselves, govern their own affairs, or establish their own norms of performance.... As a ... group they are not highly paid, nor do they seem to have prestige.[1]

Since Porter wrote, the average education has increased, journalism schools have become more acceptable (especially in broadcasting), and the American Newspaper Guild and the National Union of Journalists have succeeded in improving salaries and hours of work. During the seventies, groups of journalists within French Canada were active in work practices and disruptions designed to boost reportorial independence and win greater status and recognition.

While limited achievements are notable within Quebec, elsewhere in North America journalism as a self-governing profession remains a legal non-starter. Another field which was once equally low in popular regard, medicine, now exercises enormous legal power, affecting relationships between patients, physicians, and hospitals. One would look in vain for a comparable independent influence on the definition, gathering, and processing of news and other mass media products. The occupational norms of journalism derive almost entirely from the institutional employers.

Fish-Farming or the Beat System

Much of the world and its doings are not newsworthy, which may be just as well. Journalists, and especially TV executives, like to say their job is simply holding a mirror up to the world for us to see. The analogy is false. The limits of time and space make that quite impossible; journalists must select and they do so at two levels. The first and least conscious of the selection devices brought into play are the wideangle binoculars of liberalism. This way of seeing the world is something that editors have in common with most of their viewers, readers, and listeners. The second filter used in the selection is the mesh of news and production values discussed earlier.

Filtering the world through the journalist's lenses produces many quirky results. They fascinated A.J. Liebling who commented on journalism for the **New Yorker**. His book, **The Press**, provides a splendid anecdotal survey of the facts, foibles, and fantasies of newspaper life as he saw it. Central to that vision was the reporter-creator, not the editing process. Like many writers, he thought it too complex and overemphasised. The result was an analogy. "The American press makes me think of a gigantic, super-modern fish cannery...with tens of thousands of workers standing ready at the canning machines, but relying for its raw material on an inadequate number of hand-line fishermen in leaky rowboats."[2]Liebling's comparison was a simple, romantic one. The problem of assuring a steady supply of news to feed the press machinery had been solved decades before by opening 'fish farms', as Philip Elliott put it. By that, he meant the system of regular checking of standard information sources--the 'beat' system--but he thought that agriculture offered a better analogy for news production:

> News is produced by journalists cultivating regular beats around recognised news sources, which have their own interest in making information available. Stories and features come in known sizes and varieties, so that an editor has a good idea of the crop he will reap when he plants the seed and sends a journalist [to bring it in].[3]

City editors are like police superintendents: they divide the known world into bits and pieces and send their staff out to patrol the beats and keep them under control. City hall, labour relations, health and education, police, courts, transportation, environment. All the institutional sources and other types of news are divided into functional areas to be expertly fished by the same angler for news. The precise array of beats depends on the character of the community, the special interests of the paper, and the number and talents of reporters available. Outside the metropolis, the hinterland is chopped into geographic chunks for patrol by a district or suburban reporter or sometimes by a part-time correspondent. A few staff members are on general assignment in the news room, ready to deal with singular events as well as those that are truly unexpected. Carving the local world into functional areas worthy of full-time attention (and necessarily slighting others in the process) reflects long-established conventions of journalism. Their effect is to predict what kinds of news will be seen to be happening, where, to whom, and who will usually be providing information about it.

The advantage of assigning reporters to particular beats is that they become subject specialists. They cultivate close contacts with the relevant authorities and get inside tips and other information denied to outsiders who are not trusted. Where legal matters are involved, the beat reporter is better able than many lawyers to walk the narrow paths required. Despite these and other advantages, city editors shift their beat reporters around from time to time and even change the whole system of beats. Why shift the reporters? It is because they become too sympathetic with their sources and are in danger of being 'captured'. During even relatively short general election campaigns, correspondents who have been assigned to follow one party leader's fortunes will be switched to watch another camp. Like other journalists, beat reporters are seldom there to see news happening. They collect data after the fact from those involved. Their raw materials are the "selected and selective accounts of others--his sources," as Steven Chibnall has put it. After a study of law and order reporting in Britain, Chibnall came away much impressed with the 'capturing' or socialising process. He asserts:

> Most professional communicators feel their job is to collect and process the accounts of their sources, casting them in a conventional news form for rapid dissemination to their readers. They may recognise that the process of creating news from source accounts inevitably involves elements of interpretation and selection but this is seen as a form of intellectual craftsmanship which creates a predominantly neutral product.[4]

Although put too broadly, the central point is a sound one.

News Sources and their Nature

A lot of potential editorial material comes to the city desk by messenger and postman, the product of self-publicity efforts. Few editors admit using copy taken directly from professional public relations agents, but it serves at the very least as tips for staff reporting and for photographic ideas on slow days. Television stations looking for local features that will not be dated seem to use far more 'P.R.' (public relations) material than do large dailies. Smaller papers publish more of the copy submitted by hobby club and social group correspondents but usually only after varying amounts of checking and rewriting. What the 'club copy' lacks in immediacy it makes up in mention of local names. Its publication also serves a self-advertising function for the mass media outlets that use it.

Where the production of editorial content deserves close attention is in its sources--where the news comes from. Most of the sources of public affairs news are found in institutions, many of which exercise authority. Even when broadcast 'live and direct from the scene', what news comes over the airwaves is almost invariably created and organised by somebody. If that somebody is not a political party, planning commission, or legislative committee clearly in the public sector, it will be a business corporation or social group which has a president/chairman, treasurer, secretary, 'who gives speeches' or interviews.

Unexpected and unplanned news does happen. It has slightly less of this institutionalised character but not as much as newsmen like to think. Survivors or victims of marine disasters, highway crashes, and hotel blazes will be personally interviewed. Reporters will give overviews and pictures of the general scene if they get there themselves. Soon, however, even those events will come to be told in terms of institutions, their 'official assessments', and what they are doing or failing to do about the situation. Other qualities of news will be considered later once the process as a whole has been outlined.

News for the World

In their reporting, both the journalists in the street and those on the news desk are supposed to remember that various people in other parts of the world might be interested in their work. In many cases, that interest is slight. Whatever it is, most papers try to satisfy the demand by supplying their stories in advance to the local or nearest office of the cooperative news agency: Press Association in Britain, Associated Press in the U.S.A., the Canadian Press, and similar national agencies owned by participating newspapers (and sometimes broadcasters).

Great volumes of copy flow from local newspapers into the agency's regional and head offices. Items of wider interest are selected, edited, occasionally checked or rewritten, and then distributed to all member-subscribers through the teletype network. That system may include specialist 'wires' for state or provincial, financial and stock markets, national political, and national general news. News specially written for broadcast outlets may also be offered. Political and sports reports supplied by capital city newspapers are often highly local in their orientation. To supplement it, the agencies have small reporting staffs of their own.

The general news wire carries foreign and international reports as well; these the agency gets through exchange agreements with comparable agencies in major foreign countries and supplementary special reports produced by a few staff correspondents stationed abroad. To reduce costs and the number of exchanges at any one level, the major agencies take responsibility for passing on news of their 'satellite' countries. In consequence, British newspapers, for example, get virtually all their news of Canada through the American-oriented filter of the Associated Press. In addition to the news cooperatives, there are privately-owned counterparts, which must generate their own copy from both their own reporters and rewrites of domestic publications. United Press International, Reuters, and the New York Times service are the most general in coverage although smaller and more specialised services are also available. Profit-oriented and cooperative agencies exist in the broadcasting sectors as well, albeit on a geographically more restricted basis. Even though the larger mass media organisations will subscribe to one or two privately-owned services, those like Associated Press and Press Association are preeminent in the supply of news. Perhaps far more significant is their central role in fixing ideas of what is important and unimportant in the minds of news editors everywhere.

In newspapers, copy moves fairly continuously. It has elements of both batch and continuous flow manufacturing. While the speed of the flow varies during the day, depending somewhat on the number of editions, the usual system sees a steady sequence of copy deadlines so that inside pages are closed and 'put to bed' progressively from the back of the paper forward to the front page, which takes the latest, important stories and last minute revisions of details and the headlines. The passage of today's last deadlines simply signals time to start preparing material for the early pages of tomorrow's paper.

Broadcast News

The flow of news copy in radio and television is similar. While both media tend to function on the 'batch' principle, the process is relatively straightforward in radio. The most impoverished radio news operations depend on 'rip and read'--two, three or five-minute news bulletins taken right from the broadcast news-service machine. Local news will be tid-bits taken from local newspapers, more or less rewritten, quick telephone calls to the police station, and news tips from listeners. The more ambitious the station the more it will have newsroom personnel like that of small newspapers. Tape recorders simply replace the pad and pencil and prominent officials will be brought into the studio to make personal statements on air or in a pre-recorded tape. Reporters make on-the-spot recordings at public addresses, on the scene of accidents, and sometimes at important public hearings. The more 'actuality' tapes and the more reports staff members can make that bring in on-location sounds and voices, the better radio it is considered.

FIGURE 4 - 3
Organisation of BBC Radio Newsroom*

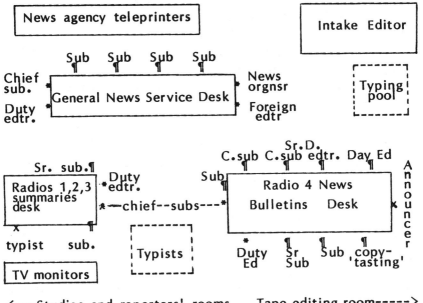

<---Studios and reporters' rooms   Tape editing room----->

*Following Philip Schlesinger, Putting Reality Together.

For the most part only radio networks attempt substantial
newscasts running up to 30 minutes. Like a paper's news
editor, copy chief, and makeup man, the radio news producer
has the job of selecting the items to be broadcast, deciding
their length and form, and fitting together actuality tapes,
staff recordings, and announcer's scripts and continuity, to
make an interesting and intelligible program. The British
Broadcasting radio newsroom (Figure 4-3) illustrates what is
for many radio people an ideal setup. The BBC divides the
tasks of preparing short newscasts and longer news programs
between two separate desk organisations. Few other
organisations devote similar resources to radio journalism.
It is usually a poor cousin to radio's major concern for
music and voice entertainment programs.

Creation and Handling of Copy

Popular stereotypes like the Hollywood movie suggest that the reporter is the key figure in the mass media picture. If so, what do all these editors and other people do? Some of the answers can be indicated by sketching the routines of generating editorial content and the flow of copy-processing through to the reader. The model shown as Figure 4-4 holds good for the broadcasting industries as well, although with several important variations.

Most newspapers compartmentalise their editorial and news content along the lines indicated in Figure 4-2. The editor or managing editor will assign specified numbers of pages or editorial columns to each department and expect the departmental editors and reporters to handle all but the most unusual news stories within those pages. Sports is the obvious example. Individual departments have their own opinion columnists. All other 'in house' expression of comment and opinionated interpretation--and particularly on public affairs--comes under the control of the editor of the editorial page. He and his staff almost invariably devise and present the paper's institutional views in close consultation with the editor and publisher. This is the area of content that the publisher supervises most closely on an issue-to-issue or daily basis. Sometimes it is the only one, particularly if the publisher has little background in journalism and no interest in politics.

The general news department is by far the largest. Inputs come from many sources: staff reporters, staff and agency photographers, part-time writers, foreign correspondents (if the paper has any), national and international news agencies, and a multitude of press releases and statements 'over the transom' or through the door from people and organisations seeking publicity. As mentioned before, staff reporters are assigned to particular tasks by their city and regional editors and submit their copy directly to them. The typewriter has been the standard instrument of the craft of

FIGURE 4 - 4

The Flow of News Copy

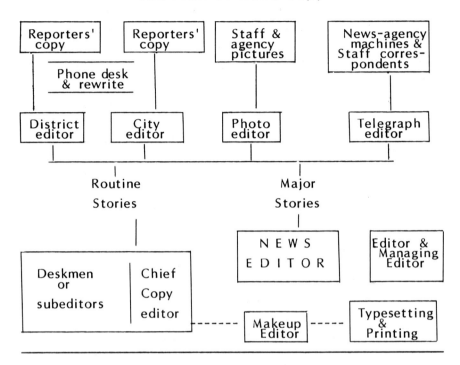

journalism throughout this century and copy has always made
its way from the writer, through the editors, and on to the
mechanical processes as typed sheafs of paper, often much
annotated. Technological change is rapidly overtaking this
tradition as well. Typewriter and paper are giving way to
the video display terminal (VDT) linked to the same central
computer that sets the newspaper in type. On up-to-date
newspapers reporters type their stories into a computer
through a VDT. This machine, which looks like a typewriter
keyboard connected to a television screen, allows journalists to correct, rewrite, or insert sentences and paragraphs
and to move them around with great ease. Reporters submit
nothing physical to the city editor. The editors also have
VDTs and simply call up particular stories from the computer

memory whenever the time comes to deal with them. Except for layout, nearly all editorial process operations are carried out on the video display units before the whole is despatched for mechanical reproduction. Elimination of the physical flow of bits of paper seems not to have changed the routines of copy processing very much--except to make them easier at almost every stage.

If dissatisfied with a reporter's copy, the city editor will call on either the original writer or somebody from the 'rewrite' desk to check facts or interpretations, to change phrasings, or to change the order of presentation. That done, if the story is considered important because of its news value or some special sensitivity, it will pass to the news editor. He makes judgements about the kind of prominence and typographical display the story should get and passes the copy on to the copy desk chief. Most stories will go directly to the chief of the copy desk. He decides what place it will occupy in the general news columns--front page, main local or international pages, or buried deep inside--and pass it to a copy editor or subeditor with instructions about length, type of heading or headline, and sometimes special points to watch for.

Though popularly supposed by reporters to be checking only such mundane matters as spelling and grammar, the subeditor occupies a crucial role in the process. Although earlier processors in the chain will have been watching out for matter that is potentially libellous or dangerous in some other legal way, the subeditor has the final responsibility before the item finds its way into print. The copy desk chief will check the work roughly, and particularly the suitability of the headline, but the subeditor will be blamed for any errors or problems with the copy in the areas of 'common knowledge' or the newspaper's policy. The latter will include things such as mentioning suicides, dealing with trade names, and characterising students as 'highspirited' or 'vandals'. (This subject is explored in more detail later.) Clarity and consistency in treatment and explanation are also on the subeditor's shoulders. He it is who actually cuts the length of stories, harmonises several pieces on similar topics, and combines stories from a variety of sources into one should that be what the news editor or copy chief requires. Editorial copy makes its way to the news editor and the copy desk in the same way from the regional or district editor and from the special bureaus and telegraph desk. A makeup editor works closely with the news editor and the copy desk chief to fit the pieces together. The objective is an arrangement that is easy to read, expresses the paper's personality, and gives every item the importance due it in terms of news values.

Television News Flow

The basic sequence of news flow through a large television newsroom (Figure 4-5 next page) is much the same as that in a large newspaper. That comes from the similarity of functions to be performed: collection, sorting, selection, editing, and preparation of the news contents for the technicians to print or broadcast. Geographically, the input side is less complex. Where newspapers are concerned with international, national, and local news, a television newsroom has only a part of this. If it serves a national network, it leaves local news to the affiliated stations. Sometimes it may not even touch local news without 'nationalising' it. If the TV newsroom serves a local area, it takes whatever national and international news it wants as a 'feed' from the network and inserts them into its own bulletins. Figure 4-5 shows the flow of these contents through a large-sized television newsroom and illustrates the variety of sources from which the materials come.

The physical forms of the materials to be handled are more varied in television than they are in newspapers. They include videotape (often taken from different types of machine), movie film in both amateur and professional sizes, teleprinter and typed stories, still photographs, sound tapes, music in various forms, and a great variety of

FIGURE 4 - 5
The Flow of Television News

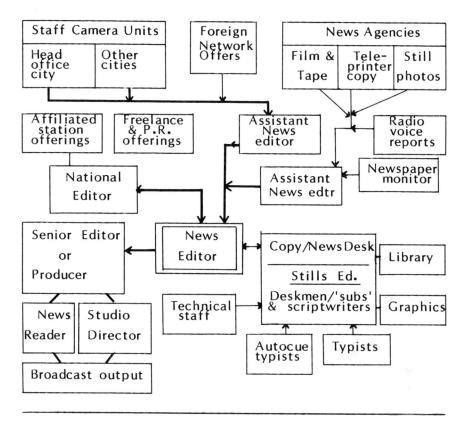

graphics such as figures, diagrams, animated cartoons, and captions. Different levels of lighting and sound must be coped with; colour adds a whole range of complications unknown to the newspaper journalist.

A television news broadcast requires a number of complementary skills. Even in reporting, teamwork is important to ensure the efficient disposition of reporting units day by day and event by event. Reporter/correspondent, field director and cameraman must agree on the news values

and be able to work together in many different
circumstances. Once the materials have been passed to the
general news desk, they must be assigned (if they are to be
used) to a particular place in that day's 'running order'
and assigned to a deskman or subeditor for preparation.

In preparing his segment of the newscast, the subeditor
decides what is to go into his segment of the news broadcast
and edit the film or videotape (usually with the help of a
technical assistant). He fills his time slot with a number
of different 'packages' of materials depending on what is
available and on the news editor's preferences. These
packages include some, or all, of: typed scripts to be read
by the announcer/anchorman or by a correspondent (either in
the field or in the studio), studio tape of interviewees,
diagrams or other graphics, videotape by staff reporters and
cameramen, purchased still photos with 'voice over', voice
reports from radio reporters and telephone interviews, and,
of course, occasionally live transmissions from the site of
the news happenings. The deskman or subeditor works under
the close supervision of both copy chief and news editor,
usually with time limits specified to the order of
'ninetythree seconds', 'two minutes ten', or something
comparable. The 'running order' of items to be broadcast is
usually established four to six hours ahead with the time
given each item being kept flexible right up to air-time.
Some items will be prepared with an eye to dropping one or
more should better film or more gripping news turn up later.
In most cases, the major evening news program is built
around two to four items prepared by staff crews a day or
more in advance. Late developments or unexpected happenings
will be handled in a newsreader's script based on news
agency copy or by telephone reports from staff members.

What needs emphasis about television news is the number
of hands through which it passes prior to broadcast. The
creation of even a ninety-second item usually involves an
assignment editor, a field crew of three, assistant and

general news editors, copy desk chief, deskman and technical assistants, program producer, and finally the studio director and the news announcer. It is a manufacturing process with a multitude of extraction and refinement steps between the raw material of the event and the consumer product eventually reaching the viewer.

The news flow through a mass media organisation has been compared to a series of gates each with its own keeper. Rather like the angel with a flaming sword who guards the portals of heaven, the wire copy editor, for instance, examines all comers, decides which nine of the ten items to turn down, and passes but one on to the next stage. Probing the reasons given for each judgement, sociologists tried to deduce the editor's news values and assess the influence on them of policy guidelines laid down by the editor or publisher. Further research has expanded the approach to almost every step of the news system. The big picture this methodology gives us is that of a giant distillation process, which expertly squeezes life's happenings down to their very essences and offers them up as a daily potion of 'l'eau de vie' for the readers' delectation and enlightenment. The metaphor is flawed. In some ways it is positively misleading. It does have the virtue, however, of representing the ideal prescribed by the canons of objective journalism. Like other ideals, it is seldom, if ever, attained in practice, and newsmen know it.

Newsroom 'Policy'

Broad agreement on what makes news and what must be done to bring it to the reader makes it possible to characterise the flow of news in general terms. The contents of those news currents are, of course, more diverse. In large part, that is because they are aimed at different audiences, often the simple result of geographic considerations. Where, however, similar media are in competition within the same marketplace, their owners try to create news products which manage a distinctive flavour without losing market appeal.

Broadcasters seek such goals by varying the entertainment mix. In newspapers the effort shows up in news policies represented as the paper's 'traditions' or 'personality'. The Times, The Guardian, and The Financial Times are as distinct from each other in London's quality market as they are from 'down market' publications like The Sun and the Daily Mirror. Similar comparisons can be found elsewhere.

Where media of the same type are not in competition, publishers' policies are less evident and show up only when advertisers cannot be offered near-saturation coverage of the market. Otherwise, there is no economic incentive to produce anything more than the service that results from the relatively unhindered application of general news criteria.

While ownership policy dictates the audience sought, such policies may also operate on the non-economic level. Where publishers are assertive and feel their public philosophies strongly, their papers reflect it--provided it has no ill effect on circulation. What is more common is that as an area loses competing dailies, the survivors' policies grow to express publishers' personal foibles and fads more than political preferences. The trend probably says more about the kind of person who becomes an owner-publisher these days than anything else. Whatever the cause, ownership 'policy' in content trades on the latitude inherent in editorial judgement about the amount of news interest in particular events. Campaigns are launched against door-to-door peddlers because the publisher's wife once suffered a fraud. Meetings of associations in which owners or publishers are members receive more publicity than those not so favoured. A private school board meeting may be covered because of an 'old boy' connection. A small oil spill in the harbour gets reported 'because the boss is a nut about water pollution' while a much more obnoxious public nuisance may well go unnoticed. 'Sacred cows' like these are pastured in most publications. For the most part though, the coming of TV, has made newspaper publishers much more hesitant about imposing policies violating journalism's 'professional' standards.

General policy statements are rare in the mass media--
except for the documents of broadcasters seeking licence
renewals. While editors issue formal memoes on individual
topics, most policy is implicit. New staff members must pick
it up as part of their 'training'--socialisation into the
organisation by the more experienced. Here supervising
editors play the key role commenting on the reporter's
performance and editing his copy prior to publication. Copy
editors have major responsibility for maintaining the
paper's personality, its continuity, and its sacred cows.

Routine judgements on newsmen's performance arise in two
ways: the daily news conferences of the chief editors and
regular bouts of daily 'tear-sheets' of the main news pages
marked up by the editor or managing editor. This is a
distinctive process of social control, which has been
examined by a number of scholars, most notably Warren
Breed.[5]While squabbles erupt on occasion and the odd
reporter quits in a huff and moves on, such events are not
often interpreted in terms of high principles. Being largely
implicit, the whole policy system seems almost invisible.

Academic observers seem surprised that practitioners do
not experience journalism as the predictable, value-ridden,
and routinized activity that sociologists have 'discovered'
it to be. But that is not every journalists' worklife.
Reporters often work alone, away from the office. They are
expected to use a great deal of initiative and imagination,
and they are forever trying to cope with strange and unusual
people and circumstances. Time is against them and nobody
but another reporter sympathises with their lot. The editors
charged with processing copy are quite different from such
reporters. Their hours are regular and worked in a
consensual atmosphere. The forms and deficiencies of local
and news agency copy are predictable, heading type spaces
and page size are inelastic and deadlines march on in
inexorable succession. They complain constantly about the
copy, the routine, and the bosses' herd of pet bovines.

NOTES TO CHAPTER FOUR

1. The Vertical Mosaic, Toronto: University of Toronto Press, 1965, 485.
2. 139.
3. In George Boyce, James Curran, and Pauline Wingate, eds., Newspaper History: from the 17th century to the present day, London: Constable, 1978, at 186.
4. Steven Chibnall, Law and Order News, London: Tavistock, 1977, xiii.
5. "Social Control in the Newsroom", Social Forces, vol.33 (1955) 328. See also: Bowers, D.R. "A Report on Activity by Publishers in Directing Newsroom Decisions", Journalism Quarterly, vol. 44, 1967, 50; Walter Gieber, "Across the Desk: A Study of 16 Telegraph Editors", Journalism Quarterly, Vol. 33, 423; Walter Gieber, "News is What Newspapermen Make It", in Lewis Anthony Dexter and David Manning White, People, Society and Mass Communications, New York: Free Press, 1964, 175, and David Manning White, "The Gatekeeper, A Case Study in the Selection of News", in Dexter and White, 160.

In allegorical time, all of Creation took six days and six nights. In our time, creating just one day's slice of life takes journalists somewhat longer. In place of a sense of humour and comparable imagination, network television substitutes a mixture of frenzy and more planning. Not surprisingly, the result is inferior. The mass media's daily versions of reality are less the product of spontaneous combustion captured on film and more the bastard offspring of nineteenth century journalism seduced by twentieth century commerce and technology. Impugning reputations this way, even metaphorically, calls for some examination of the circumstantial evidence, even if not the bloodlines.

As we turn from the newspaper version of today's reality, which it calls the news, to radio's version, and from there to television's version, we find they are all different. What is most striking is that all three media seem to be living in, or at least looking at, rather different political worlds. How and why are important questions.

Although they may appear similar because of their shared liberal outlooks, radio, newspapers, and television speak to us through different grammars and concepts. Some people call these specialised languages the ideologies of professions and occupations. The phrase 'technological bias' is more specific, seems somewhat less likely to be misunderstood, and so will be used here to refer to this phenomenon. As each new communications technology came on the scene, the people pushing it made almost identical claims. They hailed it as the ultimate means of improving man's direct experience of distant events freed from the distortions of any intermediary. Alas, each technological change or new communications institution has simply created new sets of golden images or stereotypes to stand for those things we cannot see, feel, or hear for ourselves. None of the media gives us the equivalent of direct personal experience.

Regular consumers of the mass media adapt easily and unconsciously to these ideological biases. Whole series of habits and perceptual assumptions are set in train by the simple act of picking up our regular daily paper to read. These comprehension routines Anthony Smith calls "accepting the special codes of the newspaper genre."[1] Depending on the newspaper's usual format, which is an important part of its 'personality', we expect to find on the front page the major piece of news from every field: international, national, local, financial, or sports. If the publication lacks this type of 'shop window' first page, we usually know where to find the different items. So too, we expect headline type to draw our attention to news stories and in the process we interpret the jargon and ignore their incompleteness. The relative sizes of headlines and stories combine with habits of display or makeup to convey other messages without our consciously working them out. We assume news stories will report events with detachment rather than partisanship. For the latter, and for other kinds of opinionated interpretation, we look to different parts of the newspaper. We do this even though, as Smith says, we know that:

Each sliver of the infinity of reality at which the reporter thrusts his attention reaches the reader through a haze of motives and intentions—those of the journalist, subject, editor, censor, printer, government—which are all the more insistent for being less evident.[2]

Clear distinctions between facts and comment are found naturally neither in private conversation nor in early journalism. Alongside the first newssheets of scandal and gossip there developed those specialising in the latest 'intelligences' from abroad which might be useful in business dealings. To establish the reliability of such information was essential to its commercial utility if one were to despatch goods for sale abroad or make similar commitments for purchase in hope of later resale. Journalists sought to ground their statements on what then passed for 'usually reliable sources', more often than not the assertions of government officials.

Speed began to vie with authority as a desirable element in news and the famous Jacob Reuter got a technological leg up on his news business rivals by using carrier pigeons. Another leap forward came with the invention of shorthand. Readers could be freed from dependence on the always challengeable paraphrasings of an official's speech or statement. His very words could be reproduced free of any intervention between speaker and reader. Smith calls this development the first of a "long series of journalistic techniques which at first seemed to promise the reader the complete recovery of some semblance of reality." Jacob Reuter's employment of pigeons in his foreign news service had reduced the news delay between major European centres from days to hours. The invention of the telegraph was even more significant. Its importance went beyond making long distance communications almost instantaneous. It made them two-way. For the first time, those with access to the system could check up on the alleged facts of far-off happenings.

Accelerating the pace of news communication affected
political institutions in a number of ways. Among them was
the slow conversion of foreign embassies from the primary
functions of specialised local newsgathering and diplomatic
negotiation to agencies whose prime purpose was
interpretation for the home authorities of the news they
already had. In domestic matters, the consequences were
striking. Metropolitan newspapers grew much better informed
about their own hinterlands and about the world as a whole.
Departmental prefects and regional governors of all kinds
lost their monopolies of timely information. With them they
lost most of their discretionary powers over local affairs
as rulers in the national capital tightened control over the
whole country. Centralised government became possible on a
much larger scale.

To the invention of railways and the telegraph was added
that of 'wireless telegraph' or radio broadcasting, which
extended the geographic range of these effects. Many of the
most important uses of the new technologies were stimulated
by the voracious demands of commerce for information about
price changes and similar 'hard facts' shorn of opinion. In
the positivist philosophy of the nineteenth century, both
businessmen and politicians were in no doubt that given the
facts they themselves could decide their real meaning.

If the elites of the Victorian age were excited by news
of marketplace economics and liberal politics, these matters
were neither institutionally conducted nor reported in ways
likely to interest the masses. The increases in literacy and
wage levels, however, brought millions into the newspaper
marketplaces. Very early on, the serialization of fiction
like Dickens' novels had demonstrated the much greater
popularity of personalised journalism compared to 'serious'
news. The latter gave way in the popular papers to that
combination of crime sensations, horrific disasters, sexual
scandal, comics, and other trivia known as 'yellow
journalism'. Somewhat purged by law and cleaned up, this
form of journalism is with us still in major metropolitan

centres. Modified a little more and given a dash of politics to pacify the regulators, the same genre of content has become the staple diet of commercial network TV news.

A variety of socio-psychological attempts have made to classify 'hard' and 'soft' news. One of the earliest is Wilburn Schramm's distinctions using the idea of reward for effort. 'Immediate reward' news gives immediate pleasure, it requires little concentration or effort, and it appeals to our emotions. The category includes news of crime and corruption, accidents and natural disaster, human foibles, and social quirks. Elements of conflict or notoriety, familiarity, prominence, mystery, or surprise are common. A sense of reader involvement or of immediate relevance may be promoted. In contrast, 'delayed reward' news postpones any such feelings. The benefits if any are longer range, or come as a sense of being more generally informed and prepared for the future. What importance the event has is in terms of the political or social system rather in terms of any one individual. 'Serious news' like politics, the economy, social problems, science, and education requires more conscious reader effort and often a greater sense of social duty in acquiring it. While reporters are customarily encouraged to work as many 'immediate reward' elements as possible into virtually all their writing, a reader's experience of copy as primarily one or the other type varies directly with educational level. Audience appeal is a major criterion of assessing newsworthiness and much referred to when newsmen attempt to justify decisions. Curious it is, then, to discover that, while print journalists know their paper's circulation and broadcasters know the advertising ratings for their programs, both groups know little or nothing more than that about their various audiences. Readership surveys and audience research come into being almost exclusively to promote the medium as a sales tool. Very little effort is put into discovering the audience's likes and dislikes about the mass medium's product for the guidance of the journalists charged with producing it.[3]

News Depends on the Medium

While audiences place quite different degrees of trust in the three major mass media, most seem blissfully unaware that industry and technological biases practically determine what each medium calls and presents as 'news'. By now, most news consumers have been socialised to go to one or the other channels for different things. To learn the bare facts of the most recent happenings, we look to radio news. To get a larger, detailed picture of the world's happenings over a longer period, we buy a daily newspaper. If we prefer to 'see for ourselves' what a few of those events looked like, we turn to a favoured television newsreader for an impressionistic reconstruction on film.

News was the invention of printer-journalists and their work provided the definitional framework for early broadcasters. While radio and television have profoundly affected their contents and presentation styles, newspapers remain to this day the only specialist information medium of the three. Their peculiar method of organising individual news reports originated in two late nineteenth century technical practices. That method is known as the 'inverted pyramid' style. It calls for jamming all the most important facts of a story into a brief first paragraph, with the next most important information in the second paragraph, and further data similarly ordered in subsequent paragraphs.

The 'inverted pyramid' construction persisted for many decades of daily newspaper practice and is disappearing from general use only now. Although not previously known to English literature, the form was admirably suited to the technical conditions of the telegraph and early newspaper printing processes. Telegraphy was expensive and in the early days its sending/receiving circuits were highly unreliable over sustained periods. Whatever the natural, chronological order, the most important event had to be communicated first. Explanatory details could follow later if money and the technical connection allowed.

Once the stories had been despatched from the scene and from the newsroom, they still had to be set in type and that brought into play the second important influence on the inverted pyramid style of presentation. Although words were first pieced together letter by letter, the invention of the 'linotype' machine meant they could be cast from moulds, line by line, to be arranged in columns within individual iron frames the size of a page. When any one story proved too long to fit physically into its place within the page frame, and time was pressing, the last few lines of type in the story could be thrown away. So long as the top-heavy inverted pyramid style of writing had been used, the abbreviated story would lose little of importance. The system was mechanically convenient. It saved time and expense in the technical process and, from a news point of view, it made it much easier to provide space for late news items or important additions to stories put into type earlier. The effect on content was fairly predictable for newspaper personnel—even if not for the readers. Long after technical changes made the inverted pyramid no longer necessary, journalists continued to use this unusual method of conveying information, often through sheer habit and disinclination to change their literary style. More than reader comprehension was affected. The combination of emphasis on 'hard facts' that could be confirmed, a telegraphic news style, and composing room convenience and economy brought us a definition and type of daily news that was fragmented and episodic, ahistorical, superficial, and primarily focussed on events with a brief lifespan.

Whatever their deficiencies, as information media newspapers have a unique claim to comprehensiveness. That quality developed as something of a side effect of their origins as make-work for printers. From their earliest days newspapers offered two types of information—news/comment and advertising—although they were not always distinguished from each other, and both soon came in greater quantities as demand was stimulated. The consequences are with us today.

Wherever retailers great or small wish to buy their usual acres of printed columns of advertising, great tracts of intervening white space are created. If only to keep the ads from rubbing together, but certainly in order to decoy our attention closer to them, news and editorial matter of every flavour and size is created. Journalists, of course, have a different rationale for their efforts and the provision of an all-inclusive and timely account of major events is a major part of it. Comprehensiveness of news reporting was and is the newspaper's strongest claim to the informed citizen's patronage. To avoid discouraging the dilettante in public affairs, lighter, more entertaining fare is added to the basic menu of politics and economics.

Comprehensiveness is a feature not only of nationally distributed newspapers but of the hundreds of dailies that are locally-oriented both in geographic fact and service ambition. Wide coverage meets the needs of the voracious consumer of news, true, but its functions go further. It partially satisfies the hundreds of interests and pressure groups, commands the attention of the mighty, and manages to offer something for everyone. Printed information can be taken at individual speeds, promotes comparisons, allows complete audience freedom of selection, can provide large amounts of detail (such as budget tax tables), and is readily available for rereading or reference. The printed form confers a certain aura of authority as well, although this is highly culturedependent. With such advantages, the concern governments have had to control printing may be understandable.

Newspapers have considerable ability to indicate the comparative importance of today's flow of news and of the various items in it. Although advertising broadly decides the size of the 'news-hole', the manufacturing technology makes it easy to expand or contract editorial space as events dictate. Even greater flexibility arises from the use of different typefaces, photography, artwork, and other makeup techniques to give the reader precise visual signals of the relative newsworthiness of different stories. With access, even outsiders with low technical skills can use the medium to put across a message as is demonstrated by the letters to the editor columns. The lack of licensing means managements need have comparatively little concern about prohibiting the expression of a variety of partisan opinions in their news and opinion columns.

Speed in bearing the latest tidings was for long the proud boast of all dailies. Speed was the life and breath of competition between them. Two changes put an end to this speed emphasis: the proliferation of cheap, portable radios, and the city-by-city elimination of competition between newspaper businesses. The boom in television put central city newspapers under tougher financial pressure than most had faced during this century. Their costs were mounting rapidly, their plants were obsolete, and their circulations were plummeting. As readership fell off, so did advertising. Deserting the dailies in droves, retailers were themselves desperate to fathom and to win favour with the glamorous and apparently more effective upstart that was television. As bankruptcy and mergers swallowed up traditional rivals, liberals bemoaned the terrible things that were bound to follow. What happened in fact was often not what had been forecast. In the fight for economic life (even where there were no rival newspapers), the survivors underwent personality changes by the hundreds. After brief attempts to expand their photographic coverage as a partial 'answer' to TV, they abandoned the tabloid-style journalism that many had once wielded as their chief battle weapon in the old circulation wars. It was impossible to have the big news first (except for the rare 'scoop'). Once freed from the frantic haste that had marked every production stages, editors began to stress reliability instead. 'Radio might get it first but we'll be the ones to get it right' became the symbolic battle cry. Radio, being competitive within its own industry, often didn't dare take time to check facts and newspapers found a comparative advantage in the news field.

Many have commented on the changes they think reduced competition between dailies have made in newspaper content and practice. The comments have nearly always been highly critical—and based on hypothetical rather than real situations. Too many commentators stressed the theoretical reduction in diversity and, when they did remember previous situations, they usually thought only of the liveliness and the contention of rival party viewpoints fiercely put. They did not notice the general reduction of partisanship and the adoption of more 'common carrier' or public service attitudes. These changes—largely since the second world war—opened up both the news columns and the opinion pages to the publication of highly diverse views. The foibles of human nature make it unlikely that even conscientious scholars would notice, let alone document, performance improvements in newspapers.

The Kent Commission seemed aware of the problems in assessing monopoly situations when it reported on the Canadian situation late in 1981. Despite a three million dollar research budget, it produced little reliable evidence on what differences reduced competition makes in the content of surviving 'monopoly' newspapers. The best it produced in its main report were average figures on newspaper expenditures on editorial functions and the relative rankings of different newspapers. The figures could be used to 'prove' almost any case one wished—for or against multiple newspaper organisations.

Radio Picks Up Speed

If speed was abandoned as a general newspaper objective, it was joyfully exploited by radio news. That, however, was not really widespread until after the second world war. State broadcasting monopolies (where they existed), newspaper ownership of the major news agencies, and the dominant conception of radio as commercial entertainment combined to inhibit its growth as an important news medium. In this field radio enjoys several major advantages. The first is immediacy. Where newspapers are produced in batches, radio programming is continuous in production form and can shift much more rapidly to news information than can either of its rival media. The character of both its technology and its economic support adds to rather than detracts from radio's flexibility. From the technical or reproduction perspective, whether the sound is music and voice or paid advertising is immaterial; all are very similar sound waves and take no more personnel or resources to broadcast. An emphasis on selling commercial spots of thirty or sixty seconds rather than on sponsorship of whole program blocks facilitates 'magazine' programming that incorporates broadcasting news bulletins every hour or even more frequently. When it came on a big scale, radio news killed newspaper 'extras' except as promotional gimmicks.

News ages and becomes 'olds' faster on radio than with the other media. The emphasis on immediacy amounts to an occupational obsession. It is evident in many ways and is reflected in the infection of the airwaves by inane phrases and cliches like 'the very, very latest developments', 'up to the minute and up to the second news', and, 'this is Station X-Y-Z, your NOW News station'. The immediacy obsession is a hangover from commercial radio's desperate (and successful) attempts to regain lost ground and find a new role after the spread of television. The pressure of news competition within the industry led radio to repeat and even to emphasize many of the worst features of competitive newspapering. Ahistoricity and lack of context may be only the slightest of these. So great is the urge to convey the latest developments that unless you have been listening to the radio fairly constantly you may be left completely mystified about the original situation which led to 'the latest developments'.

The start of radio news broadcasting was marked by great excitement about its verisimilitude, its power to let people hear with their own ears. Citizens could hear and judge politicians for themselves free of distortions introduced by journalists. And so it has proved, but to a far lesser extent than had been anticipated. A number of politicians developed considerable abilities in using radio. Franklin Delano Roosevelt and Adolf Hitler were two of the best-known public figures who exploited the power of radio effectively. There were many others, especially in the religio-political field like Father Coughlin and William Aberhart. Few, however, were the traditional politicians whom radio broadcasters or audiences could, or would, tolerate in the oratorical lengths to which most were accustomed. The broadcasting of legislative debates was much discussed at one time as well but not until efficient and cheap tape recording became possible were politicians' voices generally heard on radio news. The use of 'news summaries', of course, put the reporter-mediator back into the scene.

Auditory impact is a major criterion of newsworthiness for radio. Its news personnel remain solidly devoted to the exploitation of something called 'actuality sound'—the voices of participants and ambient noise from the scene. Delegates are interviewed amidst the convention hubbub, the police sergeant against the noise of the Liverpool riot, and firefighters with flames crackling in the background. Such is the acme of 'good radio'. Items incorporating 'actuality sound' have almost infinitely better chances of making the newscast lineup than do those without. While most political offices content themselves with bushels of printed 'news releases'—which make little impression in radio newsrooms, the Ontario government showed during the seventies what those who understand the media can achieve. Every day they made their own 'actuality tapes' of this cabinet minister or that explaining the cabinet's proposals, policies, and projects and sent them to all major radio outlets. They blanketed the opposition for months on end. Not only was the government supplying voice material but it was in the most appropriate shapes and sizes: 15, 30, and 60-second snippets which were easy to use to liven up political items.

Simplicity and brevity are other keynotes in radio. Complex stories simply cannot be told, because listeners usually pay scant heed and, in any case, they cannot go back to clarify or amplify points they may have missed. One consequence is a preference for action, for declarative rather than conditional statements, and for point and counterpoint presentations. Subtlety, humour, sarcasm, and many other forms of modulating political discourse have little or no place in radio news coverage. Spectacles formed the public substance of imperial politics in some eras but their modern manifestations are not a favourite radio form. It is reporting play by play action within the hockey rink or on the football field, where immediacy and 'actuality sound' combine, that radio newscasters are happiest if visual action must be described.

As an information medium, radio is more pervasive than most. Although driven from the living room by the television set (except for music purposes), radio dominates other rooms of the house, plays an increasing role in automobile commuting, and invades public places like beaches, football stands, and even what lovers' lanes remain. Its potential audience at any one time is enormously enhanced by the low demands it puts on its listeners. By comparison, newspapers demandnot only almost total involvement from its consumer-readers but a high degree of skill as well. As a form of auditory wallpaper, radio is a constant companion to millions, one capable of disseminating simple, direct messages to wide and dispersed audiences at any time.

TV: Newsreels in a Box

As location sound is the distinguishing characteristic of radio news, so 'talking pictures' are to television. Where newspapers were mainly in the business of reporting news, television news grew up, in Edward R. Murrow's phrase, "as an incompatible combination of show business, advertising, and news." A major influence was the newsreel, which was developed during the thirties to add to the entertainment offered in film theatres. Narrated in a breathless voice to convey some sense of immediacy, the newsreels concentrated on dramatic presentation of visual spectacles which could be shown for weeks after the event was over. The burning of the Hindenburg, thousands of storm troopers in splendid martial arrays at Nuremberg, and the dive-bombing of refugees during the Spanish Civil War were all newsreel episodes which might well have been proudly featured on network television news broadcasts forty years later. A similar point was made bluntly by Reuven Frank, then executive editor of NBC Evening News, in a 1961 staff memo: "the highest power of television journalism is not in the transmission of information but in the transmission of experience...joy, sorrow, shock, fear, these are the stuff of news."[4]He rejected the idea, then common in British television but soon to disappear, that television should be expected to reproduce newspaper stories on film.

Neither the immediacy of radio nor the priorities of print journalism were adopted as the criteria of television newsworthiness. Robin Day, one of the earliest British television personality newscasters, reported in 1961:

We quickly learned how television affects the selection and arrangement of news. The fact of yesterday's air disaster may no longer be top news tonight--but the first film of the scene may well merit first place in this evening's television news.[5]

The extent to which the visually exciting dominates the significant and socially important is debated by defenders of the industry and its critics. Practices vary considerably. At times, the BBC's major stories seemed to reflect the 'quality' papers' front page headlines. But this reflection of newspaper news values is much weaker than it was ten years ago. Similarly, the Canadian Broadcasting Corporation's major television news lineup sometimes looked much like that of the **Globe and Mail** of Toronto, the headquarters of CBC News; at other times only two or three leading items were the same. The major commercial networks showed even less agreement in news judgement with comparable newspapers even though both print and television journalists tend to work in 'batch production' fashion. Some, of course, would debate the fairness of the significance test implied by the comparison. While daily papers and the news agencies which depend on them provide the starting point for network TV newsroom, the consensus displayed by rival print media does not extend to the U.S. broadcasting networks. Edward Jay Epstein monitored the main evening newscasts of the three networks over a six-week period during the seventies. Of the 431 filmed stories shown, only 13 per cent (57 items) appeared on all three networks, and only 97 items were shown on two networks. Newsworthiness here depended on whether visual material was available and dramatic enough. Epstein's findings on immediacy are also worth noting:

> A four month analysis of the logs of the NBC Evening News showed that 47 per cent of the news film depicted events on the day they occurred, while 36 per cent of the news film was more than two days old, and 13 per cent was more than a week old. None of the news stories during that period were live, and on some days as much as 70 per cent of the filmed news was more than a day old. A similar proportion of news film on the CBS and ABC Evening News was also delayed.[6]

Newsfilm and videotape that appears fresh may look that way because TV uses a series of situational cliches to give that impression. "The rain-soaked industrial or political correspondent stands outside TUC Headquarters or No. 10 Downing Street and assures us that negotiations are going on at that very moment." Schlesinger's BBC study goes on:

> At this point, when X tells us that he is at a particular spot, and if he has a television [Outside Broadcasting] unit, actually shows that he is there, we enter the realms of the absurd. But it is an absurdity which is broadcasting's own.[7]

Technical tricks are often used to heighten the illusion of immediacy. That staff reporters are actually on the scene may be suggested visually by putting them in studios with library film or videotape of the distant location projected behind them. Or the former sound track is wiped clean and a staff correspondent's voice is used as 'voice over' reading scripts drafted from topical wire despatches.

Most television news is neither spontaneous nor unexpected. It is planned. While news programs are cheaper to produce than almost any other type of television content, network directors seem to keep news directors on a very tight financial string. The constant bedevilment about expense and efficiency inhibits imagination and promotes conservatism and tight control. Technical advances in telephone networks, microwave systems, and satellite communications have made a very high degree of immediacy possible but cost considerations have been the controlling factors. Only the most extraordinary events or those long planned and guaranteed to produce huge audiences (like a royal wedding) warrant immediate transmission over any distance. The advent of a few imaginative TV news programs early in the eighties showed that large audiences could be won, that money could be made, and that, maybe, TV news might grow into something more than a poor cousin but general reform is still to come.

The careful deployment of camera crews many days or even weeks in advance originated in the extreme difficulty of shooting on-the-scene or away from the studio in the early days of television. The clumsiness of the equipment made elaborate preparations absolutely essential. The habits of mind fixed in place at that time die hard--even though the possibilities have been revolutionised by modern 'creepy-peepie' (portable) video cameras and the like. Schlesinger's study of BBC news in the seventies reported that 95 per cent of advance diary arrangements were held right through to the day of shooting and that 70 per cent of the items shot were broadcast. The evidence suggests that once a TV camera crew

has been assigned, an event is almost bound to make news—
whether anything significant really happens there or not. In
the United States, Epstein found the National Broadcasting
Corporation, "which advertises itself as the largest news
organisation in the world" used ten crews stationed in five
cities as the basis of its "full coverage" of the entire
United States. In one five month period, the Canadian system
used even fewer crews to 'cover' an equally huge country. To
create an illusion of greater coverage, a CBC news producer
had a map of Canada backprojected in a studio with locating
dots lighting up in turn as an announcer's script reported
news squibs from smaller cities and towns. (Only after
several years did they get around to using more or less
'timeless' bits of film/tape to illustrate the places where
the alleged news was taking place.)

Much network television coverage comes from 'news
opportunities'—events specially staged for the mass media.
These are press conferences, interviews, briefings, and
ceremonies that are specially staged to provide prominent
people with television or photographic coverage. Daniel
Boorstin has aptly labelled these 'pseudoevents'. Other TV
news items may be more genuine in origin but they are no
less well-planned and anticipated: commission hearings in
Canada, senatorial investigations and criminal trials in the
United States, and 'doorstepping' on labour negotiations in
Britain or Australia. Even events open to the public and
press are seldom recorded live. That takes time. Instead,
the camera crew takes participants outside the legislative
chamber to be asked questions that are edited into a
newly-created event and telecast in place of the original.

Even when permitted and technically possible,
broadcasting live and directly from the scene is unpopular
with many television news producers. The content is too
uncontrollable. The networks and the producers, after all,
have their particular operating rules and styles to be
imposed on the content. The NBC memo by Reuven Frank
illustrates the point:

Every news story should, without any sacrifice of probity or responsibility, display the attributes of fiction or drama. It should have structure and conflict, problem and denouement, rising action and falling action, a beginning, a middle and an end. These are not only the essentials of drama; they are the essentials of narrative. [8]

The consequence of these practices is that the natural or historical order is seldom the broadcast order of presentation, even for specially staged affairs. Standing in opposition to the notion of providing live coverage is the argument suggested by Robert MacNeil in his book, The People Machine.[9]'Untrained witnesses miss significant details: journalists are witnesses trained to recognise what is significant in a series of events.' He goes on to say that only reflection after the event is over can yield the significance of what went on. Against this point stands the primary claim television news makes for its credibility: viewers 'seeing' for themselves without intermediaries.

The standards of excellence an occupation or profession uses may be revealed in those the group uses in singling out fellow practitioners for commendation or annual awards. David L. Altheide has reported those he found in American broadcast journalism as represented by the Radio-Television News Directors' Association.[10]Timeliness and accuracy were not high among the standards applied. What counted was sophistication of technique and technical skill. Why? Among other reasons suggested is that news producers had only a layman's understanding of the substance of the news; they were incapable of informed judgements about politics, economics, scientific discoveries, and so on. No wonder, then, that 'virtually nothing was said about substantive errors, misinterpretations, and the like.' But much was said about the way equipment was handled, the quality of editing and scripts, clever use of graphics, and strategies of presentation. These were the qualities of 'good television news'.

Pictures in Our Heads

Political image-making, or stereotyping, masquerades as a new phenomenon but it is not. Half a century ago, Walter Lippmann noted that some stereotyping was essential to nearly all communication. Journalism, however, had become so fond of creating and using such 'pictures in our heads', he warned, that it could even imperil responsible government. Today stereotyping gives promise of being the single most widely used shortcuts of political reporting. Television, the most visual of all media, has brought it to full flower.

Potentially, at least, print and radio reporters can draw on the whole English vocabulary to make verbal statements just as particular or abstract and generalised as necessary. Precision is relatively easy. Television, in contrast, is enormously dependent on symbolic representation. The destruction of a primitive hut and one widowed mother weeping is a scene that might represent any number of events. Used several times successively in the same way and it becomes television's way of representing a feature of the war in Vietnam. Neither the complexities of that war nor its general implications could possibly be shown visually. Oversimplification and symbolic representation was all that television could do. Social, political, and economic developments of all kinds must be tackled on television news and in visual forms. How can it be done? Producers use iconic cliches, stylized scenes fixed into 'pictures in our heads', images. One housewife's shopping basket and a ringing cash register symbolize inflation. Two views of widely separated automobile crashes tell us 'Scores die as holidayers jam vacation routes'. One well-dressed politician and a grizzled member of the miners' union voting tells us that 'Fate of government hangs in balance as nation votes'.

Journalists often take pride in not having an expert's knowledge of the things they report. Their interviewing techniques and outsider's approach allows them to perform as expert interpreters to the public. They translate complex situations and events 'down to the working man's level', making common sense interpretations where they can and relieving the reader of further concern about the matter. The simpler and more visual the explanation sought the greater the burden thrown on to conventional interpretations and familiar images.

As conventional interpretations, stereotypes are highly convenient tools for journalists working under pressure of deadlines. Assignment editors tell their camera crews what pictures to come back with—before leaving the office. Margaret Thatcher must be caught in shrewish disagreement with a unionist, Ronald Reagan acting tough, and Pierre Trudeau being either arrogant or petulant.

When governments change taxes, reduce social allowances, subsidise shipbuilding or aircraft production, the mass media try to personalise the story. They usually try to do this by seeking out reactions from members of the public. Local stations may use a dozen people from the local service area. Network television, however, is much more restricted and its examples many fewer. One person must stand for millions. TV news viewers know they are only watching individuals. If, however, time after time, foul-mouthed and slovenly youths are picked to speak for students, well-educated businessmen are heard giving the taxpayer's reaction, and blacks or Indians or people with foreign accents are shown as welfare recipients, powerful, generalised images become fixed in the public unconscious. Good metaphors, images that convey ideas swiftly and succinctly, are valued in all forms of communication. The hardest of all to find or invent are visual ones in the field of politics. Once found, and commended by network executives, television news soon overuses particular images and adds them to its store of handy stereotypes. When first used, such images do convey a little information. Repeated use, however, changes the stereotype in something that ends up transmitting a whole interpretative framework.

Reporters for all mass media learn to see and classify the world in terms of the established images. In his study of television news, Edward Jay Epstein devotes a full chapter to the stereotypes that dominated American network reporting at the time. These images included California Bizarre, Europe in turmoil, Vietnam war as hardware and isolated actions, Congress as institutionalised detective agent, the mystique of the presidency (a deliberate contrivance of White House staff), and apocalypse on the campus now! All of these images have made their way into the TV news of other English-speaking countries as well.

While using stereotypes does help reporters to make the strange and unintelligible a little easier to understand, both creator and consumer of news run serious risks. First, the reader may never see anything new. As Chibnall observes:

...fresh thought about new phenomena becomes unnecessary, they merely require locating within the existing frameworks of press ideology and to this end the newspapers help their readers by supplying 'cues' and 'signs' for correct identification and location. [11]

Second, the journalist's news judgement may fall victim to his own image-mongering. An Illustrated Classics comic book does provide acquaintance of a type but it cannot substitute for knowledge of the masterworks. Reporters who deceive themselves about the extent of their own knowledge mislead us more than do those who know the extent of their ignorance. Third, misrepresentations and outright lies that seem to confirm accepted images are much more likely to be published and circulated than they are to be carefully investigated. David L. Altheide and Robert P. Snow have amply demonstrated this point with their study of how the U.S. official, Bert Lance, was hounded from office in 1977.[12]Fourth, while stereotypes begin life as half-truths at best, and sometimes not that at all, the expectations they set up may lead them to become self-fulfilling, at least in the eyes of the mass media and their audiences.

One of the best cases to illustrates how stereotyping works in the news business comes from Britain. There, James D. Halloran and associates reported in 1970 on a detailed study they had made of the whole course of preparation, data gathering, and reporting techniques that the British mass media employed for the 1968 anti-war march in London. During the fifties, Britain had had dozens of huge anti-nuclear protest demonstrations. While most had resulted in very little violence, they left a lingering impression of extremism. Early in the runup to the 1968 affair, the national newpapers evidenced uncertainty and differences of opinion on what the demonstration would 'mean'. Eventually, Halloran reports, "the newspapers defined the event as likely to be a violent confrontation of the forces of law and order (as represented by the police) and the forces of anarchy (as represented by the radical groups participating)." Although it too turned out to be a generally non-violent affair, the confrontationist image persisted and coloured most of all the subsequent reporting.

Media Pictures of Politics

The picture of the world of politics presented in newspapers is much more detailed than that in the broadcast media. While not as exciting, it is more comprehensive. In reporting budget estimates and similar financial affairs, newspapers are at their best and television and radio at their worst. Print media are ideal for presentation of figures and graphs. Historical comparisons often abound because print makes for easy reader reference, for easy institutional storage, and for easy retrieval as well. Reference libraries for TV news are difficult to organise, expensive, seldom found, and seldom used. Fear of the regulators together with the low visual qualities available leads television to present material like government budgets and new legislative proposals either naively and very cursorily, or by means of a **pas de deux** of public personalities.

Politicians   provide   a   free   cast   of   performers   for
broadcast news producers. The minister comes on the screen,
is challenged to say what it is all about in 45 seconds or
less, and then is replaced in perfect point and counterpoint
by the leading opposition critic who does an equally terse
job. Whether such summaries can be intelligible or accurate
is   beside   the   point.   That   there   could   be   numerous,
legitimate criticisms is something only newspapers can take
into   account.   Broadcasters   feel   obliged   to   balance   one
government spokesman with one opposition member, not because
of the news but, because of public relations reasons.

In its liberal, night watchman version, politics is not
about taking action, but about winning general agreement
prior to governments doing something. The idea of talk,
talk, talk was built into parliamentary government from its
very beginnings. Our politics is all about ideas, and often
subtle and complicated ones. Where newspapers were virtually
invented to serve the needs of those discussing public
affairs, broadcasting was not.

The discursiveness so characteristic of politics makes it
poor   fodder   for   television.   Despite   the   hopes   of
broadcasting's pioneers, that medium came to institutional
maturity primarily for purposes of commercial entertainment.
Small wonder, then, that its operational values are those of
mass entertainment: romantic narrative, dramatic action, and
pop star adulation. No wonder either that TV political news
always exaggerates physical actions.

Because they represent organised action, arranged and
announced in advance, events like strike pickets and
demonstrations play a much bigger role in the TV version of
political news than in any 'reality'. Cameras always close
in to show action: people shouting slogans, milling about,
and waving signs. Any slight scuffle will merit far more
attention than a dozen serious speeches. The script will
spend more time telling what the police are doing than what
the issues seem to be and why.[13]If all it has to offer is

pictures of action, an industrial dispute will often not figure at all in a newspaper's reconstruction of the day's events. All journalists, though, like the excitement of conflict and one incident on the picket lines is more likely to make news in all three mass media than ten labour-management agreements at the negotiating table.

The degree to which political news is reported objectively (in journalism's terms) varies according to its type. Good news, like that of governments lifting restrictions or increasing benefits, tends to be reported with more accuracy than bad news. 'Soft news' of humanistic developments, societal change, and public policies toward the arts not only gives way in space and time priority but is reported less completely than hard news. Warren Breed has reported that individuals or groups attacking sacred cows like progress, patriotism, family relationships, and elite groups tend to receive poor coverage. He and other scholars have also observed that objectivity is found less often in reporting news that tends to disrupt the stability of small communities. Their research led the same scholars to conclude that the willingness of the mass media to deal with controversies that threaten community cohesion and integrity is inversely proportional to the geographic proximity of the issue.[14]

Events and developments in public affairs vary in their newsworthiness in terms that are more relative than absolute. The ability to reflect this depends in part on the medium. To see how it happens, watch for a slow news day. The occasion when little or nothing seems to be happening is the bane of all journalists. The weeks of slow news days that mark the summer give rise to 'the silly season'. That is when we have report after report of dogs biting men, flying saucers, frying eggs on sidewalks, and other 'human interest' stories. Reporters go around desperately trying to find public figures who can be irritated into saying something provocative or foolish, and editors try anxiously to find lead items for their front pages or first broadcast story. How much distortion results from the news creation processes depends very much on the medium. A few newspapers have a 'personality' or makeup style that dictates puffing up one or two stories, no matter how weak, to make them seem suitable for a prescribed headline display. Tabloid or half-size newspapers are more likely than most to do this. Most, however, match headline type to story newsworthiness.

However wide or subtle the variations made possible by the technology, the result in news display encourages readers to infer a certain set of priorities for their society. Newspapers, as we have seen, rank politics relatively high. The priorities that news ordering suggests are not those of government, but of the press as an institution. Different inferences about politics and its components might be drawn from the broadcast media.

In contrast to newspapers, radio and television have difficulty in suggesting orders of importance for their stories. On very big news days, the whole broadcast may be devoted to only three or four important events, but producers dislike the practice. The half-hour network newscast carries no more information than one front page of a newspaper like the **New York Times** and TV producers want to use the time they have to offer something for everybody. Most television viewers have little patience with politics unless offered well spiced. On the slow news days, though, even politics will do and changes in public affairs or errors in judgements, which might be ignored on most news days, may well get extended treatment with greater public attention in consequence. The Conservative government elected in Canada in 1979 might well have survived much longer than nine months had it not been for several minor incidents that got greater-than-normal TV attention during the slow news days of the summer. How many scandals were exposed, political reputations made and ruined, or policy campaigns disrupted because the irregular flow of events distorts news values we can never know.

Special occasions aside, crime and deviance do not constitute part of our 'normal' political picture of the world. They should, if only because the maintenance of civil order is said by Hobbes and his many followers to be the primary duty of the state. Alternatively, if politics is about 'the good life', then criminality indicates the relative success of public policies. The definition and official handling of deviance points to the various weights that a community attaches to values like personal security, sanctity of property, social amenity, equality of treatment, and group integrity. The importance given to each value adds up to a major part of the political culture. Close analyses of the treatment of social deviance would enable us to fill in some more of the features in the mass media pictures of politics.

Crime reporting engages the attention of the various media in varying degrees. We can only guess at the different nuances this gives to their pictures of the political world.

'Siren car news' represents the major focus of local radio broadcasting. Superficial stories about the latest holdup or smash-and-grab raid told in a breathless voice help to maintain the industry's stress on immediacy. Punctuating these reports with those of prison terms imposed adds a touch of gravity. News items like these are easy and inexpensive to gather. To go much further would strain the resources of most radio newsrooms without adding much. The actuality sound opportunities are limited and the usual brevity of radio reporting would also mean running unacceptable risks of trouble with the trial courts. The reporting that is done would seem, inevitably, to portray a world in which the values of the sober majority of citizens are under constant threat by the lawless. Apart from the broadcasters', the only 'real world' voices we hear are those of occasional victims and the ever-present authorities. Whatever the overall balance of reports, radio's picture owes more to Hobbes and Hogarth than to the pastoral painters.

Network broadcasting devotes less attention to reporting crime than to fictionalizing it. Generally, network news prefers criminal events of a high order: elite sums of money, high status individuals, or narcotics on an equally large scale. Occasionally, official statistics and authoritative spokesmen will permit some large or small number of incidents to be cobbled together into a 'crime wave'. The shortage of continuing picture opportunities makes these crime waves notoriously short lived. Whatever the offence to 'public decency and morals', television prefers to deal with it at the time of trial and judgement. That point in the life cycle has the double advantage of being easily predicted for assignment diaries (making camera work simple to arrange), and it minimises the potential trouble from judges and lawyers.

Overall, if one were to judge from network television news, the average citizen need worry very little about most forms of crime; they take place outside his ken. But one clearly must make that judgement on the basis of television news of social deviance. Crime and violence provide the basic and very substantial fare for consumers of television drama and entertainment. Portraying crime as a major part of social life and in almost entirely fictional terms must have significant implications for the viewers' impressionistic picture of the civic system. Unfortunately we do not know what they are.

Surveillance reporting of criminality and its prosecution on a routine basis is regularly found only in newspapers. Their relative freedom from extreme pressures of time, technical preparation and staff numbers makes them better placed than the broadcast media to set social deviance within particular perspectives. Chibnall's British newspaper study provides a good overview of crime reporting as a showcase of the medium's ideas of the good, the bad, and the ugly. The pictures are all of stark contrasts. In the columns of law and order news, morality comes across with very few shadings of grey. To quote Chibnall: 'Heterogeneity

and diversity of meaning are concealed by a reporting
technique which continually projects reality in the same
form of binary opposition, particularly, 'good threatened by
evil' and 'order threatened by chaos'.'[15]The occupational
bias for humanising the news so that all can follow and
identify with it is exploited in the cops-and-robbers
approach. Simple explanations of life are preferred.
Sometimes they appear in abstract form. Moral decline or the
evil of violence are the roots of social deviance. At other
times human agencies are blamed: the mafia, a criminal
mastermind, or communist subversives. But always, whether
they stand as social interpretations or excuses for
institutional failure, the explanations are simple, all
embracing, and almost unchallengeable.

The attention newspapers give to law and order news
depends on the publication's self-image and on management's
conception of the audience to be reached. Frequently they
add up to the same thing, but not invariably. Whatever that
combination adds up to and despite the occupation's
professional cynicism, most dailies are humanist in staff
perspective and middle class in the views they project.
Chibnall calls newspaper ideology 'profoundly liberal'.
Fortunately he tells us what he means. We live in a
pluralist society, suspicious of absolute truths but
genuinely devoted to achieving justice and other common
goals. Legitimate debate is about the nature of consensus
and the best means of incorporating it into gradualist
reform. The latter is most likely to be achieved through the
established agencies which, with all their limitations,
remain devoted to liberal values. While there is good and
bad in most people, there are a few misguided persons who,
by their own selfish actions, place themselves beyond the
pale. In the eyes of the reporter serious crime is highly
individualist rather than systemic, and episodic rather than
historically situated. While more work is needed in the
areas, Chibnall's observations confirm those of other
observers and seem generally reliable.

All three mass media impart to the world of politics very much more structure and rationality than is exists naturally. John G. Diefenbaker, a prime minister of Canada, once started complaining bitterly that the press did not report his speeches accurately. Infuriated, Ottawa reporters began doing just that, reporting his speeches word for word, stumble by stumble, and grammatical error by error. Although a great orator on the stump, Diefenbaker was the despair of parliamentary shorthand reporters and the press was soon revealing to all and sundry the good reasons for their difficulty. After a few days of punishingly accurate reports, Diefenbaker called a truce. The press went back to its occupational habit of selecting, ordering, and improving the literary form of public speeches.

The reportorial practice of improving on reality is encouraged by editors who judge speeches and actions 'that make sense' to be more newsworthy than those that do not. Radio reporters use more selection processes to give reality a better shape. In seeking 'actuality sound' for a news report, they choose the articulate over the inarticulate speaker almost regardless of the degree of involvement or responsibility. As spokesmen , they seek people with pleasant voices in preference to those with better information or greater authority. The parallels in television news will be obvious. News editors everywhere bring more order out of politica confusion than do all the committee chairmen in the world put together.

What are the implications of representing the political scene as more ordered than it is? The question is hard to answer. The process may confer undeserved dignity and security on the powers-that-be. It probably makes liberal institutions look less human than they are and therefore less representative. (It may even put off an 'inevitable' collapse or the revolution of sanity.) According to the press, our society is neither terribly complicated nor backward looking, but it is 'progressive'. There is a great deal of patterning to social events and although history may

not be all that relevant we can safely rely on a few
familiar images and stereotypes to reduce the novel to the
understandable. Above all, our life is individualist and our
interests personality-oriented. Authorities are only human
too but they generally do their best for us. Systematic
dissent is unusual. Crime and other deviance is the work of
a few troubled individuals who, having rejected the chance
they once had, do not deserve much consideration by the
majority. Such is the picture of life that is most easily
inferred from the mass media.

One element remains to complete this sketch of the
political world in the mass media: elections. Even though
they usually decide the who rather than the what of public
affairs, elections and politics are almost synonymous for
some people. That impression comes in part from early
socialisation into our civic duties. A large measure also
results from general elections being so intrusive and so
disruptive of our mass media habits. Even the most apathetic
citizen cannot escape being made aware of general elections.
Newspapers have always gloried in reporting the battle for
votes. So blatantly partisan were their accounts in early
days that scholars devised many varieties of content
analysis to provide 'scientific proof' of electoral bias.
While modern analyses are often sophisticated in their
manipulation of statistics, the 'proofs' produced depend
critically on the definitions of bias that are adopted.

Despite important improvement in our descriptive ability,
scholarly disputes over categorising value inclinations are
many and complex. As a reliable technique, scientific
content analysis remains outside the competence of most of
those who attempt it. In the meantime, the original subject
has been changing and the area of concern broadened. With a
few notorious exceptions most newspapers have adopted news
agency standards of objectivity for reporting election
campaigns. Whether the readers notice or not, most papers
profess to reserve partisanship for their leading editorial
articles and opinion columnists. Many will carry columnists

openly supporting the election of a different party. The rise of television to election prominence brings new concerns. Very few social scientists have been trained in 'reading' the grammar and vocabulary of this new medium and earlier problems and disappointments seriously inhibited the development of reliable television content analysis. General agreement is lacking on techniques which will even describe televised content adequately. Despite the claims made by the many election consultants even the most scientific analysis of content tells us nothing by itself about viewer effects.

Newspaper pictures of elections are in line with general would expect from the earlier discussion of politics in the mass media. One important difference should be noted. Both in law and in real life, a general election consists of whole series of individual contests. Party leaders go about the country trying to help local candidates. Without the mass media show there would be no national campaign. It is the collection and juxtapositioning of individual reports that constitutes the national political campaign. What does it look like? In one careful study,21 major newspapers were analysed on 13 sample dates. They published a total of 1,940 articles about the campaign, an average of seven per issue. Almost four-fifths of the stories printed were about national events and they were chiefly concerned with the national leaders' doings and sayings. The study's authors observed: "It is clear that the leaders' tours and the the speeches that are made during them are the primary source of news that is reported to the public."[16]   Western election laws usually stress that citizens vote for individuals, most of whom represent particular districts. But in the study reported, only 15 per cent of the items even referred to people other than the party leaders. News photographs published in the survey periods favoured local campaigns somewhat more (29 per cent) but more than half were of leaders and their families with another 16 per cent devoted to other prominent national party leaders.

NOTES TO CHAPTER FIVE

1. "The long road to objectivity and back again: the kinds of truth we get in journalism," Boyce & Curran, 153.

2. Ibid., p.154.

3. See especially investigations on this point by Steve Chibnall, Law and Order News, London: Tavistock, 1977. Edward Jay Epstein, News from Nowhere, New York: Vintage, 1974, Philip Schlesinger, Putting Reality Together: BBC News, London: Constable, 1978, and especially, Michael Tracey, The Production of Political Television, London: Routledge, Kegan Paul, 1976.

4. Quoted in Epstein, 39.

5. Television: a personal report, London: Hutchinson, 1961, 69-70.

6. Epstein, 15.

7. 87.

8. Quoted in Epstein, News From Nowhere, 4-5.

9. New York: 1968, 8.

10. RTNDA news award judging and media culture," Journalism Quarterly, 1978, 164-7.

11. Law and Order News, 35.

12. Media Logic, Beverly Hills and London: Sage, 1979, c. 5.

13. Glasgow University Media Group, Bad News, London: Routledge, Kegan Paul, 1977.

14. I de Sola Pool and I. Shulman, "Newsmen's Fantasies, Audiences, and Newswriting," Warren Breed, "Mass Communication and Socio-cultural Integration," and A. Edelstein and J. Schulz, "The Leadership Role of the Weekly Newspaper," all found in L. A. Dexter and David Manning White, People, Society and Mass Communications, New York: The Free Press, 1964. See also: Canada, Special Senate Committee on the Mass Media, Report, volume III, 202.

15. Chibnall, xii.

16. Harold Clarke, Jane Jenson, Lawrence H. LeDuc, and, Jon Pammett, Political Choice in Canada, Toronto: McGraw-Hill-Ryerson, 1979, 279.

"The problem of newspaper effects, like the call of the mermaids of antiquity, has proved haunting yet elusive to the author. For the past six days, he chased without finding. Only last night did it dawn on him that the effects of the mass media—unlike the quest for the Grail (which was found at the end) and unlike the squaring of the circle (which was insoluble)—might be akin to the riddle of the Sphinx; it could not be solved literally, but could perhaps be untangled."

— Michel de Salaberry

In much of the heated debate about the power of the mass media, one critical factor is neglected: the audience. Is anybody paying attention? Never mind the number of papers sold; perhaps they all went for fish-and-chip wrapping.[1] How many people actually read the biased headline? We wonder whether they read it the same way we did? Did a TV interviewer take that campaign promise out of context? Even if we all agree on that, much more information must be sought. Was the biased item ever telecast, and when? Was it at peak audience times or early, early Sunday morning? Our questions are many and the necessary answers slow in coming.

Analysis of the content of the mass media will tell us something about the institution, about its apparent biases, its processes, and the production results. It tells us little about political communication as a process. For that we must look at the message receivers, the readers, listeners, or audience. While indirect effects can be imagined, our store of information and attitudes is not directly affected by messages to which we are not exposed.

In general, political messages directed to mass audiences cannot achieve their intention:

1 if the message misstates the intended communication, or,
2 if the message is not received, or,
3 if received, it is not absorbed, or,
4 if absorbed, it is misunderstood, or,
5 if understood, the receiver rejects the message or fails to act in the desired way.

We do have statistics on how many and what kinds of people pay attention to certain kinds of information in the mass media. We have relatively little trustworthy data on how closely they attend to that information or what they do with it. Knowledge of this sort is essential to building a better understanding of the public opinion process. As it is, all we have is a lot of rhetoric, a number of theories, and a few maps (of varying reliability) that show how sample populations respond to survey questions. Changes in public attitudes toward elected politicians and their actions were thought for a long time to be the natural result of changes in the mass media's political content. From such speculation came a long series of studies. Many of them were postulated on a 'hypodermic effect', the idea that particular changes in mass media messages would bring about specifiable changes in voting behaviour. Increasing sophistication eventually took research workers into more complex enterprises and into wider fields than voting behaviour. The concept of mass media effects itself changed and much recent investigation has focussed on non-governmental areas.

While there are inquiries into both elections and policy making, the current work of greatest interest to some students of politics is agenda-setting. This concept leads to explorations of the relationship between the issue priorities of the general public and those of the mass media. In doing so, we must remember that the audience for mass media content is highly varied. Besides the generalised publics, there are specialised ones, like the decision-makers. What effect do the mass media have on them? A few of the answers and somewhat more of the hypotheses will be touched on later in a detailed report of one such inquiry.

Using the Mass Media

Much of the fear-mongering about the mass media's social consequences seems to begin with a picture of members of the public as helpless pawns of the message controllers. That picture might seem justified on the basis of 95 to 99 per cent television coverage of all households in countries like Britain and the United States. The big national newspapers sell about 15 million copies and the provincial dailies almost as many again to the 20 million British households. Americans and Canadians own more radio receivers than there are households and while multiple ownership obviously accounts for that datum, fewer than two per cent of all homes are without a radio at all. Virtually the entire population is covered by the three major media. Even remote and isolated settlements in the Arctic regions are reached by satellite and cassette television. In terms of access, radio and television broadcasting are virtually classless media. Significant differences by income group come only in connection with daily newspapers. Table 6-1 on the next page illustrates the point. Similar data has been reported many times for the United States and Britain. The close correlation between income and educational attainment, and the probability that levels of functional literacy are declining somewhat, does make newspaper consumption somewhat

TABLE 6 - 1[2]

Income and Daily Newspaper Receipt

Income	$0-4000	4-6000	6-8000	8-10,000	10-12,000	12,000+
% households taking paper	75	82	89	89	92	95

more class-restricted than the broadcast media. It still is worth noting that the lowest income group listed in Table 6-1 had relatively high access to newspapers—75 per cent of all households.

People also use the mass media a great deal. Most of them, almost 90 per cent, pay some attention to at least two media, and a majority attend to all three. Not surprisingly, the more channels an individual uses, the more he is aware of current events. There are, of course, differences in who watches which media, what they select, and how much time they devote to it.

Women tend to watch more television than do men. Males spend more time on newspapers. Groups with higher income and/or more education rely more on newspapers than television, a difference that reverses as one examines lower income groups. Newspapers are read more by the old than the young, and more in urban areas than rural. What is read and how closely is also worth noting. Our information comes from an extensive national survey. Like all surveys, it suffers from a number of necessary qualifications. It represents an average of all newspapers. As has been pointed out earlier, however, newspapers vary considerably in their 'personalities'. Some publishers will stress sports, some local and regional, while others emphasise financial/ political news. If there is a choice, people select a

TABLE 6-2[3]

Minutes Spent Reading Newspaper Sections
(Average Time)

	Sex		Age			Education	
	M	F	15-25	25-44	44+	Second.	Coll.
Front page	7	6	5	6	8	7	7
Internat'l news	7	6	7	6	7	7	8
Editorials	6	6	4	5	7	6	7
Sports	7	3	5	5	5	5	4
Women's	2	7	4	5	5	5	4
Classified ads	4	4	4	4	4	4	3
Travel	3	3	3	2	3	3	3
Financial	4	2	2	3	3	3	4
Other	4	4	4	4	5	4	4
TOTAL TIME	44	41	38	40	47	44	44

newspaper that appeals to their interests most. Another important qualification to this set of data is that it is based on what those interviewed say in response to a set of questions put by an interviewer. Much better would be readership surveys that incorporated methods of checking the respondent's answers and impressions made on them (by testing them for story recall and knowledge). Unfortunately, few reliable surveys of this sort have been conducted and made available. Even then, they are restricted to the one newspaper involved.

According to some studies, the average adult spends almost as much time in a week watching television as he does in paid employment. There is some connection between viewing

TV and education level (and income level as well), but not as much as is often thought. While 30 per cent of those with college level attainments watch only a little television—five hours a week or less, almost as many well-educated people—25 per cent—fall into the heavy viewing category. That means watching sixteen hours a week or more. The same heavy viewing category accounts for 44 per cent of those who are less well educated. Audience research also leads us to believe that urban-dwellers spend more time viewing than do rural people, females more than males, poor more than rich, and those aged 20-44 years more than those over 44 years.

Much has been made of the idea that general television should offer something for everybody. That has been two rather different things in practice. Commercial broadcasting in the United States, in particular, has seen the networks competing for the same mass audience at the same time. Hour by hour in peak viewing periods, one network's successful adventure series had to be met by another network's proven situation comedy and the third network's 'Big Movie of the Week'. Only when one prime time show was thought to be 'unbeatable' would another network offer genuinely 'alternative programming' like a public affairs production aimed at a particular minority audience. The success of commercial television in capturing mass audiences led the British Broadcasting Corporation to divide its efforts into two in 1970. It did battle for the allegiance of the masses with its first channel, successfully, and maintained and enlarged its service to minority interests through programs on its second channel.

Much attention has been devoted to patterns of political news consumption during national election campaigns. At such times, television news continues to attract bigger audiences than do the other media. The visual medium also has the broadest appeal, cutting across income, education, and social status levels. Because it is a passive medium, much of the TV audience is exposed to campaign news regardless of its interest. So too with radio. By contrast, seeking news through the print media takes effort, and researchers have found a high correlation between interest in elections and newspaper reading about them. Newspaper consumers of campaign news are also more highly educated, somewhat older, more prosperous, and more likely to live in big cities. Their high interest level also leads them to follow campaign news in the other media as well. Some evidence exists, although it is not conclusive, that newspaper followers of election news are more interested in campaign issues than are broadcast audiences. Mass media use information of this type must be treated with caution. It is survey data and consists almost entirely of the answers people give when they have been questioned. While social scientists have techniques to compensate for some respondent distortion (the tendency to lie or exaggerate in interview situations), such techniques are not often devised for the mass media parts of the study. Generally, then, we cannot know for sure how many people actually read yesterday's front page story, or watched the TV election roundup, when they claim they did. Without knowing that, we cannot make confident estimates about what the public learns, if anything, from its direct experience of campaign news in the mass media.

One of the few investigations that actualy used the rare but highly desirable device of cross-checking was reported in 1969 by Serena Wade and Wilbur Schramm.[4] They looked at four U.S. surveys of knowledge about public affairs and its source between 1952 and 1964. Fewer data were available for science and health knowledge areas in the study. Their work led them to an important distinction in mass media political news. During election campaigns, most voters' information comes from events, like conventions, debates, and talks, which are carried on television and permit vicarious audience participation. "When a campaign is not under way, however, public affairs are more likely to be represented in the media by news stories and interpretations than by televised events; newspapers can cover a wider spectrum of this news, and in greater detail."

Wade and Schramm propose that these factors might explain those studies of intercampaign periods which showed newspapers ranking higher than television as a major source of national political news. In a summary, Wade and Schramm pointed to the increasing dominance of television as a news source for all groups during election campaigns with education and life style determining how much regular use people made of the print media for that purpose. They also concluded that those who used print media as their major source, rather than television, were likely to have more information and be more accurately informed.

Elite Communication

The most avid consumers of political news are senior civil servants and elected politicians. While egoism accounts for a little of their attention, functional necessity dictates it. The mass media are an essential and major form of communication among decisionmakers. Outside the limited interests of their particular department, civil servants are only slightly better placed than most citizens to keep up with the innumerable activities of the leviathan that government has turned into. And they have much greater need of doing so. The consequences of those activities are liable to be reflected directly and often immediately in the conduct of their own day-to-day business. Officially prescribed consultation can never fill half the gaps that exist, and it seldom covers the doings of other governments and quasiautonomous agencies. Many a mockery has been made of hierarchies when the chiefs of large enterprises have learned from the press for the first time about some otherwise unknown activity going on in the distant or lower divisions of their own organistion. Civil servants depend on the press to keep track of civil servants.

Public officials also use the mass media to find out what is happening in the world they are governing. The press is the only comprehensive, continuous, and more-or-less objective monitor they have. Potentially at least, every disaster, accident, or similar event can call for some governmental response and such responses are set in motion by mass media reporting. Official despatches come later.

Of equal or more importance are reports on the apparent adequacy of social and economic programs, discussions of the effectiveness of new laws or old, and stories on the emergence of social changes of all kinds. Civil servants are as concerned as politicians, sometimes more so, to see what reception the public gives their actions and programs. No matter how well designed or administered new policies are, many of them will lose considerable effectiveness if they fail to win acceptance. The first section of the public to react to policy change is the mass media. That reaction is shown through the amount of attention, mode of presentation, general characterisation, and expressions of editorial opinion. Next comes mass media reports of the policy's reception by issue-oriented and other special publics. The politician's attention to the mass media is more personalised and more anxious than the civil servants'—they will give more weight to it than to official information—but otherwise the similarities are more striking than the differences. The biases of their knowledge base and their personal involvement makes it inevitable that governmental audiences will be much more critical of mass media political content than is the general public for which it is primarily designed.

Models of Public Opinion

In popular understanding, the major justification for freedom of the press is its role as an agent of public opinion. It provides a two-way flow of information about general sentiments in the country and the conduct of public business. The multiple feedback systems make government easier, more efficient, and more likely to be in line with popular wishes. While members of the public have personal experience they can draw on in order to assess some areas of government performance, they depend on the mass media to

monitor, report, and help interpret performance in other
areas such as foreign relations, criminal law, and general
economic management. Those reports contribute significantly
to the public's opinions about government, they stimulate
messages to the legislators, and eventually they lead to
re-election or defeat of the governing group. Some, more
idealistic versions of the model go further and expect
public opinion to dictate the contents of policies and
decisions to the government. Otherwise, it is said, our
politics are 'undemocratic'. In all cases, public opinion is
the critical, linking concept, but in no case are its
meaning and operational form agreed.

The deficiencies of the three-way model—public, press,
and government—are many. In its simple form it ignores the
institutional character of the press, which is also an actor
in the process. It directs too much of our attention to the
views of the citizenry and not enough to the influence of
those views on the administrators and how it is exercised.
Proper understanding of the system needs examination of
governmental attempts to anticipate and shape the public's
opinions. Neither do we know enough of the mediation of
information relations that takes place through political
parties and interest groups. Perhaps, above all, we need to
improve on the typical model of the public that is used. The
'public' is considerably more complicated than a mass of
single individuals whose separate opinions and attitudes can
be summed up in a few simple statistics like 55 per cent
'for' and 45 per cent 'against'.

At heart public opinion is a mixture of basic value
structures, attitudinal inclinations, and discrete issue
opinions. In most cases trying to cut it all down to two
sets of yes-no figures grossly distorts reality. That effort
is reasonable in only two formal instances: referenda or
plebiscites and some elections. The mass media undoubtedly
play a role in these processes but they are very crude
indicators of public opinion. The issue orientations that do
go into voter decisions are terribly elusive as to their

number, identity, intensity, and importance. To those points must be added the complications of past versus future judgements and nonissue considerations. If we can draw any agreed conclusion from the myriad election studies, it is that individual voting decisions are an unknown compound of party, leadership, issue, and local candidate influences. Extracting any 'mandate' from the public opinion expressed in elections is a work of sheer political artistry and never one of science.

Public opinion studies have thrown up a large literature and only a little useful knowledge. Two perspectives dominate the field. The early writers, such as Dicey, Lippmann, and Bryce, were concerned chiefly with ethical and moral aspects. They discussed such things as the citizen's duty to be involved in the public process for the 'common good'. That idea flourishes today among groups worried about civic behaviour. The other perspective has been that of students who shrugged off civic morality and plunged into empirical investigations. Unfortunately they lacked even theoretical ideas of what maps would look like for the unknown land they were trying to explore. Their finds had only the order of ragbags. What were they looking for? They were not agreed. The idiosyncracy of their definitions brings Lewis Carroll to mind:

> 'When I use a word,' Humpty Dumpty said, in a rather scornful tone, 'it means just what I choose it to mean—neither more nor less.' 'The question is,' said Alice, 'whether you can make words mean so many different things.'

Despite the general lack of clear research orientations, there was a great deal of spadework done which yields three definitions of interest. During the twenties, R. H. Gault argued that public opinion should be seen as "a certain apprehension of common and fundamental interests by all members of the group."[5] Even though newspaper commentators have usually been ready enough to take on the burden, the problem, then as now, was to determine whose version of the public interest deserved the most respect. The issue was difficult enough without tackling the proposition that under-classes often did not or could not know their 'true' interests. Representative government had set up a variety of ways for communicating many private opinions on public affairs, and elected politicians staked their places on the accuracy of their intuitive reading of public sentiment. Despite the claims of the press, most politicians soon learned to distinguish between **published** opinions and the climate of opinion in the general public, a distinction that manages to elude some commentators even today.

The invention and slow development of systematic public opinion polling eventually gave rise to one reasonably precise definition: "Public opinion consists of people's reactions to definitely-worded statements and questions under interview conditions."[6] Bolstered by the marriage of scientific sampling and machine readable data, this conception rapidly elbowed aside almost all others. Today it reigns almost unchallenged as a major piece of apparatus in the political ideology of the mass media. Unfortunately the 'research' that is undertaken for media organisations is almost always an inquiry into the public's views on sharply controversial issues, or, "those opinions held by private persons which governments find it prudent to heed" to use V.O. Key's definition of public opinion.

This development has given us an enormous body of opinion data in which the issues examined shift from problem area to problem area and almost month by month. Historical changes are difficult if not impossible to study. The American public, for example, may well have had certain attitudes toward Southeast Asia prior to the sixties and U.S. military involvement there but we have no idea what they were. During the Suez affair, British public opinion was very divided but what different people's attitudes were before it ever arose, or after it subsided, we cannot tell.

Why are changes over time so seldom explored? The data we rely on are nearly all supplied by commercial organisations. Many of the public affairs questions they ask are "free riders" hooked onto polls commissioned for product marketing purposes. When they stand on their own, public opinion surveys must be immediately saleable. That depends crucially on their newsworthiness, or at least timeliness. Most polling organizations cannot worry about much refinement. They are always short of trained interviewers (necessary for standardized interviews), their questionnaires are often leading or superficial, and adequate pretesting involves costs that customers resist paying.

With all their inadequacies, why are the commercial polls so accurate? Or are they? The question is much debated among some scholars. The claim to accuracy is very much a matter of selective advertising, missing evidence, and contending definitions. Almost all the non-electoral reports we see concern opinion distributions on public issues. A series of individual responses is usually treated as virtual responses to election ballot totals. The sums are then transformed into a type of mass media reality: 'Americans demand action over Poland' or 'Quebecers want new constitution'. They may be wholly artificial constructs but such commercial polls have become major factors in the resolution of controversial issues. Apart from the more reliable surveys conducted for academic purposes, most published opinion polls give us little evidence that can be cross-checked. Few commercial survey firms test the public pulse on the same issue at the same time and if they do, their questions, timing, and methods inevitably differ.[7] While this allows the companies room to explain diverse results, it still does not give us any proof of the overall reliability of most of the readily available polls on contemporary issues. The reported findings usually escape challenge because it is seldom in anybody's interest to question them.

The commercial polls' claim to reliability in political fields rests almost entirely on forecasts of elections.

Here they are usually on more solid grounds, particularly in two-party situations. Even then, we should note that the claim to reliability is made in terms of the polling company's own advertised standards. Before the predictions are made, there is a lot of profitable polling business to be done during the campaign. Parties, candidates, and mass media all commission their own polls. The quantity and especially the quality of the work performed depends on the depth of the clients' pocketbooks and the polling company's care and skills. The great variety of figures announced during the campaign are applauded by the leading candidates, disparaged by those trailing, and turned into news by the mass media. The poll figures are treated as indicators of trends and changes leading up to the final figures announced by the pollsters: how the election will turn out, IF.... The conditions then follow. While every survey company notes the proportions of those interviewed who do not indicate a voting preference, most mass media assume the undecided will vote the same way as those who have decided. (An unsafe assumption.) The accuracy claimed for the forecast is in terms of the company's specified standard—to which nobody pays heed: 'The Galloping Groper Survey Company said today Party A would get X per cent of the popular vote, Party B would get Y per cent, and Party C would get Z per cent. The survey design allowed a confidence level of 95 per cent and a margin of plus or minus four percentage points.'

A few mass media polling organisations and commercial organizations have been trying to incorporate into their work some of the sophisticated techniques used by social scientists for attitude surveying. This is an attempt to get beyond the superficialities inherent in ordinary opinion polling. The great problem in assessing attitudes accurately is imperfect communications. Ask a respondent a question and he automatically interprets it in light of his own experience. Such subjective distortion cannot easily be measured. If care is taken, one can measure an individual's attitudes with some consistency, but the diversity of personal experiences (and therefore of interpretative frameworks) makes comparisons between different individuals' attitudes almost impossible. Where three people hold roughly the same attitude, for example, favouring improving the condition of the poor, they could still give us different responses to the same question that is more specific. Ask the three if they approve of higher welfare payments. One person will answer the question 'no' (possibly because that person prefers non-cash assistance), a second might refuse to answer (because he is undecided about the best method) while only the third one will answer it 'yes'. The opposite also happens: three individuals give similar answer even though they hold diverse attitudes toward the same subject. Other difficulties in attitude studies arise from sample design, question administration, and conceiving the group structure thought relevant to the particular study. Coping with problems like these is expensive, takes time, and is liable to delay results past media deadlines.

Where individual opinions come from has been a matter for much inquiry and debate among social scientists. All would reject the nineteenth century liberal notion—perhaps held seriously only by popular writers—that people might arrive at opinions as the deliberate product of rational consideration. That our opinions arrive from some combination of predisposition, current socialisation, and the influence of forces like the mass media does seem to be agreed. Many of those opinions are held only passively, even unconsciously. It may take the polling agent's query to activate them. The chances are, though, that they will be counted exactly the same as views which are strongly held. The random sampling procedure used in polling tends to force a picture of society as an aggregate of disparate individuals with public opinion being represented as a quantitative distribution of individual responses. In failing to distinguish different kinds of opinions, varying degrees of influence, and leadership factors, the procedure ignores much of the opinion-making process.[8] The gaps in our knowledge of that process mean we know even less about the role of the mass media. Two sets of considerations merit particular note. First, there is a lot more to public opinion than simple aggregations of individual reactions to controversial aspects of public affairs, and, secondly, much of the press institution's influence on private lives is mediated by social communication structures.

Whatever it might once have been, today's public is neither a single, homogeneous mass nor a conglomerate of millions of isolated individuals at the mercy of the media manipulators. Those simple-minded conceptions of the 'public' were inherent in some primitive versions of the idea but they should be abandoned. In their place we should visualise a variety of social groups or specialised publics each clustered around particular sets of attitudes or issue areas. These orientations are undoubtedly related to a people's basic value frameworks but attempts to incorporate those values into the process as 'latent' or 'channelling' opinion is both too confusing and unnecessarily ambitious. To be part of public opinion, views must not only be held privately but they must be expressed socially. This approach has prompted Elisabeth Noelle-Neumann to argue that 'public opinions are those in the sphere of controversy that one can express in public without isolating oneself.'[9] Even if the implications of that take the student of politics and the press, for example, outside the narrow field of research interests, the concept usefully alerts one to its larger and often neglected context of other opinions.

For some people, politics is the country's most fascinating spectator sport. But they are few in number and so are those who pay close attention to the general run of public affairs. Far more people keep close watch over small bits of government—the pieces that seem to affect them directly. The very appearance of a political issue means at least one set of mass media audiences that will follow it intently and perhaps another group or two that will keep in touch with it generally. Most of the population, though, will have no concern about the controversy or even awareness of its existence. The 'opinion public' for each issue can consist entirely of isolated individuals who have only their special newspaper reading in common. So organised is our society, though, that the members of most opinion publics will be aware of others sharing their particular interest and will often comprise social groups like unions, hobby and sport clubs, ethnic associations, and business groups. Issues often stimulate formation of special organisations.

Not everyone in an opinion public becomes an immediate consumer of the relevant mass media content. Many people depend for information and appropriate attitudes on others within the group. As often as not these opinion leaders do not hold executive office but influence the views of others because of personality attributes and a keen interest in new information. Research work documenting informal information structures led Elihu Katz and S. J. Eldersveld to their 'two-step flow of communications hypothesis', which was found to work for a number of opinion fields besides public affairs. Sometimes the chain extends beyond the original reader/listener and their immediate audience and now the literature speaks of a multistep flow of information which is only initiated by mass media content. The lightning-like spread of the Kennedy assassination news was only the most dramatic demonstration of the power of our widespread but informal communication chains. These structures can be most efficient in communicating simple matters of facts—like a presidential death—as well as polarised orientations like approval or disapproval of specific actions or proposals. In other respects, the efficiency rating must be a low one.

All direct consumption of media contents takes place through highly selective screens that mark everyone's attention and relative inattention to things about them. We read and watch only what we want to or think we should. Of that they absorb only a part and interpret it in light of their own background. The imperfect perceptions of the first consumer are not only passed on but are themselves altered by the perceptual biases of each person in the communication chain. The socialising effects of the transmission structure may be quite strong. It has such power that scholars have found secondary traces of its influence in the secondary 'exposure' that people get through the person-to-person system. Far from acting directly and predictably to sway public opinion, mass media messages have to compete for influence with all the forces of individualistic experience and the formal and informal structures of society. In the short run the mass media can exert power only when their content deals with completely unknown topics and neither arouses nor challenges existing interests or values.

Electoral Effects of the Mass Media

Without the mass media, there would be nothing recognisable as national election campaigns. Unless electoral districts were considerably reduced, even local contests would be very different without the presence of newspapers and broadcast media. In essence, all our major political campaigns are mass-mediated. Only a very few highly politicized citizens are able to perceive anything of the candidates, party leaders, issues, or parties except by means of mass communications.

In liberal societies, any institution that has the effect of weakening the directness of the relationship between voters and their representatives has been denounced as unhealthy for democracy. That was the case with the growth of factions and political parties and later with newspapers after they shrugged off partisan controls and developed independent mass audiences. Radio and television proved no exceptions. So now we have two major institutions —party and media—standing in the way. It may be, though, that rather than helping our political parties in their roles as citizen-government go-betweens, the mass media are replacing them in that function. The evidence available does no more than support the suggestion as reasonable middle-term speculation about the future.

Politicians have always been good customers of the press.
Giving little credence to its information function, they
believed greatly in its power to propagandise. That is why
in early years they bought newspapers, worried later about
losing their support, and now seek to buy as much of
television and radio as they can manage. We, however, must
not make the common error of assuming that the heavy use of
mass media in politics demonstrates much about their
effects. It does not. Mass media advertising, for example,
is about selling goods and nothing has been better sold than
advertising itself. The super salesmen of our time are the
advertising managers. Everywhere they have persuaded
parties, politicians, and governments alike that they could
sell soap in a box—and most of them sold the politicians a
pig in a poke. The cash-product transaction is a very
slippery analogy for the processes of shifting public
opinion or winning votes; selling soap is easier than
selling ideas. Whether the political content of the mass
media has been purchased or provided free as news and public
service matters little at the moment. Hard proof of any
effectiveness is still needed. Mass communications research
in the field of politics has been extensive and frustrating.
Evidence that goes any distance at all beyond common sense
impressions is difficult to produce as a review will show.

Just what are the political effects of the mass media?
The question has been keenly debated for half a century and
longer. Politicians like F. D. Roosevelt and Adolf Hitler
'discovered' radio during the thirties with apparent
consequences that disturbed people in many circles. A radio
drama broadcast in 1937, Orson Welles' 'War of the Worlds',
sparked further concern. Its fictionalised news bulletins
about aliens invading the earth sent hundreds screaming to
the police for protection and alarmed thousands of others.
Despite these and other examples, elections were seized on
as one of the most promising research fields and early work
concentrated here. The initial emphasis—perhaps as a
heritage of wartime propaganda efforts—was on persuasion.

Messages were expected to change attitudes, which in turn would lead to changed behaviour. 'Mass media effect' was soon equated to conversion. Working with something of a rational man conception of electoral choice, investigators went haring over political fences and platforms everywhere looking for voters who had been converted from Party A to Party B as a result of exposure to political content in the print and broadcast media. The three major American studies of the period were those conducted in Erie County, Ohio (1940), Elmira, New York (1948), and the 1952 national election—the first in which television was widely used. Each inquiry indicated that the mass media exerted only a minimal influence on the voter, either in terms of helping the uncommitted to a decision or changing the minds of those who had an earlier predisposition.

Above all, the early voting studies wiped out the idea of the public as a mass of alienated or atomised individuals. As one summary put it:

> ...it appears that communications studies have greatly underestimated the extent to which an individual's social attachments to other people, and the character of the opinions and activities which he shares with them will influence his response to the mass media.[10]

Discovery that most of the voters were not easily persuaded meant this 'failure of effect' had to be explained. (What had really failed, though, was not the mass media but the research hypotheses.) To help out, a version of dissonance theory was borrowed from psychology: people seek out information that conforms to their predispositions and that supports them; they avoid or reinterpret any contrary and non-supportive messages. British research showed that three-quarters of the audience for party political broadcasts comprised sympathisers of the party making the program. Selective screening and selective perceptions provided formidable barriers against any generalised persuasion through the mass media.

Throughout mass communications studies it had been found that people who are highly exposed to one medium tend to be highly exposed to other media. Even they seemed almost immune to conversion. While some of the less-exposed members of the audience acquired new information about issues and parties, the effect was not general and, in any case, new information did not mean changed attitudes very often. Later work showed that high exposure to political content corresponded to high interest in politics and usually committed partisanship. The intensified information output during campaigns serves more to expand the data base for conscientious citizens than it does to widen the proportion of informed voters.

Other efforts were made to explain the 'failure of effects'. Election campaign messages could not even reach certain sectors of the population because of social and cultural attributes, factors like lack of formal schooling, low economic status, age, and place of residence. There was little challenge in 1960 when J.T. Klapper pointed to the flood of socio-economic influences that voting research had turned up and concluded that "mass communications functions far more frequently as an agent of reinforcement than as an agent of change."[11] But reinforcement was far from universal. A study by the Leeds Centre for Television Research on the 1964 British general election reported that reinforcement "occurs selectively among those who look for it or whose prior attitudes toward the content of a communication encourage a reinforcing result."[12] The effectiveness of transmitted information depends on more than the selectivity of the receiver according to Karl W. Deutsch, a political scientist working in communications theory. For there to be an effect "at least some parts of the receiving system must be in highly unstable equilibrium, so that the very small amount of energy carrying the signal will be sufficient to start off a much larger process of change."[13] Unfortunately other researchers did not follow up this line.

If the reinforcement approach could deal with only part of the 'problem of effects' the reason was in the problem definition as much as anything. Conversion of individuals is only one kind of effect. If we think about political consequences going beyond individuals—to groups, institutions, social subsystems, and society itself—the range of possibilities opened up is much broader. They could include reform in legislative procedures, public demonstrations, increased levels of activism by the elderly or young, changed voter turnout patterns, and so on. Streams of mass media messages eventually could supplant party loyalties altogether as a major organizing framework for the public. Few of these possible effects would be caught by either conversion or reinforcement approaches.

Here as elsewhere in social studies are seen some of the consequences of working in open-ended systems. We are trying to investigate both the phenomenon of mass communications and its percussions on the environment, which is itself dynamic. In discussing television or any other medium, James Halloran points out that "we are not talking so much about the influence of an electronic medium as about the influence of a social institution."[14] As such, their organisation and information outputs will vary from political system to political system. The institutional focus reminds us, as well, that the concept of politicians using the mass media to use people can be a little misleading. People use their institutions. That has been demonstrated by a number of studies. The 1964 British survey mentioned above found some members of the audience reporting they watched the campaign coverage because it was an exciting event, and provided entertainment. Other respondents, almost half of the group surveyed, said they used the mass media to keep up with things—a general surveillance function. American studies have shown that campaign workers attend closely to the mass media not simply because of their interest but because it is useful; it provides them with ammunition, ideas, and arguments they can use in their interpersonal canvassing. [15]

'Good media coverage' also keeps up the sometimes flagging spirits of party workers and candidates alike.

The institution and environment of political mass communications evolved rapidly during the nineteen-sixties. Unable or unwilling to rebuild life as it once was, the generation that had painful personal memories of experiencing widespread unemployment, distress, and world war lost social pre-eminence. The one-time 'TV kids' came to maturity and questioned the status quo. 'The box' was a more natural part of their lives than 'the paper'. The growth of television politics was difficult for many to cope with at first but its certain triumph as the medium of the masses in the seventies had a number of consequences.

In the early eagerness to safeguard television against the excesses of their party opponents, legislators wielded a sword that cut two ways and maybe more. The requirements for balance and objectivity in broadcasting led to considerably more exposure and prominence for third parties like the Liberals in Britain, the New Democratic Party in Canada, and for independent candidates in the U.S.A. Voter shifts in attitudes favouring these groups seemed greatest among those with generally weak interest in politics. The balance in broadcasting rules required programming to be 'above all politicking' and, resulted in presentations that implicitly diminished all traditional partisanship, and probably its overall legitimacy as well. There is a strong correlation, if not a clear cause-and-effect relationship, between the growing pervasiveness of television nonpartisan politics and rapid declines in party loyalties in the general public. Virtually every western country has reported the phenomenon. in 1975, G.J. O'Keefe claimed that television had reduced the salience of political parties in American public life. In Canada, perhaps the most communications-dependent polity in the west, only half the electorate reported always voting for the same party. Nearly one-quarter of them voted for different parties in the 1972 and 1974 general elections.[16]

Television politics has also increased the involuntary
exposure of indifferent citizens to campaign content. It
comes to their attention simply because "it's on the tube."
While some scholars speculate this has meant a significant
enlargement of the effective electorate, others have pointed
to the development of what they see as a more persuasible
electorate. J.G. Blumler has written: "Since lukewarm
viewers tend to be the least informed and the least
politically formed part of the electorate, their internal
defences against persuasion are liable to be relatively
frail."[17] The same writer, together with other colleagues,
has reported a relative decline in selective viewing by
partisan members of the audience. Because "each party
support group was exposed to more materials from the other
two main parties combined than from its own side of the
political fence," the slight differences in partisan viewing
time that had persisted until 1975 were overridden.

The evidence for mass media exposure changing voting
intentions is not at all clear cut. In the Butler-Stokes
study of British voting in 1964 and 1966 the panel of
respondents tended, as we would expect, to read the national
daily newspapers that supported their own partisan
predisposition. The readership pattern changed little over
time. But more of those who did not support the party
preferred by their newspaper tended to move toward the
paper's policy positions on issues than away from them. Up
to onequarter of that group also changed party vote
allegiance to that of the newspaper's. In the United States,
editorial endorsements seem to exercise more influence on
voting in local government elections in which partisan
guidelines are absent.[18] Endorsements also seem to be of
some help to candidates for state legislatures. An extensive
Canadian voting study, however, casts doubt on the
applicability of of these generalisations for that country's
electors. As elsewhere, the amount of attention to
newspapers, radio, and television reporting is related to
individual interest in politics, degree of personal

TABLE 6 - 3[19]

Attention to Media Reports of the 1974
Election   Campaign,   by   Selected
Attitudinal and Behavioural Variables
(Pearson's r)

	Newspapers	TV	Radio
Interest in Politics	.45*	.37*	.25*
Interest in 1974 Election	.50*	.39*	.27*
Intensity of Partisanship	.02	.04	.01
Stability of Partisanship	-.13*	-.15*	-.10*
Consistency of Partisanship	.00	-.04	-.03
Participation in Politics	.39*	.31*	.26*
Participation in 1974 Elctn	.39*	.34*	.26*
Vote Switch, 1972-74	-.01	.07	.02

*Significant at .01 level.

involvement, partisanship, and socio—economic variables.
"None of this necessarily means, however, that attention to
the media is related to changes in voting behaviour from one
election to another." They could not find a single
significant relationship between vote switching and mass
media attention. (See Table 6-3.) The same study goes on to
say that those who saw no programs or party advertisements
on television and "those who did not read much about the
campaign in the newspapers were just about as likely to
change their votes from the previous elections as were those
who avidly followed the campaign." Among those who did
switch parties, they found leader effects (images?) were
stronger among low interest citizens and issue—effects
stronger among the high interest voters. The 'flexible
partisans', as this group was called, tended to make their

decisions later in the campaign and on the basis of more information taken from the mass media. In general, this study, which was impressive in its methodological thoroughness, settled for an open verdict on the effects of the mass media on party choice.

Vote shifting could not be connected to levels of political information in an earlier U.S. study but there was a high correlation between knowledge levels and voter turnout.[20] If this is an effect it is as likely to flow from the mass media's ability to generate interest as it is from its persuasive powers. As the tendency grows for broadcasters to abandon 'straight' reporting of election campaigns in favour of emphasising their drama and excitement, television interest generation effects may be expected to increase. Traditionally, the mass media have influenced the attention given some issues rather than others. Newspapers were devoted to the practice in the days when partisanship dominated news reporting. They tried hard to challenge the bases of various party claims and sought information that would expose their weaknesses. Broadcast journalism was inhibited in doing this right from the start. Investigation of rival party issues was politically dangerous to begin with and courted legal trouble in the difficulty of maintaining 'balance' while engaging in such exercises. With the possible exception of some British national dailies, most newspapers seem also to have abandoned issue-challenging during campaigns. Perhaps that was out of fear that such activity would undermine their newly acquired claims to public service neutrality. So far as broadcasting is concerned, trying to deal with a long list of issues runs contrary to 'good' broadcast standards. In consequence, modern campaigns nearly all see a rapid winnowing of issues down to only one or two—especially if judged by the television reporting.

The permeation of politics by the TV industry's technological biases are evident everywhere although there have been few systematic studies.[21] A party's selection and nomination of candidates for election is only one of the most obvious effects. Delegates to party conventions cannot avoid, whether consciously or unconsciously, thinking about their candidate's ability to present both himself and his party on television. Personal characteristics such as general appearance, informality, warmth, and quip-shooting have been turned into more important election assets than good judgement, sound information, and ideological commitment. It is difficult to think of a more important effect that the mass media exercise on electioneering.

'Image-mongering' and 'presidentialisation' of general elections are two effects generally attributed to television. The focus on central personalities is unmistakeable in the content analyses of campaign coverage. M. Harrison has reported that in the rigorously controlled British broadcasting news, more than half of all the time devoted to political figures was devoted to the two major party leaders. Only 4 of the 1,837 candidates in the 1970 election were mentioned in the news bulletins.[22]

The general weakening of party identification among electorates in the west means party leaders must 'run ahead' of their party in public opinion if either leader or party is to have much hope of winning. A detailed study of one electoral district in Hamilton, Ont., disclosed a significant relationship between perceiving a party leader favourably and intending to vote for his party's local candidate. There was some evidence of a correlation between a favourable image of a local candidate and intention to vote for him. In both cases, the intention to vote in a particular way because of a favourable image was most pronounced among uncommitted voters and party-switchers.[23] We can only speculate that when voters have not formulated their voting preferences or are wavering in their intentions, the normal selective exposure and perception devices do not operate to mediate the flood of campaign information in the mass media. Each candidate's personal appeal and image competes for the voter's attention with

non-political events. Television stereotyping—which favours
those of other candidates and with personalisation so
strongly—has had its consequences for the other media as
well as for voters. Even daily papers, which apart from the
British nationals are highly local in orientation, now give
far more of their news and picture space to national party
leaders than to all other aspects of election campaigns.

One of the most famous early attempts to use television
in order to change one's political image deliberately was
the Checkers speech of 1956. In the light of Dwight D.
Eisenhower's apparent rectitude, Richard Nixon's candidacy
for the vice-presidency was seriously challenged on moral
grounds. A clever television performance using the family
pet, 'Checkers', gave Mr. Nixon's image the necessary
whitewashing. Almost unknown until 1968, Pierre Trudeau
bounded on to the Canadian political stage and swept the
voters of that year with an image compounded of suaveness,
excitement, intelligence, and a little adventure. Faced with
an overwhelming Trudeau charisma, his opponent, Robert L.
Stanfield, achieved a private fame with members of the press
in deriding his own image. As the 1972 general election
approached, he said, no, he thought this one should not be a
personality contest—"it would be too unfair to Mr.
Trudeau." After a third defeat, he retired with a comment
about his mass media image. "If all the fellows of the press
had seen me walking on water, they'd say it was because I
couldn't swim!"

The first two decades of voter survey research led to a
neat summing of mass media influences in the reinforcement
theory. It said that individual voters were enmeshed in such
a web of socio-cultural variables that served to filter all
perceptions of reality that mass communications would act
chiefly to reinforce rather than to convert people's voting
predispositions. Overall, it was concluded in the early
sixties, the effects must be minimal. Mass media influences
were shunted from a central to a peripheral position of
concern as voting research went on for another two decades.

Social and communications change went on as well. Today we find the process has given us a surprising accumulation of evidential bits suggesting that mass media currents must still be reckoned with amid the muddied tidal waters of democratic elections. As yet, it seems impossible to knit those bits into a theoretically coherent pattern. That may have to await completion of the larger task of a satisfactory theory of the electoral processes themselves.

NOTES TO CHAPTER SIX

1. This hypothetical explanation is, alas, only an historic allusion now that the European Community has outlawed this fine old English tradition.
2. Table 75 from The Senate of Canada, Special Committee on the Mass Media, Good, Bad, or Simply Indifferent, vol.3, pt 1 of the Report. 1970.
3. Ibid., Table 32.
4. "The Mass Media As Sources of Public Affairs, Science and Health Knowledge," Public Opinion Quarterly, v. 33 (1969), 197-209.
5. Social Psychology, New York: 1923, 176-7.
6. Lucien Warner, "The reliability of public opinion surveys," Public Opinion Quarterly, v.3 (1939), 377.
7. For a fascinating and rare attempt to cross-check poll results with each other, see T. W. Smith, "In search of house effects: a comparison of responses to various questions by different survey organisations," Public Opinion Quarterly, v. 42(1978), 105-114. See also: "Did they get it right?", The Economist. May 5, 1979, no. 271, 20.
8. See Herbert Blumer's "Public opinion and public policy," in D. Katz and S. Eldersveld, Public Opinion and Propaganda, New York: Dryden Press, 1954, 74.
9. "Public Opinion, Classical Opinion: A Re-evaluation", Public Opinion Quarterly, v. 43 (1979), 143-156.

10. Elihu Katz and P. D. Lazarsfeld, Personal Influence, New York: Free Press, 1955.
11. The Effects of Mass Communications, New York: The Free Press, 1960.
12. J. G. Blumler and Denis McQuail, Television in Politics: Its Uses and Influence, London: Faber, 1968, 215.
13. "Communications models and decision systems," in Charlesworth, Contemporary Political Analysis, New York: The Free Press, 1967.
14. "Mass-media effects: a sociological approach," in Mass communications and society, The Audience, Unit 7, 21, Milton Keynes: The Open University, 1977.
15. Kenneth G. Sheinkof, Charles K. Atkin and Lawrence Brown, "How political party workers respond to political advertising," Journalism Quarterly, vol. 50 (1973), 334-339.
16. Harold D. Clarke, Jane Jenson, Lawrence Leduc, and Jon H. Pammett, Political Choice in Canada, Toronto: McGraw-Hill-Ryerson, 1979.
17. "The political effects of mass communications," in The Audience, Unit 8, Milton Keynes: The Open University, 1977.
18. Angus Campbell, et. al., Elections and the Political Order, New York: John Wiley, 1966, 139.
19. Political Choice in Canada, 290.
20. Elections and the Political Order.
21. A major exception is found in chapters 3, 4, and 5 of David L. Altheide and Robert P. Snow, Media Logic, Beverly Hills and London: Sage, 1979.
22. See his chapters on campaign broadcasting in D.E. Butler and Anthony King, The British General Election of 1966, London: Macmillan, 1966, and D.E. Butler and Michael Pinto-Duschinsky, The British General Election of 1970, London: Macmillan, 1971.
23. See G.R. Winham and R.B. Cunningham, "Party Leader Images in the 1968 Federal Election," Canadian Journal of Political Science, v. 3 (1970), 376-399, and R.B. Cunningham, "The Impact of the Local Candidate," C.J.P.S., v. 4 (1971), 287-290.

For all of their importance to the party control of government and their place in the civics of liberalism, elections comprise only one part of democratic politics. Our systems of elected representatives do stand as ultimate protection against tyranny by government. Beyond voting, however, lies a lot more to political life than the press and political scientists might sometimes lead us to believe. Since the early sixties, political scientists have placed an extraordinary emphasis on the study of elections to the nearexclusion at times of other aspects of political life. Modern news media have a comparable fondness for interpreting as much of politics as possible in terms of its probable impact on the electoral fortunes of political personalities. One result has been a terrible neglect of our need to explore the non-electoral connections between democratic politics and the part played in them by mass communications. Legends abound in this field, particularly with respect to local newspapers and local politics.

Politicians and historians are prone to blame or credit newspapers for any number of exercises of press power which exposed political and official corruption, stimulated or dictated particular decisions, inspired new policies, or frustrated the adoption of new programs or legislation. The Hearst press has been blamed for starting the Spanish-American war and the Pulitzers praised for 'cleaning up' various city hall regimes. The Daily Mail is blamed for the Zinoviev Letters affair, and Ontario daily newspapers credited with making the provincial government drop the notorious Police Bill of the nineteen-sixties.

Few of the thousands of newspaper histories and journalists' memoirs that have failed to chronicle many such exploits. Unfortunately, not many of them have been examined systematically and carefully enough to establish a substantial causal link between press report and political happening. Among the few reliable sets of materials available in such areas are the case studies in Colin Seymour- Ure's The Political Impact of the Mass Media. Apart from that we have a surfeit of works that demonstrate to the complete satisfaction of the author (and those similarly predisposed) that TV or the press was responsible for any number of policy changes in public life. Television's effect in bringing the Vietnam war into American living rooms night after night is one favourite subject of such assertions. Most of them tend to ignore the presence of other contributing factors, which are usually so numerous or intangible that they make it impossible to single out the influence of any one factor such as television.

If it is to convey anything useful for the study of politics, 'power of the press' must mean publishing activity that leads individuals and governments to act politically in ways which they would not otherwise have adopted. The publishing activity takes in fact, opinion, and mixtures of the two. For analytic purposes its nature does not matter. It all consists of information bits weighty enough to tip some person or institution along a particular direction. The process may be immediate or cumulative, direct or indirect. The political activity may be a specific decision or a 'non-decision', that is, an agreement, spoken or unspoken, not to deal with some area of public life. The long-time party leader, W. L. Mackenzie King, once asserted that politics consisted as much in what was prevented as in what was accomplished. The range of mass media effects on the audience goes beyond decisions and non-decisions. Potentially, it takes in the whole of social attitude and behaviour learning. Political sociology is a vast territory and for critical commentators it is here that the mass media has its most important influence, one that continues past childhood and in some societies may not even cease until the grave. As we saw earlier, scholars can use tools like content analysis to illustrate the value-laden frameworks of mass media reports on industrial relations, sexual stereotyping, protest campaigns, criminal deviance, and so on. Demonstrating the influence of either the actual content or the social habit/institution of the mass media is another business altogether. The variables are so numerous and the process so complex that positivist research is near-impossible. What one cannot disprove, others cannot prove. We are then thrown back on 'common sense evidence' to substantiate what are essentially ideological propositions.

Ideological propositions about the global impact of the mass media on politics are not confined to leftwing critics of managed capitalist societies. Disappointed liberals and cynical conservatives are equally likely to hold forth about television's trivialisation of politics at the cost of high purpose and principle. Substantiation is equally hard to produce and the effort is made only infrequently. A few serious investigators, however, have mustered some evidence that certain features of news media reporting have contributed to a decline in popular trust in elected politicians and civil servants. Most impressive of this work was a study reported by three U.S. scholars in 1976.[1] They looked at two sets of newspaper readers, one set of which

subscribed to daily papers that content analysis revealed
were noticeably more critical of governmental institutions
than were those read by the other group. Readers of the
highly critical newspapers scored much lower on 'trust in
government' scale than did the readers of relatively
uncritical newspapers. Apart from isolated instances like
this, worthwhile work on mass communications and
socialisation remains at the level of disciplined
observation and speculation. Outside the field of electoral
behaviour, empirical inquiry has largely centred on
political bias and public opinion distributions.

So commanding a role has the concept occupied in western
liberalism that initially the press was presumed to exercise
its power through the medium of public opinion. The model
depicted in Figure 7-1 persisted even when politicians
seemingly short-circuited the process by acting immediately
they saw press content. That was usually 'explained' by the
law of anticipated reactions. Academic inquiries into the
first set of relations (press to public) seem to have been
inspired by an idealised vision of the press as a 'clear
channel'--a wholly objective medium of communication.
Whatever the inspiration, interest soon developed in
political bias and the effects of editorials, slanted
stories, and misleading headlines. In many cases classrooms
provided the laboratory. In an experiment at the University
of Idaho,[2] for example, two professors were able to 'plant'
thirty bogus editorial items in the pages of a local paper.

FIGURE 7 - 1

Press Influence: the Standard Model

| Press Content | ----> | Public Opinion | ----> | Government |

Half the items were favourable and half unfavourable in their discussion of the former prime minister of Australia, William Hughes. A prior test showed none of the 203 subjects had prior knowledge of Mr. Hughes. Half the students were exposed to the favourable editorials and half to the unfavourable as an incidental part of their reading. After two months during which Mr. Hughes was supposedly touring the region, the readers were tested for their attitudes toward him. As expected, those who read the favourable editorials were well disposed toward him—98 per cent, and 86 per cent of the other group was ill-disposed toward the man. The same attitude distribution still persisted four months later.

In this way social experimentalists built a body of evidence which was later exploited by students and practitioners of propaganda under wartime conditions. What was not generally realised until much later was that one could feel confident of such biasing effects only in the case of individuals who had had no relevant predispositions or firm opinions.

Agenda-Setting

Walter Lippmann's pioneer work on public opinion made the first suggestion, in 1922, that there was a close connection between the newspapers' political contents and the mass public's political images. The early American voting studies tried to probe this but without much success. A more important development came in the mid-fifties when Elihu Katz and Paul Lazarsfeld developed the 'two-step' theory of communication in their **Personal Influence.** Lippmann's notion was taken a good deal further in 1961 by V. O. Key jr. in his **Public Opinion and American Democracy.** He noted that the evidence for a stimulus-response model of the power of the press was weak and contradictory at best. The more profitable area to examine might be the link between the mass media's selection and presentation of political news and the set of issues being discussed by the general public.

The press cannot tell us what to think. By the mid-sixties, most scholars were agreed there were too many mediating factors for anything like that to happen. Perhaps, Key suggested, what the press really ends up doing is telling us which issues to think and talk about. The idea was not unique to Key but his discussion of it was very influential. The proposition was put in more dramatic terms by Theodore White in The Making of the President 1972:

> The power of the press in America is a primordial one. It sets the agenda of public discussion....It determines what people will talk and think about—an authority that in other nations is reserved for tyrants, priests, parties and mandarins. [3]

It was some time before these propositions were carefully examined. Virtually all the major voting studies of the nineteen-sixties paid some attention to the mass media but most simply described the campaign content and partisan editorial stands. Others tried testing some version of the old stimulus-response model. A few turned up, almost incidentally, suggestive correlations between the reporting priorities of the mass media and the relative salience of particular issues for the mass publics. What appears to be the first study specifically tailored to test the concept of agenda-setting was reported by Donald L. Shaw and Maxwell E. McCombs in 1972. During the 1968 presidential election, they had found, in Chapel Hill, N.C., for instance, that among undecided voters there were close relationships between the political issues which the news media emphasized and the ones the voters saw as key issues in the election. Even though the three presidential candidates had placed widely divergent emphasis on the issues, these voters gave essentially the same kinds of emphasis and priorities to the major issues as they found in the press coverage as a whole. This suggested to the authors "that voters—at least undecided voters—pay some attention to all the political news in the press regardless of whether it is about or originated with a favored candidate.[4] This conclusion contradicts the basic concepts of selective exposure and selective perception, ideas which, as McCombs and Shaw point out, "are central to the law of minimal consequences."

The field of study blossomed during the seventies with different attempts being made to define and expand the boundaries of the notion of agenda-setting. McCombs' definition, now fairly widely accepted, specifies the concept as a "strong positive relationship between the emphases of mass communication and the salience of these topics to the individuals in the audience." [5] Many studies assume a causal line running from the mass media agenda to the public agenda, but without extensive time-lag research it is difficult to demonstrate. Some interdependence and 'reverse flows' have also been suggested. The projects that have been undertaken encompass the contents and presentation schedules of different communications media and varying, non-comparable time periods. The most common approach looked at television, daily newspaper, and/or radio broadcasting in one particular locality over a fairly short time-span. The public agenda varies in content somewhat more. Two political scientists, for example, say that

> The public agenda consists of all issues which (1) are the subject of widespread attention or at least awareness, (2) require action, in the view of a sizeable proportion of the public; and (3) are the appropriate concern of some governmental unit in the perception of community members. [6]

That is the most closely specified definition of the public agenda. More partial ones are used increasingly as much of the work is carried out in the field of communication studies and not political science. One consequence is that the bulk of research attention is drawing away from studying public issue attitudes. The focus is shifting to the cognition of specific items by members of the general public, as awareness is necessarily antecedent to opinion-holding, that is, 'if you haven't even heard about it, you can't have an opinion on it.' The items examined range far beyond the political to include all kinds of mass media contents. A few studies have looked at particular strata or types of audiences rather than at the public as a whole. Other work has looked at a series of single topics across a variety of community types, different media, and over varied time periods.

The research has confirmed important aspects of the agenda-setting hypothesis. There are distinct connections between the prominence the mass media give to certain politicians, issues, and data and the importance that people in the audience attach to those items. We cannot, however, speak of a generalised effect. Once again, characteristics of audience members determine how much the mass media will affect their scales of importance. Those most vulnerable are people whose partisan attachments, political convictions, independent knowledge, and general interests are low or non-existent. With people like these, the range of influence seems to vary with the amount individuals are exposed to mass media content, their use of the various channels, access to other information sources, and technological features of the arrangement and presentation of various items.

In what may be an excess of scholarly caution, Shaw and McCombs have suggested that 'the major political role of the mass media may be to raise the salience of politics among the American electorate every four years.' Only then, presumably, are enough voters paying close enough attention to political happenings in the mass media that agenda-setting influences begin to operate. In the early weeks of the campaigns studied by Shaw and McCombs, newspapers seemed to be the more powerful agenda-setters with television coming on to a stage of equal influence much closer to the election date. Once again, the better-educated tended to agree more with the newspapers' agendas of issue salience and the lesser-educated with television agendas. The report on this research project went on:

The differential effects of the two media also depend on the nature of the personal agenda. Newspapers have more influence on the intra-personal agenda of issues, those issues considered personally most important, while television has more influence on inter-personal agendas, what people talk about with each other. This is compatible with the earlier evidence that newspapers wield long-term influence while television fills a short-term influence role. [7]

The study of agenda-setting and similar phenomena is complicated by the previously unsuspected existence of dynamic mechanisms in social intercourse. One such is the 'spiral of silence' series of effects reported by Elisabeth Noelle-Neuman.[8] Despite differences over public affairs, for example, most people prefer to have harmonious relations with their peers. Noelle-Neuman points out that a constant process goes on in which an individual tests his reactions and opinions against those of his peers. He learns which topics are 'worth discussing', deduces the range of tolerable agreements and disagreements, and begins adjusting his own conversational agenda so as to maximise the comfort of his social relationships. It is yet another process of reducing social discomfort. In all of it, the press may play little or no direct role (except possibly for the provision of potential topics), but the mechanism undoubtedly conditions agenda-setting possibilities.

Bureaucratic routines and time limits written into financial and other measures are responsible for putting many of these matters on the schedule for debate and decision. The communication networks of individual decisionmakers generate other items on the schedule but in what proportion they arise from the various mass media, public representations, and private approaches we have very little idea.[9]

The research has centred on the functional relationship of the mass media to the political agenda of the community.

Political scientists, however, need particularly to discover the relationship between the press and the established structures of political discussion and decision. That would also help us to pick out and examine the two analytically separate political roles of the press to which this approach draws our attention to The first is as a communication channel serving general and elite audiences. 'Agendasetting' is only one of a number of indications that this is not a clear channel like a telephone line. The process always affects the message. The second role is as an actor who influences the subjects and direction of authoritative decisions whether intentionally or unintentionally. Because, among other things, neither role is very often adopted openly, it is difficult in practice to distinguish the two roles. Quite apart from the question of its utility to political scientists, the agenda-setting work suffers another weakness. Too often it simply describes a relationship between information source and information recall. It may amount to little more than a test of certain psychological propositions about information retention and learning and communications.

Whatever the distributions of politically relevant opinions among the public, they must be important to the study of popular government. But we must take care. In its present raw and mushrooming state, the concept of public opinion is rather indigestible. If it does provide the yeast for our system of government, nobody can yet tell us how it works. Agenda-setting research is telling us something about the first relationship—press and public. So far, we know little or nothing about the second relationship. All we have is the dubious assumption (which most definitions of liberal democracy actually require) that there is a connection between mass opinion on the issues of the day and decisionmaking in popular governments. The character of that connection is likely closer to the speculation of V.O. Key than to the notions behind the fad for public opinion issue surveys. Key's thought was that the public would generally

FIGURE 7 - 2

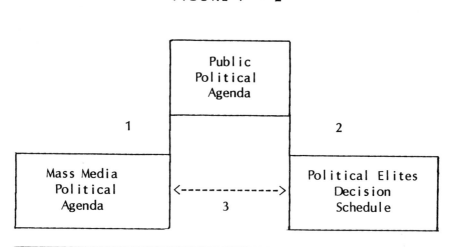

acquiesce in decision-making by the elites so long as their decisions did not stray very far beyond the society's broad set of fundamental values. Even those values were subject to some manipulation and could be seen in the process of changing over time. Although much mass communications inquiry has focussed on the press' functional relationship to society's political agenda, the usual model needs a third link. The first two are, of course, those connecting the mass media's political agenda to the public's political agenda (1), and the public agenda to the decision-makers' priority list (2). The important connection which has been relatively ignored so far (numbered 3 in the diagram) is that tying together the decision-makers' agenda and the mass media's political agenda. The reciprocal nature of this third connection is particularly noteworthy.

Debate and Decision Schedules

If the press does have some success in telling members of the public what they should be thinking about, how about the decision-makers? The simple democratic model (earlier Figure 7-1) suggested elected representatives took their cues and political agendas from the citizens. But even a cursory examination of parliamentary or other legislative agendas shows that they are markedly different in their concerns from those on the political agendas of either the public or the mass communications institutions.[10] Cabinet ministers and their deputies do not spend much of their working time talking about the same political issues as do members of the public. Why not? While cynical responses are easy, we do not know very much of the real answer.

Students of legislative and administrative processes have shown that bureaucratic needs dictate a large part of all governments' decision schedules. This is especially the case, of course, where 'sunset' laws are popular or where legislatures traditionally keep spending departments on a short financial string. Trying to implement even a few of the innovative ideas that newly elected politicians bring into office with them will also occupy a good deal of the decision time long after public opinion has passed on to other interests. We should recognise as well that the representation of public opinion at any one time is completely dependent on the questions that are asked of the public by the polstergeists, as Marshall McLuhan has aptly termed the survey industry. There are, then, good reasons why we should not be surprised by a discontinuity between the preoccupations of government decision-makers and those matters which commercial pollsters report are preoccupying the general public. But what of the other relationship—that between mass media agendas and those of the decision-makers?

The least complex of the possible sets of mass media and political elite relationships are probably those at the local level. To explore some of the questions involved in those relationships a research team at Queen's University, Canada, mounted a project focussed on three small Ontario cities that seemed roughly similar to each other and were partially insulated from outside mass communication flows.

Primary attention was given to the relationships between the press agenda and the schedule of issues that the city councils and their chief executive officers dealt with over a twelve-month period. While a city council agenda is also referred to as a political agenda at times, the less confusing term of civic decision schedule was used instead. A close look at details of the study may make both the problems and possibilities of this sort of research evident.

Focussing the inquiry on the decision elite allows researchers to avoid some of the difficulties encountered in using mass public agendas. First, the principal actors have personal access to the information reported in the press as well as the ability collectively to change their own agenda of debate and decision. Second, focussing on principal actors at the local level makes it easier to approximate a whole population than does a sampling system. Besides improving logistical efficiency, the method helps to raise the significance of the findings. Third, the focus on decisions and those taking them helps to reduce confusion between the agenda-setting and the data circulation functions of the press, a confusion that has beset some studies using mass public opinion agendas.

The Ontario inquiry distinguished between two types of agenda elements—the item and the issue. An item was a story or story element arising from routine surveillance of civic events. Perhaps more importantly, it evokes no particular emotion in the reader (apart from the so-called 'human interest' story ,which was not issue-relevant. Such matters were usually items of routine administration, introduced to council meetings, and passed with little or no comment.

An issue is more important and complex. Schattschneider taps the heart of the problem in singling out issues by reminding us that "an issue does not become an issue merely because someone says it is. The stakes in making an issue are incalculably great. Millions of attempts are made, but an issue is produced only when the battle is joined."

An issue involves some polarisation of opinion as well as some degree of commitment to a particular course of action or viewpoint. Schattschneider's discussion of these points draws our attention to other attributes of issue conflict:

In the competition of conflicts there is nothing sacred about our preference for big or little conflicts. All depends on what we want most. The outcome is not determined merely by what people want but by their priorities. What they want more becomes the enemy of what they want less.... Political conflict is not like intercollegiate debate in which the opponents agree in advance on a definition of the issues. As a matter of fact, the definition of the alternatives is the supreme instrument of power; the antagonists can rarely agree on what the issues are because power is involved in the definition.[11]

Of special relevance is the way issues arise from within local structures of political controversy. These social sets need not be explicitly political for nonpolitical structures of controversy can play significant, if not determining, roles in the degree of influence actors exert on the content of the civic decision schedule, that is the elite agenda for debate and decision. Any influence the mass media may exert on the decision schedule will similarly be related to the degree of access and legitimacy the media enjoy within the local system of political controversy. That access and legitimacy may vary dramatically from one city to another. How that influence varies depends on a whole constellation of cultural, personal, social, and historical factors.

The press seldom has continuous legitimate access. It may win a voice within those structures in at least three ways:

1 through appeals to the symbolic universe of community traditions and preferences,
2 through legitimate actors operating within the structure, or,
3 through the influence on legitimate actors of moral suasion or what they perceive to be public opinion.

Where access is neither continuing nor automatic, we may expect to find mass media content aimed at gaining entry to the structure. It must be borne in mind that the press acts as both suitor and maid, as an instrument pressing its own interests and as an instrument of established community interests and institutions.

The Research Project

The three cities selected were all in Eastern Ontario, had population bases under 70,000 and one daily newspaper each. They were Kingston (population 61,870) with The WhigStandard (circulation 36,000), Belleville (34,500) and The Intelligencer (17,300), and Peterborough (64,500) and The Examiner (23,700). The three cities are fairly modernised communities and difficult to characterise along class lines in either subjective or objective terms. They lie outside the main information currents of the Toronto and Ottawa metropolitan centres and are very different from them. The three cities have broadcast media that seemed more interested in their entertainment than their news function. They appeared neither to spend substantial resources on covering city politics nor to exercise much impact on them.

For the print agendas, each paper's major newspages were catalogued for a full twelve-month period beginning in December 1977 and timed to take in the city general elections. Stories were listed by subject, headline topic, page, and display characteristics. Excluded from the final list were reports of coming community events, and human interest stories outside the jurisdiction of the city councils. A jury of three persons familiar with the paper's reporting for the year aggregated items into principal issue areas. Reports on these issues were ranked in terms of the proportion that front page stories bore to the total of all news stories on city politics. (Differences in display habits might preclude this type of comparison for other newspapers). The result was three sets of print agendas.

TABLE 7 - 1

Comparison of Press and Elite Agendas: Belleville

Issue	Press Salience	Elite Salience
Mayor/Ald. Meeks conflict	1	5
Harbour control transfer	2	4
Sports arena management	3	1
Thurlow Twp. annextn.	4	6
Pinnacle Street & traffic	4	2
Downtown improvement and Front Street development	5	2
Quinte '78 Marina project	6	4
Humane Society shelter	7	2
Courthouse & registry location	8	6
Moira R. control dams	9	5
Downtown parking	10	2
Zoning & official plan	11	3
Meyer's Mill restoration	11	5
Neighbourhd Improvement Project	12	4

The politicians' decision schedule was determined through interviews with the mayors, virtually all the elected councillors, and each city's chief administrative officer. Respondents were asked to recall the most important items of council business, the most controversial and conflict-laden issues, and the most important decisions made in council. After free association responses, recollection aids were supplied. These prompted little change. The individuals ranked the issues twice, in terms of the importance they had given them and the importance they thought the council had given them. These rankings were rationalised and aggregated to get decision schedules for each city. Then they were compared to the appropriate print agendas.

TABLE 7 - 2

Comparison of Press and Elite Agendas: Kingston

Issue	Press Salience	Elite Salience
Fluoridating city water	1	8
The quality and efficiency of municipal services	2	5
P.U.C. inefficiency & management	3	9
Waterfront planning & development	4	1
Taxi by-laws and their enforcement	5	7
Disputes in the city labour pool	6	6
Budget, finance, and spending	7	3
Development and city planning	8	2
Protection and safety of public	9	10
Zoning and official city plan	10	4

Tables 7-1, 7-2, and 7-3 show the rank orders of issues in each of the paired sets of agenda and decision schedule for the three cities. To summarise the tables, the item rankings in the agenda pairs were found to be in fairly close correspondence (within four ranks of each other in 60 per cent of the cases for two cities, and in 43 per cent of the cases in Peterborough, the third city.

Can the wide rank differences for the other items be explained? Let us take one case, Kingston (Table 7-2). Look at the divergence in issue salience between the print agenda and the decision schedule. Three of the four issues ranking lower on the print budget were routine civic business items: budget and finance, general development plans, and minor zoning matters. More to the point, the three issues all lacked high degrees of emotional commitment and failed to generate much controversy. That is another way of saying they ranked low in conventional news values. The paper did not rate them as high in newsworthiness as the decision

TABLE 7 - 3

Comparison of Press and Elite Agendas: Peterborough

Issue	Press Salience	Elite Salience
Newspaper's city hall coverage	1	6
Mayor-council disagreements	2	7
Appointment of Hospital Directors	3	6
Management consultants' study	4	5
Parking and its enforcement	5	6
Economic development programs	6	1
Controversy in the PUC	7	6
Clonsilla Street development	8	6
C.G.E. nuclear plant	9	5
CEMP construction project	10	3
Abolishing ward system	11	6
Housing development issues	11	4
Zoning and planning	12	2
Land assembly plan	13	6

elites rated them in importance. Another category, general waterfront development, was a catchall. When the researchers took the highly controversial Marina City project out of the waterfront category, the two lists came closer into line. The issues higher in the print agenda than in the decision schedule were all matters on which community opinion was significantly polarised. That made them high in news values.

The tabular data tell us nothing about the Kingston newspaper's ability to influence the decision schedule. The causal arrow could run either way—depending on the issue. The interview data did suggest a degree of influence for the newspaper but it was limited to those issues on which The Whig-Standard found itself in alliance with the recognised community interest groups. It was not the press which was responsible for getting the Marina City issue on the civic timetable in the first place. But once there the continued opposition of the pressure groups enabled the newspaper to keep the issue alive and at the top of the decision schedule long after the council wanted desperately to drop it.

City councillors reported the press had inspired three other issues that they had ranked rather low: taxis, snow removal, and water fluoridation. Certainly the politicians did little about them and some cited this as evidence of their resistance to newspaper pressure. Strong moral fibre on the council's part is only one possible explanation Although most of the elected officials had had to make some kind of comment on the three issues, they were able to shift political responsibility for them quite handily. Taxicab control was under the jurisdiction of the independent Police Commission. The quantity and quality of snow removal was decided by the vagaries of Old Man Winter and by budget allocations made the year before and which were unchangeable by that time. The third question, fluoridation, was quickly transmuted by council action into a public referendum on which the councillors did not commit themselves. The press agenda suggests two other attempts to influence the city's decision schedule -public safety concerns and industrial relations in the public utilities. The newspaper gave these items considerable prominence but not one of those interviewed freely recalled them. On being prompted, the councillors attributed little importance to the issues and less than half thought the press had exercised any influence at all on council's patterns of discussion

Council Newspaper Relations

Earlier it was suggested that the correspondence between a press agenda and a civic decision schedule would depend on the newspaper's place in the community structure of issue cleavages. Sitting in continuous assessment of that standing

are members of the local political elite. Their judgement
will provide others with behavioural cues. It will decide
the scope and direction(s) of influence between council and
press, and those may well depend on the issue area involved.

Council newspaper relations varied widely from Belleville
to Peterborough to Kingston as did the cleavage structures.
During the study period, Belleville manifested a single deep
split among members of council -not a partisan one because
party organisation is anathema to the Ontario municipal
culture. Most issues saw the mayor and six or seven aldermen
lined up against three 'non establishment' aldermen.

The long-standing battle between the mayor of Belleville
and one 'maverick' culminated in electoral confrontation in
1978. At the last possible moment the newspaper strongly
urged reelection of the mayor. The challenger was defeated
and thus removed from active politics. Even the local in
fluentials who were interviewed endorsed the common cafe
claims that the council majority represented the city's
business and industrial interests. The newspaper was said to
do the same and editorials appearing in The Intelligencer
during the study period did nothing to disprove the claim.
Most of the 'insiders' applauded the fairness and under
standing of the newspaper's approach to city affairs. As a
group, they insisted that its reporting had no influence on
their agendas or decisions. Only the outsiders had negative
opinions about the reporting of city politics.

The city of Peterborough presented a different picture,
almost a mirror image. There the mayor had recently won
office over an establishment figure and was one of the
outsiders although several of the councillors would usually
support him. "I'm just a working man myself " was one of his
frequently voiced populist notes. He spoke of his time in
office as a mission to improve the city's economic base by
attracting more industrial employment. That mission often
put him at odds with some of the established business

interests, possibly because a measure of success would tend to undermine their position. The mayor was also in direct conflict with the leading paid officials. Several of them he had criticised openly and he had tried several times to overhaul the entire administration. Legally, the mayor of an Ontario city is closer in status to a British than to a 'strong' American mayor but his direct, popular election his range of committee memberships and his casting ballot combine to give him significant political weight. The Peterborough mayor was a popular public figure. He worked closely with the newspaper, The Examiner, and sometimes gave it copies of consultant's reports and other official papers before council members had seen them.

Not surprisingly, most of the then councillors in Peterborough were anti-newspaper and critical of the mayor for conducting city business openly through the newspaper. Only the mayor and three supporters thought the newspaper coverage of civic politics was fair and professional. At one time, the majority sought to make an issue out of the mayor newspaper relationship. They proposed a motion censuring the "biased and unprofessional reporting" of the press but were dissuaded from proceeding with the issue. The councillors who were happiest about the situation were most likely to assert that The Examiner exerted no direct influence on the council's agenda. Others disagreed. The paper had too much influence in their affairs. The majority particularly complained that the paper was always stirring up the city voters to complain to them and generally making political life more troublesome than it need be.

Kingston represented a third case. All observers were agreed that the council was a heterogeneous body with no cleavage line cutting across a range of issues. A fairly even balance of power resulted. The mayor was frequently forced to use his casting ballot to decide issues. The citizenry, by contrast displayed a number of rather durable cleavage lines. Two of them provide the semi permanent division between the business professional community and the academic-artistic group. Civic battles were often joined by some of the large numbers of people in the extensive hospital and medical research establishments. Various electors and ratepayers' associations and a poor people's lobby furnished other participants in the city's lively politics. While most of these interests lacked stable communications and formal organizations, their intercourse was enhanced by common workplaces, common recreation and leisure activities, and the city's compact size. Different combinations of these interest groups mobilised from time to time to attack what was always called 'civic progress' by its promoters. A well established local family owned the newspaper and it is Canada's oldest in continuous daily publication. These roots were in curious contrast to the ambivalent status of its news/editorial staff.

In two cases, Belleville and Peterborough, the paper's relationship to factions within the decision elite gave it direct and continuing access to the arena of legitimate disputants. The Kingston newspaper seemed to lack such standing. Its access was only intermittent and had to be won (or lost) issue by issue through support and enlistment of more legitimate participants in the process or by appealing directly to the interests of community groups that enjoyed legitimate access. Generally, those interviewed in Kingston were prone to raise very direct questions about the newspaper trying to "butt into" local affairs. Charges were made that the reporters and editors lacked "understanding of community issues." had no commitment to Kingston, were "too unprofessional", and were all working toward employment in Toronto. (The numerous awards won by the paper tends to discredit the charges of journalistic incompetence). The decision makers' criticisms all turned out to be directed toward press involvement in issues which did not have the support of other legitimate community interest groups. Only in Kingston were issues mentioned on the decision schedule that did not rank on the print agenda. About those issues the newspaper published only limited surveillance reports.

Findings

The three Ontario cities study brought the research team a mixed bag of conclusions. In the Kingston situation, most elite members saw the press **qua** political actor as an outsider to be excluded from the debate. It was accorded little or no legitimacy in raising issues on its own. In Belleville, **The Intelligencer** was inside the structure. Its print agenda reflected the decision schedule. Association with the majority faction of local notables legitimated the newspaper's participation. In turn, the established groups could count on the editor to voice their concerns. In the Peterborough case, press legitimacy and validation for its agenda came from association with the mayor and the council minority who supported him.

In both Belleville and Peterborough, challenges to the newspaper's role in civic affairs came from those people in opposition situations. For students of agenda-setting, the the observation that the print agendas appeared to exercise greater influence on what the opposition elites talked about seems a somewhat perverse finding. This press 'influence' apparently worked in two different ways. Sometimes, the opposition tried to beat the governing group about the head for failing to give adequate attention to certain issues on the print agenda. At other times they tried to make the newspaper's pattern of reporting into an issue. Otherwise, the print agendas were found to correspond with the interest patterns of those in the local elites most closely associated with the press.

The ability to influence local decision schedules appears —on the basis of the interview data—to be a function of the prevailing structures of debate and decision-making. The ability may not be generally inherent in local newspaper reporting as such. Of this, the Kingston case provided the strongest evidence. There, significant effects were noted only when the press was associated with other legitimate actors. The situation conforms with some of the findings of

Robert Dahl and other American pluralists. In contrast, the Belleville situation would confirm the expectations of those social critics who see local dailies simply as the mouthpieces of local elites. The Peterborough case cannot be readily categorized in similar terms.

The tendency for small newspapers to support community notables is often said in the literature to arise as much unconsciously as consciously. The explanatory factors mentioned are many but usually include four sets

1. The publisher's vulnerability to local social and business pressure.
2. Vocational training of traditional gatekeepers (city and news editors, etc.), which leads them to omit or bury news items that might call into question the sociocultural structure and people's faith in it.
3. Reporter's reliance on authority figures for news sources.
4. The journalistic concept of professionalism which emphasises rationality, decisions rather than discussion, depersonalisation of local legislative proceedings, legal language, and respectful treatment of local notables.[12]

The three newspapers studied are small but do a respectable job in terms of most English-language local dailies. A study of three different cities and their press might well give different results, particularly if the communities were larger, more socially variegated, and exhibited correspondingly wider social representation in the political elites. Urban sociologists have not reported many such cases. In those circumstances a study like the present would have to deal successfully with even more variable influences on press agendas and civic decision schedules.

The press affects the political system in numerous ways, most of them not well understood. Into this category falls things like the media's function as a channel of inter-elite communications and the consequences of the routine surveillance reporting of governmental institutions and activities. These things, however, do not provide much of the stuff of press legendry. For that we must move closer to some of the concerns of this study. Even here disappointments are probable. Daily newspapers have undoubtedly led local politicians to particular policy decisions that the newspapers preferred and that, if left entirely to their own discretion, the politicians would not have taken. Defined that way, the power of the press –even in local affairs--is an unusual and sometime thing rather than commonplace. Even the ability to get 'City Hall' talking about preferred issues depends on the alignment of socio-political forces in the community and the place among them that the newspaper has won for itself.

NOTES TO CHAPTER SEVEN

1. Arthur H. Miller, Lutz Erbring, and Edie N. Goldenberg, "Typeset politics impact of newspapers on issue salience and public confidence " A.P.S.R., v.73 (1979), 67 84.
2. William Albig, Modern Public Opinion, New York. McGraw-Hill, 1956, 348-9.
3. New York, Bantam, 1973, 327.
4. The Emergence of American Political Issues, St. Paul, Minn.: West 1977, 8.
5. "Expanding the Domain of Agenda-Setting Research: Strategies for Theoretical Development," a paper for the Speech Communication Association, Washington, D.C., December 1977.
6. R.W. Cobb and M. H. Keith Ross, "Agenda Building as a Comparative Political Process,". A.P.S.R., v.70 (1976), 126-38.
7. The Emergence of American Political Issues, 156.
8. "Turbulences in the Climate: Methodological Applications of the Spiral of Silence Theory," Public Opinion Quarterly, v.41 (1977), 143 158.
9. For one of the few studies of its type, see Anthony Barker and Michael Rush, The member of parliament and his information, London Allen and Unwin, 1970. Also relevant is J.L. Walker, "Setting the agenda in the U.S. Senate," British Journal of Political Science, vol.7,(1977), 423 445.
10. Greater correspondence would probably be found, though, between mass media agendas and those of U.S. presidential press conferences and occasions like Question Time in Canadian parliamentary bodies.
11. E. E. Schattschneider, The Semi-Sovereign People: A Realist's View of Democracy in America, Hinsdale, Ill.: Dryden Press 1975, first published 1960, 66, 72.
12. See, among others: Warren Breed, "Mass Communication and Sociocultural Integration," in L. A. Dexter and D. M. White, eds., People, Society and Mass Communication, New York: Free Press, 1964, and D. L. Paletz, Peggy Reichert, and B. McIntyre Speck, "How the Media Support Local Governmental Authority," Public Opinion Quarterly, v.35 (1971), 80-92.

Like the universal church of old, our mass media system must fight continually for its independence. For those whose increased control the media are trying to avoid, losing means more than tolerating a nuisance. It means submitting to its dominance. Many are the battles already won by the news media. Any institution that wants to be a vital force today must reckon with them and deal on their terms. The elected are the most obviously submissive, and politicians are still busy making themselves over in the desired images. Their surrender makes it possible for the administrative and judicial institutions to resist the pressure. The major economic and a few other institutions are also holding out. Some think that new technologies will make communications impossible for governments to control. That looks like wishful thinking. Governments have enormous ability to win the upper hand and should never be underestimated. In any society proud of its diversity the struggle between institutions is a continuing one, never finally settled.

Although the language has been martial, the instruments used in the competition among institutions have been social. On the one side we see public exposure, various forms of ridicule and embarrassment managed by capitalising on technological awkwardness, and oligopolistic access to mass audiences. On the other side the weapons have been economic and judicial harassment, competing enterprises, withdrawal of patronage, monopoly control of information, legal force majeure, and, occasionally, appeal to the civic emotions of patriotism and 'the national interest'. Curiously, the most powerful weapon of all, news, has itself been the storm centre of relations between the mass media as political institution and the society's other institutions of governing influence. Exploring some of those relations will lead us to brief considerations of advertisers and economic groups, party politicians and civil servants, censorship, and varied forms of news management and manipulation.

Although all content decisions are, in a sense, political, it is as a news medium that the press has won political influence. The most important element in such influence has been elected politicians' belief in the power of news, or, at the very minimum, in their reluctance to take the chance of behaving as non-believers. Ironically, while few people will subscribe to a news story as a fair account of things we have experienced personally, almost everybody adopts mass media news as an acceptable definition and description of all other realities. Those realities include the various institutions of government.

In the days when government was small, politics was a primary experience. Mediaeval man, for instance paid taxes directly to his masters, suffered arbitrary justice, and was assured only a very uncertain peace of mind and property. He had a highly personal knowledge of the relevant political institutions. Government has magnified itself enormously today but mass media man seldom thinks of government imposts and services as politics. For him, it has been redefined. He thinks of politics as what he learns about through the news.

Most of us see politics chiefly as something experienced vicariously in the mass-mediated versions. We have far more personal encounters with government than mediaeval man ever did but we tend to interpret even this personal experience more and more through the lenses of the mass communications institutions rather than through the political viewpoints of party, elected representative, or church. American political institutions have learned this lesson so well that two authors assert "the context of media work and the news perspective it has propagated now take precedence over virtually all other contexts of meaning and logic in the realm of public presentations."[1]

What is this mass media news that so influence even the self-presentations of government and other institutions? Those in public life are the same as the rest of us in their rejection of news as a fair account of any reality they have experienced personally. But they know it will be other people's political reality. To point out, as Anthony Smith does, that news is simply another invented genre of literature (or communication) like the novel, or poetry, or teledrama, or cinéma vérité is not to condemn it. Most journalists do not claim to present detailed historical documentaries. They are offering us **news**, a particular communication form our culture has developed for organising and distributing certain kinds of information bits which will be of fairly wide interest. As we have seen earlier, news has its own rules–its own criteria of relevance and professional acceptability—but none of them adds up to a claim that a 'pure view of reality' is provided thereby.[2]

People in other institutions usually recognise this view of the news intellectually. Some recognise it operationally as well. Emotionally they dislike it and do their best to take advantage of it politically. When they cannot, they strive instead to change the nature of the relationship between their institution and that of the mass media. The relationship is seldom a direct one. It is mediated by a number of variables including occupational definitions of

the communicators' roles, their audiences, and their product
(news). The societal status of the various mass media, their
method of finance, their industrial structure, and their
patterns of ownership will affect the inter-institutional
relationship. Equally important in majoritarian societies
will be the comparative strength of the support bases of the
mass media and the political and economic institutions.

Economic Interests

If there is something everybody 'knows' about the
commercial mass media everywhere, it is that advertisers
control the news content—or at least have a great deal to
say about it. After all, advertising is the major source of
mass media income in the English language countries (save
for the state broadcasters) and 'he who pays the piper calls
the tune', doesn't he? So goes the folk wisdom. The vehement
denials with which editors and publishers greet such claims
sound just a little odd in societies that are largely
capitalist at heart and generally economic determinist in
popular philosophy. How much accuracy is there to the folk
wisdom when it comes to the specifically political
relationships between the mass media and its economic
clientele? The characteristics of the relationship are many
and complicated. For our purposes, they can be reduced to
the essentials by making a few distinctions, between:

1 Explicitly political and general non political content.
2 Program sponsorship and broadcasting spot commercials.
3 Content intervention and private system programming.
4 Ownership and management of the mass media on the one
   hand and their advertising clients on the other.

The development of mass circulation newspapers freed
journalists from their long-established dependence on party
and factional patronage. It did not mean complete freedom.
Economically, they were snared in one and sometimes two
traps. First, they had to publish a type of periodical that
would attract and hold the very high number of readers

needed to finance it- a mass newspaper. Secondly, when higher and higher news-stand prices failed to match rising costs, advertising became essential as a supplement and then as a mainstay. Journalists had to continue producing newspapers that would generate circulations large enough to keep advertisers interested. Only a few dailies were able to survive by serving a small but very prosperous readership, which could be sold to advertisers at premium prices.

Since the rise of advertising journalists have carried on a love hate relationship with institutionalised commerce. That relationship was exacerbated by the journalist's ambiguous social status, occasional radical tendencies, and streaks of perverse independence abetted by developing notions of quasi-professionalism. The larger the news organisation became, the more remote the news staff was from advertising and economic necessities, and the more zealous they grew to protect their performance standards from outside interference. They were not always successful.

Even today newsrooms are filled with stories about wicked advertisers able to work their evil ways with the news content. The examples are invariable. The police arrest of a major local retailer who was driving 'under the influence' was not reported. Another advertiser's daughter got unwarranted news space for her wedding. The manufacturer's new model cars get picture space and 'testing' by the motor editor. All examples turn on the exercise of discretion and news judgement by the managing editor or news editor. That such decisions have been influenced by non-news factors seems irrefutable on occasion. That those incidents are isolated rather than generalisable seems almost as clear, although one must take care in trying to generalise about the workings of several thousand daily newspapers.

The question of advertisers' intervention in newspaper content has been looked at in the course of public inquiries in both Canada and Australia. The Canadian Senate special report on the mass media reported that they had "heard dark hints that abuses existed, but were unable to find any cases, nor were any documented." Two Australian royal commissions (1949 and 1962) agreed that there was some evidence to suggest that individual advertisers exerted pressure but concluded that it arose "more from a conflict of commercial interest than from impropriety or any corrupt motive." Both inquiries emphasised that evidence was found only with respect to attempted pressures. As one author notes succinctly, "attempts at pressure prove something about what some advertisers will do -nothing about what the press lets them get away with."[3]

The economic fates governing newspapers are themselves perverse. The more advertisers a newspaper wins, the greater its own financial strength, and the less dependent it is on the whims and demands of any one advertiser. One fiercely independent editor in Chicago put it this way years ago.

We aren't doing an advertiser any favor when he signs a **Tribune** contract and he isn't doing us a favor. We wouldn't be selling advertising if we didn't make a profit, and he wouldn't be buying it if he didn't make a profit.[4]

That editor's case for interdependence is perhaps best made by observation of the plunges in retail sales during extended newspaper strikes. 'They need us every bit as much as we need them' has been the newsman's consolation about the relationship over the years. Not every situation meets that idealised representation of the relations between advertising clients and mass media editors. A number of newspapers and broadcasting stations as well, often those in small cities, are financially weak and are unusually dependent on one or two large advertising clients. At the very minimum, financial and probably editorial autonomy would seem to require a solid revenue base, one that cannot easily be seriously threatened by one major advertiser or some small group of them joining together to pressure the medium rather than competing against each other.

As more of an entertainment than a news medium, broadcasting has developed somewhat different relations with commerce. The financial pressures to build and maintain mass audiences were far more powerful than those faced by most newspapers. The print media could build and sell specialised audiences which even paid for the contents of the commercial product, whether news or advertising messages. With few exceptions in the early days, broadcasting could deliver only mass audiences which had paid nothing for the product (in a capitalist system!), which was fickle in its program choice, and the existence of which was itself difficult to verify. The development of program sponsorship in the American system together with the advertising 'interference' this led to has been well documented. Edward R. Murrow pointed out at the time that the sponsor of a one-hour television program was not only buying the few minutes devoted to extolling his product; he was determining within broad limits the total character of the entire hour.

The system extended beyond overtly entertainment programs to include most public affairs and documentary productions. One meat packer is said to have refused to allow a show it was sponsoring to display a mediaeval knight's traditional garb because Armour was the name of a rival meatpacker. Fred W. Friendly has reported extensively on his experience as a senior executive with the Columbia Broadcasting System (CBS). An aluminum company, Alcoa, was a sponsor of a highly-ranked documentary series, "See It Now". One of the shows was "on cigarettes and lung cancer, and both CBS and Alcoa felt the pressures of the tobacco industry which buys both air time and aluminum foil."[5] Most pernicious to the idea of mass media editorial autonomy was the general practice by stations and even networks to allow advertisers and their agencies to take the initiative in devising and preparing whole program packages. While the most obvious forms of this have disappeared, the growth during the seventies of independent companies that in the business of producing and selling programs to broadcasters is relevant to this concern. The result may simply be that today the exercise of strong advertiser influence on broadcast content has not been eliminated but simply driven underground.

Not so often noted was the early avoidance of many American practices in the United Kingdom. Its regulations prohibited specific sponsorship of programs and produced a system of almost random commercial spots, which effectively insulated the news and program producers from most individual advertiser pressure. Not all advertisers have given up. In the face of legislative and other impulses, some of the bigger ones have simply shifted the pressure points. The provision of free products for use within programs—automobiles for commuting and chase scenes, electrical appliances for game shows—reduces costs for program makers, wins excellent 'exposure', and, possibly, provides that mental conditioning which J. K. Galbraith sees as TV's chief economic function.[6] Advertisers with image problems, like tobacco firms, sponsor sporting events like professional golf cricket matches, automobile racing, and so on, which attract big audiences now or can be promoted to do so. Every mass media reference to major happenings then becomes an unwitting advertisement for the sponsor. Some organisations, like the BBC in the early nineteen eighties, fought against being used in this way (through provisions in their contracts with the Football Association) but such refusals were exceptional rather than representative.

Whatever the situation, the case can always be put that all intervention in content decisions is political. Concealing the police record of one elite member and awarding greater social prominence to one wedding rather than to others is part of the process of legitimation that supports the governing class and makes a mockery of liberalism's professed belief in equal opportunity. For all the generalised persuasiveness of that argument, it remains curious that a capitalist elite either cannot use or chooses not to use its alleged control over the mass media specifically to propagate idea-sets in opposition to those of the left-wingers they claim control the mass media. With that curiosity devoted conspiracy theorists will have no difficulty. They find adequate explanation the mass media's continuing need to market a commercially viable product.

The greatest influence the commercial establishment exerts on the mass media and its political content arises from conceptions of the marketplace. With only a few exceptions, the sellers of goods and services want to be loved as well as profitable, and particularly when they perceive the two qualities going together. Institutionally, that has meant a wish to avoid association with public affairs controversy or unpleasant programming that disturbs the audience. Coincidentally, commercial network program directors came to the fortuitously compatible conclusion that building big TV audiences could best be advanced by a similar avoidance pattern. A better recipe for producing mass media content that reinforced the status quo would be difficult to devise. It is sentiments like these rather than any direct advertiser pressure that Fred Friendly blames for the eventual death of programs like "See It Now". A few still survive, even prosper, but few of them generate more than small audiences, slight advertiser interest, and small production budgets. When a network like the C.B.C. stops worrying about building audiences to sell to advertisers and devotes reasonable resources to programs like "Marketplace", it has sometimes won unexpectedly large audiences.

The range of acceptable controversy in the commercial mass media corresponds closely to that of the legislature and its major parties. Television has defined politics for the millions primarily in terms of clashes between powerseeking personalities. Broadcasting that exploits this conception of politics fits the norm so well that few of those watching are diverted from their 'proper' functions as members of the mass audience. Neither cash nor licence security need be risked in making public affairs television newsworthy. After all, the purpose of most TV news is acting as a come-on, as a commercial for the real commercials.

While not as inhibited as television, the newspaper press has devoted relatively little attention to public affairs questions other than those thrown up by the established structures of political controversy. To most reporters, for instance, business news is boring; and their response is understandable if the phrase means only civic boosterism. News of the world of business and commerce might reasonably be interpreted as including things like automobile safety, dangerous drug products, food additives, and environmental pollutants. These and other forms of public misbehaviour could easily have been discovered and fully exposed even by newspapers with modest resources. All it took, basically, was staff time and competence to read and interpret trade magazines, academic journals, and public auditors' reports. The mass media, however, launched very few of these recent public issues. Most began life from within the accepted constitutional system. Until adopting an issue gives a major party leader promise of political gain, many such questions will continue to languish in the political wilderness and only specialist publications will report on them.

The political blandness of the mass media is sometimes blamed on their increasing entanglement in newspaper chains and multi-enterprise conglomerates. The 'cause' is more basic. It is putting newspapers and broadcasters on a sound business footing. Any advertiser that wanted to press a newspaper along a particular partisan political course would be rebuffed in most publishing houses today. Editorial integrity might have a little to do with it but good business sense would have more. Non-partisan news columns make far fewer customers unhappy than do partisan accounts. The surviving 'press barons' whose chief object is to run personal propaganda outlets are engaged in an expensive, risky vanity. They are the aberrations, not the norm.

The contribution of the business conglomerate in publishing has been to give newspapers and stations more solid financial backing and a better approach to building mass circulation and audience figures. In doing so, the chains have also preserved a number of media enterprises that were faltering and would otherwise have perished. This was the strategy that provided the foundation of the Roy Thomson international empire.

The 'business-minded' approach to newspaper publishing has seldom led to higher expenditures on news-gathering and production. Impulse sales at the newsstand were once significant factors in determining a paper's total circulation. They are no longer. Spending more on editorial resources may bring more prestige and respect but it seldom brings more business. No wonder then that newly appointed publishers or editors hardly ever turn out to be crusaders ready to do battle with Public Enemy No. 1, unless he has already been convicted by others. The Senate report on the Canadian mass media commented that "broadly speaking, advertisers, their agencies, and the media owners are all the same kind of people, doing the same kind of thing, within the same kind of private enterprise rationale."

So long as journalists continue to ply their trade in much the same kind of boats as businessmen, and so long as they base their notions of reality on raw materials furnished by other institutions, business interests will have little need of disrupting the relationship by trying to intervene directly in mass media political content. While the remark was made more than a century ago, Sir John A. Macdonald's observation seems to remain relevant: "when you see what a journalist will write unbribed, why then, there's no need to bribe him, is there?"

The Press as Actor-Crusader

The press has a strangely malleable self-image. On most occasions, its journeymen will swear an expert's devotion to polishing the mirror-to-society concept. On other occasions, they will add a pinch of watchdog-for-the-little-man notion. When the sacred spirit of public indignation really seizes hold though, the newsman will swear a never-ending crusade against the forces of evil—whoever they might be at the moment. In between stages, journalists will assert the right of all institutional citizens to offer their opinions for the guidance of others, and go on to do so with some vigour through the editorial columns. These differing roles and the impulses and behaviours they inspire add varying dashes of confusion to the relations between the political institutions of government and the mass media.

The first scribblers of early English journalism were in no doubt about their own preferred social role. They wanted to change the opinions of those who mattered. Later, there came to be far more people whose opinions mattered together with hundreds of commentators eager to enlighten them. People like John Stuart Mill glorified, even sanctified, the publication of many diverse opinions and elevated the idea into a tenet of the official ideology. News was invented as a commercial product but its potentials were missed at first. Comprehension of its significance to the governing process had to await two major social developments: the sharing out of some elements of political power among the people and realisation that the newly-developing mass circulation newspapers represented the most efficient way of reaching hordes of voters. During that time journalism was turning to a highly schizophrenic activity. It persisted in trying to play a variety of political roles and maintain equal credibility in all of them: opinion-shaper, watchdog, party propagandist, voice of the people, mover and shaker of cabinet chairs, and independent reporter of reality. In between times, journalists did whatever was necessary to make a living as well.

The press institution does not try to perform quite so many roles today as once it did. Journalists argue there is no reason today why people should mix up the analytically separate functions of news reporting and opinion-shaping. Different individuals are responsible for them and most mass media try to make the distinction between news and opinion quite clear. Confusion exists just the same. Differentiation between the two types of content is not nearly as easily made or clearly marked as journalists would have us believe. Even when it appears so, the public frequently fails to heed the marks. One of the results is lowered public credibility —especially for the print media, despite its greater detail and exclusive qualities of reference and comparability. It is an ironic comment on the faith people have that they can place greater trust in the moving information bits that television lets them see with their own eyes.

Willy-nilly the role of political actor is everywhere attributed to the press institution. Little need be said here about editorials and opinion columns, the first of the two methods the press adopts for its conscious interventions in the political system. These expressions of policy preferences are aimed at two directions simultaneously—at the general readership and at the decision-makers most directly involved. Part of an editorial's credibility with decision elites rests on suppositions about its effect on the general public, about which there is not much hard evidence. Another part of what authority it commands rests on knowledge that other influentials will be reading the same arguments and they, even if not the general public, will be able to demand appropriate answers in certain cases. Beyond that, leading articles and editorials must depend for influence on a combination of their inherent persuasiveness and the newspaper's general reputation.

The second of the mass media's methods for conscious intervention in politics is the crusade—a barrage of news and 'exposures' on a selected topic backed up by editorials and all other persuasive powers available. The 'saturation coverage' of one issue amounts to implicit admission that a good deal of deliberateness, even manufacturing, goes into the news process. Where other news outlets might think the issue worthy of one or two displays, the crusading medium suspends such normal criteria of newsworthiness and devotes far more resources to it. Every facet of the issue is examined minutely, preferably in highly emotional terms.

Impressive   discoveries   are   reported,   and   appropriate
expressions of shock, horror, and indignation are solicited
from interest group spokesmen. The publication of supporting
man-in-the-street   interviews,   news   stories,   and   editorials
is spread over a number of days 'to build for effect'—the
manipulation of opinion changes in the public and decision
groups to bring about the desired responses. What is wanted
ranges from compensation for an injured child to political
resignation to criminal prosecution. Where the crusading
medium is, unusually, a broadcaster, overt editorialising is
replaced by unbalanced expressions of sympathetic support
for the cause by community spokesmen.

Early   twentieth   century   American   daily   newspapers
achieved   greatest   notoriety   for   crusading—usually   against
corrupt city governments and 'the big interests'. Most other
countries had press crusaders as well. The tabloid press in
Britain was crusading continuously between the two world
wars and Canada's largest newspaper, **The Toronto Daily Star**,
was so devoted to campaigns in opposition to slum housing,
legal   drinking,   and   capital   punishment—that   its   founding
publisher was nicknamed 'Holy Joe' Atkinson. In many cities,
crusades provided much of the excitement of daily journalism
and probably all the legends about the immense political
power of the press.

What   inspires   crusades?   Idealism   and   commercial
calculation. So many crusades reflected terrible battles for
circulation among big city dailies that a powerful cynicism
has gripped most commentators on the phenomena. With some
justice   they   pointed   to   the   Hearsts   and   Pulitzers,
Northcliffe and Kemsleys, and dismissed all as profiteering
buccaneers who left the poor no better off, the concerned
more confused than enlightened, and the politicians more
opportunist   about   reform   than   before.   Such   one-sided
judgements could leave us as cynical as the accused
publishers. We need to remember that some people **do**
deliberately take up journalism as a weapon with which to
achieve moral and social reform. Even if a paper should make

some commercial gains through the crusading process, that by itself does not subvert the ideal; without finances, the newspaper fails and the cause may well die. Others take up journalism for the sake of political power and for that we need look no further than British press barons like Beaverbrook. The memoirs and biographies of thousands of journalists are filled with anecdotes about their political crusades and their presumed direct influence on the course of particular issues and governmental decisions.

Crusades are with us still although they have changed shape and character. In their original form, they looked much like current Soviet press exposes in which the activities of 'anti-social' individuals are revealed and castigated without much attention being drawn to the policies and institutions which bear chief responsibility for them. There were exceptions, of course. The Pulitzer attack on insurance companies and demand for their close regulation finds echoes half a century later in British press crusading on housing and rent control policies. Despite this and rare examples like the Ontario newspapers' successful campaign to defeat the notorious police powers bill in 1964, modern press campaigns seem to lack bite by comparison. The **New York Times** Christmas Cheer Fund has many counterparts: The **Star** Fresh Air Fund, the **Nottingham News** Scanner Campaign, and Save Our Hospital/Industry/School struggles everywhere public budgets are cut. Whether in terms of popular emotion, journalistic enterprise, or academic analysis, they do not seem to be in the same class of political action. So too we are likely to judge the more sedate mass media efforts represented to 'Action Line' and 'Public Defender' newspaper columns or broadcast programs aimed at righting bureaucratic wrongs.

Crusading, editorializing on public issues, raising funds for charity, and acting as mass media ombudsman are all forms of direct political activism. As such, they directly affect relations between the mass media and the political institutions. Such activities mean the press takes a position on public issues in clear-cut opposition to the government. Doing so is bound to undermine the mass media's claims to be judging political issues dispassionately in terms of professional criteria. Whatever objective reporting most staff members may attempt, the press institution as a whole is affected and leaves itself wide open to threats of regulatory reprisal. So far as they play much more overt roles as political actors than does television, newspapers will continue to lose credibility in the eyes of both government and the public. And losses in credibility weaken both a paper's influence and its news-gathering capacity.

Governmental Views of the Press Relationship

Many politicians view the mass media with a passion even more intense than the love-hate feeling journalists have for advertising. Some of this passion can be attributed to the lopsidedness of the relationship. For reporters and editors government and its denizens may be no more than so much raw material to be converted into a commercial product, news. The mass media, though, are more essential to politicians and other public servants. They are a key to long life or rejuvenation at the polls, even a drug for some politicians. Seemingly, they can mean the success or failure of any of hundreds of administrative programs which need well-informed and cooperative publics to achieve their objectives.

Those in government attribute a variety of political roles to the press. They see the major task in instrumental terms those of informing the citizen-subjects of what the government is doing for them and interpreting the significance of that activity. The mass media are also expected to protect the public interest through its watchdog function, guarding against corruption, lax performance, and favouritism toward special groups.

People with governmental responsibilities need a variety of information coming back to them from the public in great volume and quality, data about the effectiveness of existing programs and the need of new or amended ones. While the mass media do offer the advantages of fair comprehensiveness, easy availability, and immediacy, as scientific indicators of social change, they are lacking in perfection. This is the source of many of the diverse criticisms that colour the public servants' perspective on mass media performance. Journalists are said to lack experience and they persist in playing up the 'wrong' news. Both complaints may reflect no more than different viewpoints and different sets of self-interests. Premature publicity, emphasis on program mistakes rather than successes, inadequacies of technical and contextual explanation—objections like these reflect the different stakes and involvement that the two institutions have in the same events. Western governments occasionally achieve something close to their communications ideal. Consider royal weddings, state funerals, and the Queen's Speeches to Parliament. Better yet, look at the big rocket launchings by the U.S. National Aeronautics and Space Administration. They added up to splendid news of government, for government, and by government. Robert Lewis Shayon described one such event in this way:

> On the networks there were tension, suspense, bits of information, marvelous pictures, impressive simulations, and artful animation—but one would be pressed hard to say the coverage was not a fullblown commercial for the government, NASA, the space industry, and the broadcasters.[7]

A commercial for government? No wonder! Limited only by the schedules of the cosmos, governmental authorities were able to control the timing of the events, determine who would be the participants, set the stage, light it, and even control the television cameras themselves. These are unusual situations. Unfortunately, no democratic ideal is achieved at such times for network television is nothing if not a one-way medium. Even as developed in the U.S.A., the most pluralist of societies, mass television has no capacity for feeding opinions back from the people to their governors.

The exceptional event does little to relieve public officials' dissatisfaction with the mass media relationship. Instead of the direct 'hotline' to and from the citizen grassroots—which would make the work of governing both easier and pleasurable—all they have is a rival, business-oriented, institution which uses them, ignores their legitimate needs, and offers a heavily filtered communications channel only marginally better than nothing. Allowing any of this vast store of resentment to surface is guaranteed only to worsen their difficulties. Although they constitute the premier legal power in a country, those in charge of government can only swallow their pride, bury the skeletons as deeply as possible, and try to adapt their speech, presentation, timing, and public personalities.

While many politicians failed abysmally in adapting to new mass media technologies, others succeeded brilliantly. F.D. Roosevelt, John F. Kennedy, Pierre Elliott Trudeau, Enoch Powell, and some of Britain's journalist-politicians provide ready examples. So much has TV 'style' affected U.S. election campaigns that one study of the 1972 event found that the commercials for candidates actually carried more information about solid issues than did the news broadcasts.[8] Public figures who do adapt to the mass media's requirements do not get away with it scotfree. Altheide and Snow point out part of the cost in their book, **Media Logic:**

> when a media logic is employed to present and interpret institutional phenomena, the form and content of those institutions is changed. The changes may be minor, as in the case of how politicians dress and groom themselves; or they may be major, such as the entire process of present-day political campaigning in which political rhetoric says very little but shows much concern.[9]

The influence of 'media logical' presentations goes beyond style. It alters the perspective of those who must persuade the public that their policies are just. It creeps into the very substance of the choices which they settle on.

Releasing government information becomes more and more manipulative. Increasingly, it is the mass media themselves that provide the means and the arena of conflict and positional manoeuvre for the major political actors. The action may pit an interest group against a political party, the executive against an opposition, or one government department against another. The major medium for this type of conflict has been the newspaper, although growing sophistication in media exploitation will bring more television use. Press conferences and interviews show a trend in which increased enlightenment is neither the necessary nor probable result. Anthony Smith has tells us graphically how TV interviewers and politician-interviewees play cute games with each other. The one tries to be as challenging and daring as possible while the other connives at the game to try and enhance his image or situation.

The business-industrial biases of television lead it and others to assess public affairs broadcasting in terms of daring and audience—not information. Whether the exposure of so many people to their political leaders means that the citizenry knows less and less about more and more, we cannot tell. Nor do we have the data to assess the claim that the the mass media's chief political effect is to 'narcotise' the people into peaceful acquiescence of elite rule. There is evidence that the majority of us who depend primarily on TV, with its visual and entertainment emphases, do turn blind eyes toward issues turning on bare facts. Such people pay little attention to detailed criticism or abstract analysis. The developing media/politics relationship shows no signs of improving our critical capacities. And those who govern us find it hard to distinguish between what is good for them and what is good for us. The temptation to equate the fate of the government and the welfare of the community is never stronger than when the executive sees its public relations going sour. At such times threats to the 'national interest' crop up with surprising frequency. The fault is often seen to lie with a hostile mass media.

A 'solution' that enjoys increasing popularity is to get communications content under control. The crude method is censorship. The more skilful method is news management.

Censorship

People who are dissatisfied with the mass communications channels sometimes accuse the press itself of censorship. They say that is what the mass media's normal processes of content creation, selection, and editing add up to. If the word censorship refers to any kind of useful concept, it must be rather different. The complaint would hold water only if the media were common carriers open to everybody's use. They are not. Censorship is imposed on the mass media by external authority. Paul O'Higgins provides two clarifying definitions in his study, **Censorship in Britain:**

> First of all, there is pre-censorship (sometimes called prior censorship) under which legal rules confer authority on some person to examine the text of what is proposed to be said, published, performed or distributed, and only after receiving the licence of such authority is the dissemination of the information concerned lawful.[10]

Liberal societies and their mass media accept the necessity of wide-ranging censorship under wartime conditions without much dispute. Peace brings much more quarrelling about it. Some jurisdictions like the Canadian provinces set up public bodies to censor proposed advertising for beer and liquor. In other cases, industries will organise trade procedures to vet advertising for toys, tobacco, and pharmaceutical products. Although it often happens under threat of government regulations, that is not quite censorship. Cultural goods such as films for public display, theatre productions and school textbooks are undoubtedly subject to prior censorship in many places. Protection from pornography is a frequently found justification but freedom of political expression is restricted as well, and sometimes with openly declared intention. O'Higgins describes post-censorship as:

legal rules [which] do not require authorization before
the matter is disseminated but impose penalties, fines,
prison, deprivation of civil rights or damages upon the
persons responsible for the dissemination of material
which contravenes certain limits usually extremely vague,
laid down by the law.

The most dramatic example of general political censorship by
a liberal regime in peacetime comes from Canada in October
1970. It was imposed under the War Measures Act, which in
effect declared a state of emergency to deal with the
terrorism of the Front de Libération du Québec. The news
media were prohibited from publishing or broadcasting
anything that threatened national security or supported the
F.L.Q. Although there were minor challenges to the law by
student newspapers, the government and the major news media
did not come into open conflict during the relatively
shortlived crisis. American and British journalists have
certainly been subject to prior censorship since the end of
the second world war but not on their home territories; most
cases have involved battlefield situations like Korea, Suez,
and Vietnam.

The number of marginal cases is growing and will probably
continue to do so wherever urban terrorism flourishes or
cold war threatens to warm up. A classic case was the
American federal government's efforts to prevent the **New
York Times** from publishing the so-called Pentagon Papers.
Those efforts did not have the backing of censorship statues
but used the full range of weapons in the government's legal
arsenal, many of them turning on property rights (in the
papers themselves) and definitions of the 'national
interest'. Although publication was delayed, in the end the
U.S. government failed. A drug manufacturer's efforts to
prevent **The Sunday Times** (of London) from revealing the
results of its investigations into the thalidomide tragedy
achieved partial success, for publication, and possibly
justice, was delayed for some years. The British authorities
regularly prevent other news media from publishing

confidential government information by applying to the courts under the Official Secrets Act. Britain has two sets of broadcasting institutions, private and state-run, each of them regulated by a government-appointed board. The recent history of British broadcasting is replete with instances of these boards censoring programs planned by the broadcasters for which they are responsible.[11] Whether these boards are really 'external' to the institutions as a whole is a matter of debate but they do not seem to have taken their actions on explicit instruction from governments of the day.

Other censorship activities took place in Britain, in Northern Ireland and elsewhere under provisions of the Prevention of Terrorism Act which were quite far-reaching in their powers. The D-Notice system dating to the early part of this century further constrains what the British mass media publishes. Government departments seeking secrecy for particular areas of national security sent notices to this effect to a joint government-press committee, which, if it approved, circulated them to the mass media. More than sixty years of voluntary compliance gave the system considerable constitutional weight but it was violated on occasion and seen to be falling into disuse by the early nineteen-eighties. The absence of prosecution or penalty made it hard to classify such a system as legal censorship, a term more aptly suited to the draconian contempt of court powers wielded by British judges.

If crass majoritarianism is not to overwhelm legitimate minority voices, politicians in liberal democratic governments must hold fast to a number of self-denying attitudes. The operation of state broadcasting systems imposes considerable strain on those attitudes. How can they be publicly owned yet outside the government's control? The first major test for the British Broadcasting Corporation came with the General Strike of 1926. The historian, Asa Briggs, quotes a famous memorandum from the organisation's first head, John Reith: "Assuming the B.B.C. is for the people, and that the Government is for the people, it follows that the B.B.C. must be for the Government in this crisis too.' Members of Parliament opposed to the government's policy were not allowed to broadcast their views, and they were thereby effectively silenced for the daily newspapers had also been closed down by the strike.

Despite the odd beginning, the BBC gradually developed a peacetime autonomy from day-to-day governments that was the envy of public broadcasters everywhere. This came about through the device of filling the board of governors with non-governmental but trusted members of the British elites. The BBC saw itself, with some justice, as being a public corporation outside the government but within the constitution. By the Suez crisis, which split the political elites down the middle, the BBC had no apparent hesitation in providing air time for public figures to discuss and to attack Sir Anthony Eden's policy. In discounting rumours that the government was driven to considering taking over the BBC, one participant has written:

On the other hand there was real and severe pressure put on the BBC in other ways. This took several forms: attempts to impose pro-government speakers and curtail critics of the Suez policy; rows over the Opposition's right to reply to Ministerial broadcasts; the planting of Foreign Office liaison officers at Bush House; and Parliamentary measures designed to clip the BBC's wings.'12

The BBC survived that crisis but it should not be thought that it was totally insulated from political pressures. It was not and incidents involving several prime ministers, notably Harold Wilson, demonstrated the always fluid state of the political relationship. State broadcasting on the British model can be independent only within the political model of represented by established institutions. Film and time might be devoted to Scotish nationalists and Welsh devolutionists, yes, but neither the Welsh arsonists or the Irish 'men of violence' were to be allowed a TV platform.

The deepest running sore on the British body politic, the Ulster insurrection was responsible for keeping national security interests at knife points with journalistic principles for more than a decade. In this affair, it was the press rather than the political institution that found self-denying attitudes both expedient and convenient.

The trouble politicians have in keeping their hands off state broadcasting was also evident during the seventies in Canada, another country facing a strong separatist movement. There, the politicians gave into the temptation openly. The prime minister, Pierre Elliott Trudeau, had long battled independence movements in his home province of Quebec but his fight was faltering in 1976, a year in which secessionists won control of the Quebec government). He and fellow Quebec members of parliament lashed out at the 'treacherous' journalists who worked for the French language network of the Canadian Broadcasting Corporation. Where the CBC was legally charged in its charter with fostering Canadian unity, the French language network was accused of doing all it could to give aid and comfort to the separatist forces. The broadcast newsmen replied in some heat that they were only applying recognized standards of newsworthiness. The leaders of the separatist party were skilled in the ways of television. It was they, and not the federalists with their tired old speeches, who were making news. After parliamentary manoeuvres and many dark threats, the responsible regulatory authority was directed to make an 'independent' investigation. Within Radio-Canada, it found a lot of sympathy for the separatist case but no evidence of bias pervading the news. A little knuckle-rapping for everyone brought the incident to a close. Honour was satisfied all round: the journalists thought the politicians had suffered humilitating defeat and the politicians decided the news looked a lot more balanced as a result of the inquiry. During the 1980 Quebec referendum campaign the balance in news coverage given to the two forces was measurable with a fine ruler.

News Management

A condition of mass media and government relations more common than outright censorship is news management. Although its practice goes back much further, its public recognition under that name dates from the late nineteen-fifties. As held by American commentators, the concept describes a set of governmental techniques for manipulating public opinion through the news media together with implied condemnation of their use in a supposedly open society. This moral condemnation assumes a normal press relationship in which journalists are free to talk to any number of public servants and agencies, checking their accounts against each other for reliability and accuracy. Government spokesmen are presumed to be trustworthy in their statements and to welcome general disclosure and public discussion of their activities. In the absence of declared war, those assumptions may be happy ones to make if peaceful and friendly relations prevail among major powers. They do not fit the perceived needs of political leaders engaged in varying degrees of cold war or limited hostilities. The assumptions may be equally invalid if a government thinks the national interest is seriously threatened by economic problems believed to be susceptible to official exhortation.

James Reston accused the Eisenhower government of news management in its response to the U-2 crisis, the first known use of the term.[13] It came into much wider use to describe Washington's behaviour during the Cuban missile crisis of 1962. Arthur Krock wrote at the time: "News management policy not only exists but, in the form of direct and deliberate action, has been enforced more cynically and boldly than by any previous Administration in a period when the U.S. was not in a war or [on] the verge of war."[14] The techniques are most of those known to students of propaganda. Indeed the only point of distinguishing the terms may be to clarify whether the perpetrator is a liberal or not-so-liberal regime. It should be noted, perhaps, that

U.S. government news management has generally been confined
to one particular range of activity at a time—usually
military. It has involved a limitation in the number of
those authorised to give information to the press and
overall tightening of government secrecy to levels more
common to Britain than the U.S.A. The Kennedy administration
issued a memorandum to press people setting out twelve
categories of news they did not want reported and assigned
police and F.B.I. agents to track down the sources of
unwanted disclosures. Newsmen also complained police were
deliberately harassing representatives of 'unfriendly'
papers and networks. Flattery, presidential appeals to
individuals, calculated leaks of information, exaggeration
of victory, careful timing of press releases, outright
lying, and occasionally admitted suppression of unpalatable
happenings were also aspects of governmental attempts to
influence mass media reporting of the Cuban situation. This
combination caught many American journalists off-guard. They
were especially incensed by the frankness of a statement by
Arthur Sylvester, an assistant secretary of defence:

> News generated by actions of the government as to content
> and timing are part of the arsenal of weaponry that the
> President has in the application of military resources
> and related forces to the solution of political problems
> or the application of international political measures.
>
> Management of the news of the activities of the
> military establishment is one of the 'weapons' essential
> to national security, a 'weapon' made more vital to our
> arsenal by the current world tensions than ever before.

News management continued to be one of the 'weapons in
the arsenal of democracy' throughout the Vietnam war. It was
used not only against foreign enemies but against domestic
critics of government policy like Senator Wayne Morse.[15]

News management takes place in other countries that
claim to have open government. Two examples from Canada will
suffice. A meeting of the economic consultative committee of

the Commonwealth countries took place in Accra, Ghana, in September 1961. Britain's intended entry into the European Community was an important agenda item for a number of countries and especially for Canada. It seems clear that the Canadians had decided to do all they could to deflect Britain from its objective which was said to be terribly damaging to the economies of Britain's traditional trading partners. The secrecy of the discussions combined with the large number of correspondents searching for scraps of news provided the chance to manipulate news reports from Accra. Two Canadian cabinet ministers, George Hees and Donald Fleming, used off-the-record speeches and deliberate leaks by their assistants to whip up British (and Canadian) public opinion against EEC membership. Here the purpose of Canadian news management was to bring about a change in another country's policy decision. Caught out at home in misleading statements and other attempts at deliberate manipulation, the politicians pleaded the national economic interest as justification. The furore contributed to a disastrous drop in public confidence and their eventual loss of office.[16]

The mass media institution, for its part, will often abandon its arms-length distancing from public authority and connive with others' news management. City council property redevelopment is a common candidate for such treatment. The city of Kitchener, Ontario, has a farmers' market building more treasured by preservationist groups than by the city council. The normally vigilant **Kitchener-Waterloo Record** worked with city officials for months to keep quiet or misrepresent a planned redevelopment scheme. The situation was exposed three days before the critical deadline in February 1972 by a student newspaper whose story was reprinted in the nearby Toronto **Globe and Mail**.

Punishing the Press

When the mass media refuse desired cooperation, public authorities can retaliate in many ways. Those used in English-speaking states during the past decade include:

* Withdrawal of special reporting privileges.
* Prohibition of note-taking, photography, or tape recording.
* Denial of access (across police or fire lines, for instance).
* Refusal of information or program production help.
* Official inquiries into the mass media or its role in special cases.
* Measures subverting advertising revenues or boosting business taxes.
* Harassment by police, tax officials, health or building inspectors.
* Threats of licence non-renewals, anti-monopoly action, or other prosecution.
* Public campaigns of vilification (reported by the mass media).
* Launching competitive enterprises like government newspapers.

The possibilities and implications are fairly obvious so detailed reference will be made to only a few illustrations. The relations of the U.S. federal administration with the press were frequently uneasy—especially during the seventies. John F. Kennedy is much-quoted on how he wished the New York Times had not been so responsible in concealing the advance information it had about the Bay of Pigs episode. The implication is that the U.S.A. would thereby have been spared the disaster. A contrary reflection is that the newspaper would have been labelled a traitor and blamed for the invasion going wrong. Certainly television was often made the scapegoat for the mid-sixties rioting in U.S. cities. The press was also blamed for draft-dodging because of its failure to picture Vietnam as the glorious enterprise some thought it should be.

Various aspects of the mass media were investigated in the aftermath of the urban riots. L.B. Johnson's Commission on Civil Disorders was charged with discovering what effects they had had on the riots. Numerous examples of provocative and fictional reporting were found and disturbances arising from imitative behaviour were cited. In some ways the press could not win. The Commission pointed out that the news coverage emphasis was not riot scenes and looting but on law enforcement activities, with the result that legitimate minority group grievances were not brought out the way they should have been.

The culmination of a war on the press waged by Johnson's successor, Richard Nixon, was his famous 'unleashing' of the vice-president, Spiro Agnew. In a much-publicised speech, Agnew particularly attacked the three U.S. national television networks. He claimed they abused their near monopoly position of influence with the American people to peddle an irresponsible and distorted picture of political life which elevated a narrow set of liberal ideologies and denigrated the worth of traditional values and institutions. The broadcasters were also reminded that federal commissioners were responsible for all television licences. As the former counsel to the CBS network, Richard Salant commented in another context:

> The threat is always there...that if the Congressman or Senator doesn't like our treatment of an issue in which he has an interest, then he will push for legislation to license the networks, or limit their profits—or some other regulatory exercise entirely irrelevant to anything but punishment for the exercise of news judgement.[17]

Network television in the United States—unlike that elsewhere—has escaped much government control. That does not remove the continual threat that controls might be instituted, for even governments ideologically devoted to deregulation can be tempted to act in the interest of 'higher moral standards'. What is more, as the Brookings Institute pointed out, if television produced an ordinary product it would stand out as a highly concentrated industry. "Yet, paradoxically, a country uniquely dedicated to promoting competition seems to accept concentration in

its most important mass medium."[18] That opens another avenue
by which legislators can threaten television news
operations. That was made clear to them again after the CBS
network broadcast a carefully prepared exposition of how the
U.S. defence establishment spent, by its own estimate, up to
$30 million yearly on propaganda to win public support for
its war machine. Agnew labelled the program a subtle and
vicious attack on the country's defenders and U.S.
congressmen tried to subpoena the CBS president to a special
hearing. When he refused to attend, he was threatened with a
contempt of Congress citation but friends in the House of
Representatives were able to sidetrack it.

Attempts to find institutional solutions to complaints
about the mass media have been more characteristic of
Britain and Canada than the United States. Press councils
with representatives of both public and publishers have a
mixed record. In some cases they have provided a respected
forum where aggrieved citizens have been able to demand and
get an investigation and an apology at least. Journalists
have been vindicated at times and on other occasions they
have been tried and found wanting in the eyes of their
peers. The British Press Council, especially, has been a
shield useful for diverting the regulatory thunderings of
left-wing politicians who feel disadvantaged by a
preponderance of right-wing editorialists. It is hard to see
any improvement in newspaper practice that can be credited
to the press councils, although it may be there. A few
papers, like the **Toronto Daily Star**, have assigned a senior
journalist to act as an internal ombudsman, somebody who
investigates complaints against the medium and discusses
them in print in a regular column. This institution is said
to bring about changed attitudes in the newsroom but, here
again, there is no observable evidence.

In a manner comparable to the press councils, public
broadcasting boards of governors in Britain, Australia, and
Canada hear and adjudicate complaints from both individual
and institutional sources. Once again, it is easier to see

in these activities the operation of a fairly effective press protective mechanism than it is to detect any particular improvement in broadcasting habits.

While not often thought of as a media protection device, electoral or broadcasting legislation in the three parliamentary countries may be important in this role. Such rules provide for different forms of party-controlled political broadcasting. While the political institutions do get professional production assistance, the content is entirely a matter for the elected representatives of the people. Whatever their impact on voters, party political broadcasts do constitute a direct channel to the electorate and may buy a little protection for public broadcasters.

A characteristic of all relations between the institutions of government and those of broadcasting has been the assumption that only one or two megaphones are available. That being so, their use has to be rationed in some way—and all the methods tried have proved unsatisfying from the perspective of most political figures. (The print media escape most overt regulation on grounds of their plurality, real or potential.) Many of the strained relations between the political and the broadcast institutions are attributable to the consequences of the regulatory assumption, but it is an assumption that rests on either organisational or technological grounds. The Dutch and a number of other people have shown that control of the broadcasting 'hardware' can readily be divorced from control of 100 per cent of the content 'software'.[19]

Whether the power of private capital investment in broadcasting is everywhere strong enough to prevent a determined political scheme of divorce and reorganisation is a matter for investigation. Such efforts might, in any case, be somewhat futile—if the technological developments overtaking Canada are a forerunner of situations elsewhere. Cable television carrying a dozen or more channels has achieved far greater penetration in Canada than in any other country. In addition, as early as 1980, and in spite of official attempts to outlaw the practice, thousands of dish antennas were being erected to tune in different communications satellites and transmit their myriad signals to even more thousands of domestic households. These developments increased the fragmentation of mass broadcast audiences, frightening conventional broadcasters and advertisers alike who began worrying whether the mass audience might not disappear altogether.

The multiplication of broadcasting channels may well reduce, if not eliminate, much of the antagonism politicians and broadcast journalists have for each other. As they have discovered in patches here and there, what political malcontents really want is not to get their messages into print or over the airwaves. They want a chance at the mass audiences that were built up primarily for entertainment and commercial purposes. The question is how long will our channels of popular communication remain mass media? If they do survive, is there any prospect that they will carry much 'serious' political communication to the masses when it will be so easy to switch to other media choices?

NOTES TO CHAPTER EIGHT

1. David L. Altheide and Robert P. Snow, **Media Logic**, Beverly Hills and London: Sage, 1979, 192.

2. Anthony Smith, **The Shadow in the Cave**, London: Quartet, 1976, 170.

3. Henry Mayer, **The Press in Australia**, Melbourne, 1964, 167.

4. Quoted in F.C. Irion, **Public Opinion and Propaganda**, New York, 1970, 80.

5. **Due to Circumstances Beyond Our Control...**, New York: Random House, 1967.

6. **The New Industrial Estate**, New York: Houghton-Mifflin, 1967, 384.

7. "TV-Radio: Cosmic Neilsens," **Saturday Review**, August 9, 1969, 40.

8. T.E. Patterson and R.D. McClure, **The unseeing eye**, New York: Putnam, 1976.

9. 11.

10. 12.

11. See, for example, the British press for the week of May 19-23, 1980 and the the Broadcasting Authority's cancellation of Granada Television's programs on surveillance activity in Hong Kong.

12. F. R. MacKenzie, "Eden, Suez and the BBC—a reassessment," **The Listener**, December 18, 1969, 841-3.

13. Bruce Ladd, **Crisis in Credibility**, New York: New American Library, 1968, 110.

14. "Mr. Kennedy's Management of the News," **Fortune**, March 1963, 82.

15. See also Hanson W. Baldwin, "Managed News," **The Atlantic (Monthly)**, April 1963, and articles in M. Raskin and B. Falls, eds., **The Vietnam Reader**, New York: Random House, 1967.

16. Much of the story is told in Peter Newman, **Renegade in Power**, Toronto: McClelland & Stewart, 1963. See also Christopher Young, "What Happened at Accra: Mr. Fleming vs.

The Press," The Ottawa Citizen, January 27, 1962, 7, and
Canada, House of Commons, Official Report of Debates, 1961.
17. Quoted in Robert MacNeil, The People Machine, New York:
Harper & Row, 1968, 245.
18. Roger G Noll, Merton J. Peck, and John J. McGowan,
Economic Aspects of Television, Washington: Washington,
1973, 267.
19. For a description of the Dutch and other systems, see
Anthony Smith, ed., Television and Political Life: Studies
in Six European Countries,, London: Macmillan, 1979.

If you ask serious questions about the mass media, you are probably looking for moral answers.

* Do strong daily newspapers really help to keep governments more responsive and politicians more honest?

* How can we use broadcasting to improve education?

* Why is television such a weak force for good and a powerful stimulus to violence?

* Can anything be done about it?

Even explorations that seek somewhat different answers, like this one, cannot avoid moral issues. They are built into the choices of what questions are worth study and how to go about finding answers to them.

Most scholars would agree that even the most carefully formulated version of structural-functionalism cannot pretend to be either precise or value-free. It is better thought of as a useful approach to understanding society better. With all that conceded, critics will sometimes argue that structural-functionalism leads us to immoral behaviour. They claim its emphasis on learning how our society actually works implies a conservative acceptance of the status quo with all of its injustices. When academic study turns into a substitute for civic inaction, the accusation is a fair one. If reform from within is really impossible, the accusation of immorality is fair again. But if you think bringing about effective change requires first an understanding of how our society really works, then the charge against structural-functionalism is nonsense. While politics is the major means for bringing about deliberate social reform, it is itself changing—without any deliberation or planning. The chief reason lies in changes in the technology and character of the mass media as a political institution.

Saying that the press has characteristics of a political institution does not mean that is a complete description. It is not. The major news media are primarily commercial or entertainment enterprises. What we mean is that the mass media comprise groups of people who take a regular and important part in our society's governance—the process of authoritatively defining and distributing goods, services, and other valued things in our lives. Participating in that process in consistent and predictable patterns over a period of time implies longevity and organisation, both important attributes of social institutions. 'The Fourth Estate' is as close as popular expression comes to the notion of the mass media performing political functions. In using the term, we should take care not to think of these organisations as having anything like the coherence or unity of purpose we see in political institutions like the United States Senate, the House of Lords, a city council, or an established political party. Rather than standing outside of them—as the journalists' images would suggest, the mass media interact politically with these other institutions. In this respect, the British Broadcasting Corporation, for example, likes to see itself as 'within the constitution but outside the government.' That is true as well of the major daily press. Within the galaxy of politics the media differ from the other institutions; they have non-political purposes like winning audiences and making money. While they provide the communications needed to make political institutions work, they have different, and semi-independent bases of support. Their relationship with the public is voluntarist, and they are not consciously and primarily interested in political power. All are important considerations.

For the mass media as an industry, news is a commodity; news is a commercial for the 'real' commercials. For mass media as a political institution, though, news is a public service, a creative idea, and a political weapon. What it is at any one moment depends on whose perspective counts. Steven Chibnall points out:

> Professional communicators are not simply puppets on strings pulled by capitalists. Nor do they necessarily feel oppressed by the power of the machine they serve. They are men and women who exercise choice and construct their own realities within the constraining parameters set by their ideal and material interests and their professional stock of knowledge. ... While retaining a certain detachment and distance from his materials and the accounts he constructs from them, the communicator generally finds acceptable the interpretations of the reality they reflect.[1]

Opposition elements at all levels (both inside and outside the constitutional system) attack the mass media for their subservience to the governing group. What they are really attacking is the concept of news itself. Popular ideology glorifies the houses of elected representatives, but the journalists know the executive is 'where the action is', and

the executive takes the actions that make news—almost by
definition. Political activists outside the administration
have a tough time getting equal play in the mass media. They
can do it only by actions that are equally newsworthy.

The personnel of the mass media tend to treasure an image
of their institution as something of a common carrier of
political information. Such a picture is not very true to
life. The information to be shipped has to be packaged in
the technological shapes and institutional values that fit
the carrier's delivery systems. To be a common carrier—like
a telephone company, for instance—means you cannot be
actor-critic and watchdog as well. The roles are quite
incompatible. The common carrier image is appealing and
television in particular is reinforcing that image and its
popular acceptance. If the communicators themselves share
the same value-sets as the governors, that probably does not
matter. In western countries, the values held by governors
and newsmen often differ significantly. The problem is
compounded by the mass media's dependence on government for
political content. While the print media are quite dependent
enough on official sources for their definition and supply
of reliable news, the broadcast media are infinitely more
dependent on them in most countries. The relationship is
surprisingly fragile. So long as they emphasise a variety of
conflicts in their news content, the mass media are
testifying to the political elites' inability to achieve
complete dominance over our societies. If the Pollyanna or
Dr. Pangloss critique of mass media news were ever to be
realised, and all conflict-laden stories replaced by human
interest or 'good' news, that would signal something other
than the hoped-for better world. It would signal, in fact,
the triumph of a depressingly uniform set of values
favouring one elite group above all others.

As it is, the leading groups in our society still hold to
somewhat incompatible sets of preferences. You may be able
to explain these inter-elite differences in a variety of
ways but the fact of their existence remains. Taken together

the complete array of accepted values represents the boundaries of the arena within which elite groups compete. Reducing the mass media to common carrier status by wiping out their actor-critic and watchdog roles would fit in beautifully with the pure commercial entertainment function often attributed to them. One significant result, of course, would be the neutering or complete removal of one of the few autonomous actors within the political system.

During the past quarter-century the American academic study of politics has been strongly influenced by two particular approaches: David Easton's systems theory and the structural functionalism of Gabriel Almond and James Coleman. Their works stress the necessity of looking at an institution like the press in terms of the way it functions in relationship to other social institutions. Almond and Coleman suggest the existence of seven political functions together with a feedback circuit:

1. Interest articulation
2. Interest aggregation
3. Political socialisation
4. Rule making
5. Rule enforcement
6. Rule adjudication
7. Political communication

Although this set lacks something in theoretical tidiness, it does provide a useful way of examining the mass media's political relationships. In doing so, we must not let Montesquieu and other commentators mislead us. Despite labels like legislature, judiciary, and executive, the names of these institutions of government do not describe their functions with any great accuracy. The press probably plays some part in most of these political functions and it does not have a monopoly in carrying out any one of them. They are all shared with other institutions. A study of any one function by itself would require examining all political structures in society. In some countries, nonpolitical institutions would also need investigating if we wanted to track down all performance of a function. It should be noted that not all politically relevant activity can be called functional. Certain actions—such as passing and enforcing a new law—are usually said to help keep the political system going, but they do not always do that. Occasionally the result, quite unintended, is that a government is defeated or the whole regime overthrown in revolution. There we can see rule making and enforcement were actually dysfunctional.

The idea that politics and communications live in symbiosis has run all through this book. But there is a third party—the citizen-audiences. Without them, the first two are as clanging cymbals in an empty concert hall. While the mass media may be blamed for some changes in public behaviour, lines of influences are working in both directions. Changes in the audience stimulate changes in the mass media. Many people blamed television for the uprisings in Watts and other U.S. neighbourhoods. The blame was misplaced. Responsibility really rested in the institutional relationship certain parts of the U.S. audience had with their TV sets. As one official inquiry pointed out, for all the people who saw urban arson and rioting on television, and then went out and did the same, there were millions more who stayed home and kept the peace.

Think of 'Fourth Estate' as the mass media acting in its capacity as one of the political institutions. What is the role of the audience then? About this we know very little. Certainly audience tastes and preferences are neither fixed nor readily predictable—as many a former mass movie-maker can testify to his financial sorrow. The audience role in the Fourth Estate is a changeable and a constantly negotiable one. Among the most important influences here are the politically relevant characteristics of the audience. To discover these, we need first of all to consider each medium's technological requirements. Tabloids and other popular newspapers, for example, do not ask much but a minimum level of reading ability is needed. That keeps one part of the population out of the audience. To join an audience, people need the economic means—money to buy the newspaper or rent the TV/radio set. Publications like **The Times** or the **Wall Street Journal** and other print media demand higher levels of literacy. These levels are threatened constantly by television's relatively greater accessibility or ease of use. If cable and satellite systems do end up fragmenting the present mass TV audiences into smaller, specialist audiences, that would seem likely to increase rather than reduce the threats to literacy.

In addition to economic and literacy factors, the audience's political character is affected by geographic, cultural, boundary, civic, and interest factors. The geographic dimension flows naturally from the limitations imposed by the media's different technical requirements. Here we think of newspaper circulation zones, the signal strength of television stations, and so on. Political socialisation helps determine who can, or cannot, be an effective political part of a mass media audience. Richard Nixon's 'Checkers' speech, for instance, may well have been brilliant election television but before effective communication could take place viewers had to understand the relevant political culture. If their reading and viewing preferences exclude all things political, then people end up excluding themselves from participating in the mass media political institution. Citizenship qualification and political boundaries like those of the city, province, or nation-state act in similar fashion to determine the size and nature of the audience sector of the Fourth Estate.

At every juncture the people in modern western states are, consciously or unconsciously, negotiating what roles they will play in the mass media political institution. This phenomenon is important but it has been generally neglected or blurred by the concentration of research workers on the electoral functions of the mass media.

The so-called electoral functions of the mass media are a popular topic of discussion. The research so far seems to suggest that most electoral functions are performed in the

short term except in the American presidential elections
which run longer. Electoral functions are identified as:

1 Selecting and raising issues.
2 Distinguishing parties and identifying candidates.
3 Reduce the tensions and fears of party activists and
   reinforcing their convictions.
4 Arming party workers (with propaganda arguments) and
   getting them to work effectively.
5 Providing national integration of local campaigns.
6 Providing information for floating voters.

Not so often noted as an electoral function but probably of
equal importance to the others is the role the press plays
in social stabilisation. After our earlier survey of the
topic, there is no need to review the findings of mass media
electoral research here. It will do to note that genuine
party 'conversion' seems rare, reinforcement is more common,
and major change possible only in ways that do not challenge
core beliefs or extensive personal knowledge on a subject.

Opposing parties usually represent elections, however
inaccurately, as choices between major policy alternatives.
Intense emotional involvement for every citizen is
encouraged officially. If all of this were taken too
seriously, a great many voters—those whose party
lost—could not possibly accept the results peaceably. Civil
strife would result. Mass media treatment of the campaign,
however, contributes to a degree of voter cynicism,
especially about the breadth of the alternative policy gap,
and that cynicism helps prepare voters to accept whatever
changes the election does in fact bring about.

Some of the functions treated as 'electoral' are
performed in between election campaigns as well. Issue
creation and issue selection are good examples. To discuss
them fully would require a full-length study by itself. For
now, let us simply note two aspects of the mass media's role
in the issue process. first, the simple circulation of
issue-relevant information stimulates political demands.

simply note two aspects of the mass media's role in the issue process. First, the simple circulation of politically relevant information stimulates political demands. This happens as various groups discover openings and opportunities for improving their relative positions in society and try to take advantage of them. Relevant information covers a wide range but in addition to formal political news, it includes reports of interest group activities, and circulation of individual opinions through letters to the editor, 'open line' or telephone radio programs, and so on. Second are the consequences for public issue resolution flowing from the mass media's undoubted influence on the public's agenda and on official decision schedules. That is exercised through news selection, news emphases, and editorial prescriptions. Mobilisation effects go beyond campaigns as mass media reporting affects activities like party recruitment between elections as well.

Intentions of political actors are poor guides indeed to the functional effect of their activities. The collection, selection, processing, and distribution of news of all types amounts to the incidental performance of a major political function, data circulation. The journalists only intended to turn out a good paper or broadcast. Nevertheless, their 'revelation' of this tidbit or that often affects politics in ways that were both unintended by the journalist and usually completely unforeseeable. That is one reason why Tables 9-1 and 9-2, which organise the political functions of the mass media in summary form, pay no attention whatever to the intentions of those performing the function.

Whenever publishers try deliberately to direct certain events through news or editorial campaigns, as often as not the results are just the opposite of what was wanted. Few newsmen relish the idea of helping to enforce government rules and regulations. That is what they are doing, though, whenever they publicise new programs or policies, whether they deal with traffic fines, social welfare eligibility, water use restriction, or marijuana and narcotic control.

TABLE 9 - 1

Political Functions of the News Media
By Time Span

SHORT   TERM---------------->---------------->LONG   TERM

Data circulation	Legitimation	Integration
Interest expression		
Issue creation	Issue resolution	
(watchdog)	Value manipulation	General
(ombudsman)	(Opinion-forming)	political
Mobilisation	Recruitment	socialisation
Agenda setting	Decision scheduling	
Stereotyping	Context setting	

NOTE: The table is meant only to suggest the main dimensions of the
      question. In some cases, one function may be performed within
      a very discreet time period. The perfomance of others will
      take place over several periods.

News reports about the routine effects of existing programs
—police checks, income tax refunds, convictions and
sentences—all help to make known the official rewards and
punishments. In the process, these reports are making
substantial contributions to what we have called the rule
enforcement and rule adjudication functions.

Stereotyping is pinning instant images on people or
fixing new developments firmly within familiar frameworks so
we can locate them easily. It needs only a very little time.
Election campaigns are a good time to watch it happen before
your eyes, but it takes place in many other circumstances as
well. Once it was popular to blame stereotyping and the
politics of imagery almost entirely on those who chose the
headlines and photographs for daily newspapers. Now we know
a little better. Stereotyping is an integral part of all
journalistic technique serving mass audiences. It is the
major means by which the unfamiliar is made comprehensible.

TABLE 9 - 2

Political Functions of the News Media
By Role Emphasis

COMMON CARRIER	REPORTER	POLITICAL ACTOR
Data circulation	Legitimation	Integration
	Watchdog	Ombudsman
Interest expression		Issue creation
Mobilisation	Recruitment	
Stereotyping	Context-setting	Value manipulatn
		(Opinion formg)
	Agenda setting	Issue resolution
Interest aggregation	Decision scheduling	
Political socialisation		

NOTE: As before, the table is only suggestive. Clearly the performance of one function may be attributable to the mass media when they act in more than one of their roles. The comprehensive phrase political socialisation is a good example.

We are all subject to it. It is not limited to people content with a superficial grasp on what's going on around them. The influence of both stereotyping and agenda setting extends beyond the short term. They operate across all time periods although, if we think of them being performed and repeated often enough, a time comes when it is worth recognising that what they are now doing is setting the general context of our perceptions. At any one time, part of the particular way in which we see our own world comes from a mixture of our individual experiences, including previous sets of mass media images and issue priorities. Yesterday's contexts also provide the mental starting point for the journalists charged with selecting and presenting today's news. In their turn, members of the audience use similar contexts or frameworks to take in and make sense of the latest tidings. The dual rebound effect should be noted.

For all their impartiality, newsmen are taken in by their own stereotyping and context setting as their audiences are.

While some campaign managers claim to be expert manipulators of election images, professional image-mongers perhaps, we should remain skeptical both of their claims and those of their detractors. The longer-run effects of stereotyping are virtually unexplored. We also know little of the governmental aspects of agenda-setting. Our findings are limited to the process, to the role the mass media play in the distribution of public opinions and issue priorities.

What do we know about the influence of the mass media institution on government decision makers? Almost nothing systematic. We have anecdotal evidence that the press has played roles in resolving issues. We know politicians have taken decisions favoured by strong local newspapers and which it seems they would not have taken in the absence of press activity. We still need to comb the myriad journalists' and politicians' memoirs to see what firm conclusions can reasonably be inferred from them. The task is a large one but the potential pay-off is high. One attempt to explore part of this territory was the study of decision scheduling in three Ontario cities. It showed that local newspapers do affect what civic decision makers discuss. While it could not pick out the limits of that influence, the study did suggest that press exercise of this function depended critically on the community's established cleavage lines and on the relationship each newspaper had to other institutional actors in the local political system. A related question worth exploring is the qualitative impact on local politics of the professional quality, focus of news attention, and structure of the mass media serving the area.

The Press as Narcotic

A common criticism of the mass media is that over time they trivialise politics. The complaint is made by liberal commentators of all flavours and is given a more exaggerated form by marxist writers. The liberals object that the mass media focusses too much attention on the irrelevant in politics. Instead of seeking out the genuine philosophical differences and major policy divisions, the mass media fasten on personalities, their quirks, hobbies, dogs, and peanut farm connections. No longer seen to be about important issues, politics is reduced by commercialised communications to trivialities, which lack even entertainment value. Almost every flickering television show contributes to weakening the civic culture—particularly as it relates to key procedural values that constitute the touchstone of traditional liberal democracy.

The 'narcoticising dysfunction' of the press in is the way some observers characterise this trivialisation process. The phrase has its intellectual origins in Marx's reference to organised religion as the opiate of the people. What it means, briefly, is that the more attention people pay to the information explosion the more they are turned off politics instead of being galvanised into action. The real social concern they once had is spread out so widely and so thinly that it becomes wholly artificial. Writers like C. Wright Mills, Herbert Marcuse, and William Kornhauser have all drawn attention to dangers they see arising from the pseudo-environment created by the mass media. They argue that commercial mass media create a relationship between membership cadres and political organisations that is unmediated, unidirectional, and depersonalised. These writers fear that the natural result is the creation of mass media publics that are all too vulnerable to manipulation.

In some ways the citizens most vulnerable to manipulation are those most dependent on television news. They believe they are 'seeing for themselves' and assume that the institution of television news is value-free, having no more influence on content than the newspaper press has on the print journalist's contribution. Being unaware of how wrong they are in making this assumption, the TV news consumers drop their guards against the various forms of bias. Faced with a flood of information about politics that is wholly trivial, the public is more often narcotised than energised.

The dulling process affects more than just casual citizens. Concerned and highly attentive people may congratulate themselves on a lofty state of interest and information, but they seem equally subject to the fallacy of thinking they are seeing and judging for themselves. What kind of realisation have they that nothing is being done to deal adequately with the world's problems? (Whether that is possible or not is another question.) Even avid consumers of political news mistake an acquaintance with the problems of the day for trying to do something about them. While too little attention to the problems of others has its dangers, so has too much thinking. It may cripple the very possibility of action. As Shakespeare had Hamlet say,

And thus the native hue of resolution
Is sicklied o'er, with the pale cast of thought,
And enterprises of great pith and moment,
With the regard their currents turn awry,
And lose the name of action.

Political Socialisation

Mass communications in general and the news media in particular exert undeniable power in telling us how society expects us to behave and exposing those who fail to measure up. This task of implicitly reporting what these standards are is performed quite explicitly in the field of political norms. Ironically, perhaps, our press here are performing functions that are usually the responsibility of religious institutions in other societies.

Newspapers, radio, and television all delight in discovering and reporting deviations from agreed standards of one sort or another. Hence, the public demand for stern action that follows publicity given to oil tanker spills, individual profit at public expense, or special treatment for friends of those in office. By making continued evasion of the issue difficult for politicians and public officials, press exposures and repeated commentaries add up to considerable pressure favouring a single rather than a double standard of morality—at least for these groups in society. Mass media publicity closes the gap between private attitudes and public morality. In modern societies, the mass communications institution constitutes a major agency of social control. James Curran has pointed out the ways in which the modern press has contributed to the normative integration of British society.

> It links together socially differentiated and geographically dispersed groups, emphasising collective values and collective symbols of identification. It ritually affirms the rules under which the political system operates (by giving prominence for instance to general elections, by-elections, parliamentary debates and the representatives of accredited interest groups).[2]

He, too, has argued that the press tends to characterise challenges or even potential challenges to the established sociopolitical order as irrational, unrepresentative, and a threat to the majority. Examples of these practices are easy to find whether our memories and command of history are long or short: conscientious objectors, participants in the 1926 general strikes, early suffragettes and modern feminists, equal rights supporters for blacks and homosexuals, anti nuclear and antipollution campaigners, and the like. The labels the press bestowed on them and popularised are indicative: conchies, bolsheviks, gays, nukes, or peaceniks. One need not share all their assumptions to understand the concerns of people like Lazarsfeld and Merton, who have argued that increasingly 'the chief power groups...have come to adopt techniques for manipulating mass publics through propaganda in place of more direct means of control.'

Denis McQuail has pointed out that any society extensively penetrated by mass communication channels is likely to experience strong tendencies toward uniformities.

These arise both from the characteristics that have made mass audiences possible and from the public's common store of information. Although that data is extensive and rapidly changing at times, most mass media consumers have much the same information set because it is produced by a small number of news sources using similar selection criteria.

Because all these disparate groups of audiences and citizens are exposed to relatively uniform pictures of the world outside them a certain degree of homogeneity results. Since most people know very little of that world at first hand, what knowledge they have comes vicariously—through the highly-generalised or stereotyped forms of the mass media. This phenomenon may contribute to the building of some social coherence, which in turn is probably reflected in an increased degree of political unity or even cohesion. In traditional or primitive societies social homogeneity is often said to flow from internalisation of similar sets of traditional values and attitudes. In mass media societies the situation would seem to be different in some important aspects. Among them is the general dependence on sustained flows of information that are unstable as to their content and focus but essentially rooted in the same world views. McQuail argues persuasively that the capacity of modern societies to undergo rapid political change without major disruption can be attributed, at least in part, to the centralised mass communication systems, which exert integrative effects during periods of differentiation and fragmentation of former relationships.[3]

In building consensus behind leaders and legitimacy for the system, the mass media are seen to be supplying a positive form of socialisation, that is, one contributing to maintenance of the society. That result conforms, naturally, to most leadership preferences but it cannot always be counted on. The result is sometimes dysfunctional, for the press will also mirror or initiate dissent, which occasionally leads to questioning of the status quo and possibly social and/or political disintegration. Students like Karl Deutsch and Marshall McLuhan have shown how mass communications systems have inspired quite different results from those sought by elites who have been totally unable to predict, let alone deal with, unintended consequences.

In furthering the transmission of the cultural heritage as part of the socialising process, the mass media also help provide common knowledge materials, which individuals may draw on if they are motivated to identify with the political system. Why and when individuals activate that identification as citizens are questions we are only beginning to explore seriously. Clearly the mass media are of greater importance in political recruitment. This is the process of turning citizens into activists or militants who try to use their knowledge to bring about change in their common political arrangements. The skill with which citizens get and use information from the mass media and other sources largely determines their political effectiveness.

While many have urged the creation of a new democracy built on the undoubted appeal of mass television, it is not at all clear that political television operates to increase voter interest. It probably does just the opposite. There is some evidence that heavy TV watchers are more apt to be turned off politics than light viewers. That means that rather than stimulating citizen interest increasing television exposure increases voter apathy. TV commercials offer powerful propaganda for several ideas that, at base, tend to subvert political participation. First is the idea that even externally-directed people are more concerned with 'having' than with either 'being' or doing. Second is the notion that many would like to believe is true—that there is an effortless and instant solution to life's problems.

For their part, when politicians acting in a similar vein suggest in every election campaign that supporting them will offer an easy solution to whatever ails the body politic, they are equally guilty of misleading the innocently apathetic citizen. No wonder that he is alienated, or at

they are equally guilty of misleading the innocently
apathetic citizen. No wonder that he is alienated, or at
least 'turned off', when he discovers charismatic leaders do
not solve all his problems and that he is generally rather
helpless individually to affect the course of public affairs
very substantially. Politics cannot be simple because life
itself is not simple, and especially so in liberal societies
priding themselves on permitting, indeed encouraging, a
multiplicity of voices seeking many diverse and usually
conflicting objectives.

The mass media's performance not only has direct
consequences for the political system but it influences the
functional behaviour of other institutions as well. The
personalisation of politics and ever-increasing emphases on
the single person of party leaders has been a frequent
subject of comment. Not so often observed, however, is that
the ability of these same leaders to communicate directly
with the public is having profound consequences for
institutions like political parties. Once they played the
major role in facilitating intercourse between leaders and
followers, in shaping election issues, in watching for
government mistakes, and in determining the general
ideological climate. In much of this, the press seems to be
making them functionally less and less relevant. The rise in
the United States of powerful single-issue pressure groups
is only one of the many related consequences.

The traditional or 'brokerage' parties will be driven to
generalise their appeals more broadly than ever if they are
to have any hope of exploiting the wide and heterogeneous
mass media markets. Despite evanescent 'swings' to the
near-right or to the near-left, the idea that parties should
make their electoral appeals on the basis of tightly defined
philosophical grounds is almost guaranteed disappointment.
Party appeals are likely to become even more elastic than
they have been in North America. One sign of this may be
seen in the rapid rise of new complexes of public affairs
activities, which the new mass media politics has inspired.

Apart from commercial polling and media content analysis, nearly all these activities are concerned with manipulation of symbols. These include advertising, public relations, 'voter-market research', and leadership and issue perception surveying. In the political warfare on Main Street, all these tools are freely available for hire regardless of religion, party platform, or ideology.

Altheide and Snow have made one of the few studies of inter-institutional influences involving the mass media. Like many British commentators, they see mass media processes serving as a major source of legitimation for the actions of other establishments. Mass communications determine what subjects will be discussed and what is thought to be relevant for the general community. Through the development of media personalities our societies are given instant experts whose endorsement or validation other people are forced to seek. The dominant mass communications institutions—like the American networks or the 'quality' British papers—do even more than influence the way other communication channels operate. They go on to provide the whole society with criteria for evaluating any and all public figures or proposals for action that require popular support.[4] This phenomenon needs much more investigation than the little it has received if we are to understand the political role this media institution plays in our society.

Generally, press publicity for government ends up supporting the dominant system, but you cannot count on it. The news media's occupational bias favouring conflict and novelty introduces important elements of unpredictability, which are potentially very disruptive of the powers-that-be. This strong preference for the new and surprising leads Bernard Roshco to argue, persuasively, that the press has "a constant potential for subversion." The constant search and publicising of novelties means the media institutions become a device for popularising new attitudes and new opinions, sometimes even for encouraging deviant ways of thinking and behaving, much to the despair of behavioural conservatives within the elites. "The consequences are institutional change, revised social values, the restructuring of newsmen's frame of references, and the redefinition of who and what is newsworthy."[5] On the other hand, while sometimes bothersome to office-holders, the press ombudsman role demonstrates that individual wrongs can be set right within the system and so ends up supporting it. Although newsmen like to stress watchdog aspects of their routine surveillance of politics, that too contributes to society's better adherence to liberal norms. Like the BBC, the press watchdog patrols the area outside the government's residence but well inside the constitutional fence.

If the press is to act as an effective watchdog on government (and it cannot even now cover all the ground), how much independence does it need? While many observers have asked the question, very few reassuring answers have been provided. Most common among the 'solutions' have been responses depending on some theory or other of competing, pluralist elites. Counting on the elite groups to compete with each other looks less and less satisfactory as we see that the creation and production of news about politics is falling under the control of fewer and fewer elite owners. There is no problem, those owners tell us. Because they claim not to exercise detailed control, and the owners themselves sometimes see things published they would rather not, most of them sincerely believe operating control is firmly in the many hands of the professional editors. To that claim a variety of responses related to the selection of editors and reporters according to certain value standards has already been suggested. And whatever theory of competing, pluralist elites one might subscribe to, none of them manages to get around one homely observation: the owners of watchdogs seldom turn them loose on their friends.

In the concern about 'watchdogging', we may expect little help from most journalists. They do not see themselves as part of history and its social forces. They are too bound up in the daily rushing hither and yon and too caught up in the technological demands and occupational biases of the news media institutions. Many journalists still speak as though the impossible dream of objectivity might yet be realised. Almost all refuse to admit, except possibly to their own most secret selves, that the press is no mere observer of the political theatre but one of the most vital, active, and powerful actors ever exposed to an audience.

Ralph Miliband has distinguished four functions of the government apparatus. He speaks of the maintenance of law and order, the fostering of supportive consensus, and advancement of both the economic function and the national interest. He looks at differences in the ways in which these functions are performed in order to distinguish the relative degree of independence that governments might have from the upper classes in a society.[6] Comparable questions might well be posed for the mass media institution. Just how free is it it from the elites? Its freedom is almost wholly in terms of detail. While the mass media are tightly bound to the ideological vision of the elites, their technology and occupational biases instil in the institution unpredictable abilities to disturb—rather like lightning strikes in a summer storm. The randomness of the process makes even the elites cower on occasion. Image-making is at its most observable, and most unpredictable, in national politics. Whatever party opponents or advertising agents might try to direct, the images result more from the vagaries and happenstances of the news institutions and what has been called 'pack journalism'.

The nature of press influence becomes less random the more local the focus of political news interest. The number of actors and institutions is reduced and both people and players have fewer socio-psychological defences against certain kinds of propaganda. Drawing the 'lightning' down to earth will not really allow it to be captured and tamed. It would allow much better study, though, of the political effects of the mass media if more were undertaken at the local level.

All the functions that have been ascribed to the mass media are requisites for our type of political system. If the mass media were not developed, the same functions would have to be performed either in whole or at least more fully by other political processes or institutions. Whether the news media carry out those roles in ways that support the existing system, or contribute to its decline and transformation depends as well on the many other factors that interact with them. Many but not all the faults of our mass media institutions are those of society itself and we are but seeing their reflections on our television screens. As T. S. Mathews reminded us, "the press does some good, some harm, but not nearly as much of either as it is popularly supposed or as the Press would like us to think."[7]

Orthodox social science theories are so weak that we really do not know what is functional for the system, that is, what contributes to its survival and vigour, and what does not. The news media appear to lend considerable legitimacy to the conflict that elections represent. The party propaganda, policy criticism, and image construction all help to provide a normative base for the political system. All politics needs that general agreement on shared values whether the state has a single party or many, and is communist or technocratic-military at heart. In our type of society, the loadig of the overt political messages is highly critical of the party in power. Does that help to keep our governors on their toes? Or does it contribute to citizen apathy and cynicism to the extent that the chief effect of the way the mass media present news about politics is simply to postpone the day when the present system is replaced by one that is more overtly materialist or by one that truly realises mankind's higher ideals? We neither know the answers to these questions nor do we have any agreed way of establishing them.

While politics is the major instrument of deliberate and peaceful change, it is itself undergoing change without deliberation. Mass media news about politics is the cause.

The developing cause and effect relationship between politics and the mass media is a reciprocal relationship, of course, but more is involved. Without the third party—the citizen-audience—neither of the first two sets of institutions would amount to as much as an obsolete radio tube or a junked linotype machine. Both government and press institutions try to keep favour with the people. Beyond that our influence on these institutions has not been terribly visible. Perhaps we will get much more influence through some fantastic multiplication of program choices and the development of super-interactive television systems that liberate everybody from the marketable mass in one quick dose of new, cheap technology.

It must be stressed that this discussion has been based on existing systems for producing news of interest to mass audiences. Those audiences could disappear, especially in any 'national' sense. Here is where newspapers, paradoxically, may be less threatened for a time. The reduction of same-medium competition and the flight to suburban cities will allow them to exploit their traditional strength—local community orientation. Their leap into each other's arms and those of the conglomerates will give them the financial power to do what they must. The wild proliferation of program choices is fragmenting audiences everywhere there is a cable system or the possibility of satellite signal reception and decoding. The threat is obviously greatest to the commercial networks. They will be saved in one of two ways. Either they will prove their critics wrong and demonstrate that the audiences are great, homogeneous masses which do not want meaningful program variety, and so they will successfully go on producing more of the same. Or they will adapt. Being powerful economic institutions, the networks will not sit idly by while their major sales product (mass audiences) falls to pieces. What they will do, and how that will affect our political communications falls into the realms of five-year plans and social science fiction (which may amount to the same thing).

Meanwhile another problem remains with us. Our elite structures are extending their range of legal and policy instruments of control in the communications field. If eventually they manage—in our own best interest, of course—to complete their takeover of all the political institutional aspects of the mass media, then the citizen-audience will achieve neither independent influence nor moral liberation.

NOTES TO CHAPTER NINE

1. Steven Chibnall, **Law and Order News**, London: Tavistock, 1977, 224.
2. James Curran, "The press as an agency of social control", in George Boyce, James Curran, and Pauline Wingate, eds., **Newspaper History: from the 17th century to the present day**, London: Constable, 1978.
3. Denis McQuail, in J. G. Blumler and Denis McQuail, **Television in Politics: Its Uses and Influence**, London: Faber, 1968, 13.
4. **Media Logic**, Beverly Hills & London: Sage, 1979, 237,238.
5. **Newsmaking**, Chicago, University of Chicago Press, 1979, 125.
6. **Marxism and Politics**, London: Oxford University Press, 1977. See also: Peter Golding and Graham Murdock, "Theories of Communication and Theories of Society," **Communication Research**, 3 (1978) 339-356.
7. **The Sugar Pill**, New York: Simon & Shuster, 1959, 179.

Bibliography

ADAM, G. Stuart, ed., **Journalism, Communication and the Law,** Scarborough, Ont.: Prentice-Hall, 1976.

ALTHEIDE, David L., "RTNDA news award judging and media culture," **Journalism Quarterly,** 55(1978) 164–7.

ALTHEIDE, David L., and Robert P. SNOW, **Media Logic,** Beverly Hills & London: Sage, 1979.

BALDWIN, Hanson W , "Managed News," The Atlantic (Monthly), April 1963.

BARKER, Anthony, & Michael RUSH, **The member of parliament and his information,** London: Allen and Unwin, 1970.

BARRETT, Marvin, & Zachary SKLAR, **The Eye of the Storm,** New York: Lippincott & Crowell, 1980.

BLACK, Edwin R., "Canadian Public Policy and the Mass Media," **Canadian Journal of Economics,** 1 (1968) 368–379.

BLUMLER, J. G., "The political effects of mass communications", in The Open University, Mass Communications and Society," **The Audience,** Unit 8, Milton Keynes, 1977.

BLUMLER, J. G. and Denis McQUAIL, **Television in Politics: Its Uses and Influence,** London: Faber 1968.

BOWERS, D.R. "A Report on Activity by Publishers in Directing Newsroom Decisions", **Journalism Q.,** 44(1967) 50.

BOYCE, George, James CURRAN, and Pauline WINGATE, eds., **Newspaper History: from the 17th century to the present day,** London: Constable, 1978.

BREED, Warren, "Social Control in the Newsroom", **Social Forces,** 33 (1955) 328.

CANADA, Royal Commission on Newspapers, **Report,** Ottawa, 1981. (The Kent Report).

CANADA, Royal Commission on Publications, **Report,** Ottawa 1961, (The O'Leary Report).

CANADA, Special Senate Committee on the Mass Media, **The Uncertain Mirror,** Ottawa, 1970. (The Davey Report).

CHARLESWORTH, J.C., **Contemporary Political Analysis,** New York: Free Press, 1967.

CHIBNALL, Steven, **Law and Order News,** London: Tavistock, 1977.

CLARKE, Harold, Jane JENSON, Lawrence LeDUC, and Jon PAMMETT. **Political Choice in Canada,** Toronto: McGraw-Hill-Ryerson, 1979.

COBB, R. W and M. H. KEITH-ROSS, "Agenda-Building as a Comparative Political Process," **American Political Science Review,** (1976) 126-138.

COHEN, Bernard C., **The Press and Foreign Policy,** Princeton: Princeton University Press, 1963.

COHEN, Stanley and J. YOUNG, **The manufacture of news: Deviance, social problems and the mass media,** London: Constable, 1973.

CROUSE, Timothy, **The Boys on the Bus,** New York: Random House, 1973.

CURRAN James, 'The press as an agency of social control,' in BOYCE, CURRAN, andWINGATE.

CURRAN James, ed., **The British Press: a Manifesto,** London: Macmillan, 1978.

CURRAN James, Michael GUREVITCH and Janet WOOLLACOTT, **Mass Communication and Society,** London: Edward Arnold, 1977.

DAY, Robin, **Television: a personal report,** London: Hutchinson, 1961.

DEUTSCH, Karl W., "Communications models and decision systems," in Charlesworth, **Contemporary Political Analysis,** New York: Free Press, 1967.

DEUTSCH, Karl W , **Nationalism and Social Communication,** Cambridge-New York: MIT-Wiley, 1953.

DEXTER, Lewis Anthony and David Manning WHITE, **People, Society and Mass Communications,** New York: Free Press, 1964.

EPSTEIN, Edward Jay, **News from Nowhere,** New York: Vintage, 1974.

FAGEN, Richard R., **politics and communication,** Boston and Toronto: Little, Brown, 1966.

FRIENDLY, Fred W , **Due to Circumstances Beyond Our Control...,** New York: Random House, 1967.

GALTUNG, Johan, and M. RUGE, "The structure of foreign news," **Journal of Peace Research,** 2 (1965) 64-91.

GLASGOW MEDIA GROUP, **More Bad News,** London: Routledge, Kegan Paul, 1980.

GLASGOW UNIVERSITY MEDIA GROUP, **Bad News,** London: Routledge, Kegan Paul, 1976.

GOLDING, Peter, and Graham MURDOCK, "Theories of Communication and Theories of Society," **Communication Research**, 3 (1978) 339–356.

GREAT BRITAIN, Royal Commission on the Press, 1947–1949, **Report**, London: HMSO, 1949.

GREAT BRITAIN, Royal Commission on the Press, 1961–1962, **Report**, HMSO, 1962.

GREAT BRITAIN, Royal Commission on the Press, 197?–1976, **Report**, HMSO 1976.

HALLORAN, James, Philip ELLIOTT, and Graham MURDOCK, **Demonstrations and Communications: A Case Study**, Harmondsworth, U.K.: Penguin, 1970.

HOLSTI, Ole R., **Content Analysis for the Social Sciences and Humanities**, Reading, Mass.: Addison–Wesley, 1969.

HUTCHINS, Robert S., chairman, The Commission on Freedom of the Press, **A Free and Responsible Press**, Chicago: University of Chicago Press, 1947.

JENKINS, Simon, **Newspapers**, London: Faber, 1979.

KATZ, Elihu and P.D. LAZARSFELD, **Personal Influence**, New York: Free Press, 1955.

KATZ, Elihu and S. ELDERSVELD, **Public Opinion and Propaganda**, New York: Dryden Press, 1954.

KLAPPER J. T., **The Effects of Mass Communications**, Glencoe: Free Press, 1960.

KROCK, Arthur, "Mr. Kennedy's Management of the News," **Fortune**, March 1963.

LADD, Bruce L., **Crisis in Credibility**, New York: New American Library, 1968.

LIEBLING, J. J., **The Press**, New York: Ballantine, 1961.

MacKENZIE, F. R. "Eden, Suez and the BBC—a reassessment," **The Listener**, December 18, 1969, 841–3.

MacNEIL, Robert, **The People Machine**, New York: Harper & Row, 1968.

MARGACH, James, **The Abuse of Power**, London: W.H. Allen, 1979.

MATHEWS, T.S., **The Sugar Pill**, New York: Simon & Shuster, 1959.

MAYER, Henry, **The Press in Australia**, Melbourne: Lansdowne, 1964.

McLUHAN, Marshall, **Understanding Media**, Toronto: McGrawHill, 1964.

MILIBAND, Ralph, **Marxism and Politics**, Oxford University Press, London, 1977.

MILLER, Arthur H., Lutz ERBRING, and Edie N. GOLDENBERG, "Typeset politics: impact of newspapers on issue salience and public confidence," **A.P.S.R.**, v.73 (1979), 67–84.

MURPHY, David, **The Silent Watchdog: The press in local politics**, London: Constable, 1976.

NIMMO, Dan D., **Newsgathering in Washington**, New York: Prentice–Hall, 1964.

NOELLE–NEUMANN, Elisabeth, "Turbulences in the Climate: Methodological Applications of the Spiral of Silence Theory," **Public Opinion Quarterly**, 41 (1977), 143–158.

NOELLE-NEUMANN, Elisabeth, "Public Opinion, Classical Opinion: A Re-evaluation," **Public Opinion Quarterly**, 43 (1979), 143–156.

NOLL, Roger G., M. J. PECK and J. J. McGOWAN, **Economic Aspects of Television Regulation**, Washington: Brookings, 1973.

PALETZ, David L., Peggy REICHERT, and Barbara McIntyre SPECK, "How the Media Support Local Governmental Authority," **Public Opinion Quarterly**, 35 (1971) 80–92.

PATTERSON, T. E., and R.D. McCLURE, **The unseeing eye**, New York: Putnam, 1976.

PEERS, Frank W., **The Politics of Canadian Broadcasting, 1920–1951**, Toronto: University of Toronto Press, 1969.

PEERS, F. W , **The public eye**, Toronto: University of Toronto Press, 1979.

PETERSON, Theodore, Jay W. JENSEN, and William L. RIVERS, **The Mass Media and Modern Society**, New York: Holt, Rinehart, 1965.

PYE, Lucian W. **Aspects of Political Development**, Boston: Little, Brown, 1966.

ROSHCO, Bernard, **Newsmaking**, Chicago: University of Chicago Press, 1979.

ROWAT, Donald "How much administrative secrecy?" **C. J. of Economics and Political Science**, 31 (1965) 486.

RUTHERFORD, Paul, **The Making of the Canadian Media**, Toronto: McGraw-Hill Ryerson, 1978.

SCHLESINGER, Philip, **Putting Reality Together: BBC News**, London: Constable, 1978.

SCHRAMM, Wilbur and Donald F. ROBERTS, **The Process and Effects of Mass Communications**, Urbana: University of Illinois Press, 1971.

SCHWARTZ, Mildred A., **Public Opinion and Canadian Identity**, Berkeley: University of California Press, 1967.

SEYMOUR-URE, Colin, **The Press, Politics & the Public**, London: Methuen, 1968.

SEYMOUR-URE, Colin, **The Political Impact of the Mass Media**, London: Constable, 1974.

SHAW, Donald L., and Maxwell McCOMBS, **The Emergence of American Political Issues**, St. Paul, Minn.: West 1977.

SHEINKOF, Kenneth G., Charles K. ATKIN and Lawrence BROWN, "How political party workers respond to political advertising," **Journalism Quarterly**, 50 (1973), 334–339.

SIEBERT, F.S., Theodore PETERSON and Wilbur SCHRAMM, **Four Theories of the Press**, Urbana: University of Illinois Press, 1956.

SINGER, Benjamin D., ed., **Communications in Canadian Society**, Toronto: Copp Clark, 1975.

SMITH, Anthony, **British Broadcasting**, Newton Abbot: David & Charles, 1974.

SMITH, Anthony, **Goodbye Gutenberg**, New York: Oxford, 1980.

SMITH, Anthony, ed., **Newspapers and Democracy**, Cambridge, Mass.: MIT, 1980.

SMITH, Anthony, **The Shadow in the Cave**, London: Quartet, 1976.

SMITH, Anthony, ed., Television and Political Life: Studies in Six European Countries, London: Macmillan, 1979.

SMITH, Anthony, ed., The Politics of Information, London: Macmillan, 1978.

STROUSE, James C., The Mass Media, Public Opinion, and Public Policy Analysis, Columbus,O.: Merrill, 1975.

STERLING, Christopher H., and Timothy R. HAIGHT, The Mass Media: Aspen Institute guide to Communication Industry Trends, New York: Praeger, 1978.

TRACEY, Michael, The Production of Political Television, London: Routledge, 1977.

TUNSTALL, Jeremy, The Media are American, London: Constable, 1977.

TUNSTALL, Jeremy, Journalists at Work, Beverly Hills, Cal.: Sage, 1971.

TUNSTALL, Jeremy, The Westminster Lobby Correspondents, London: Routledge, Kegan Paul, 1970.

WADE, Serena, and Wilbur SCHRAMM, "The Mass Media As Sources of Public Affairs, Science and Health Knowledge," Public Opinion Quarterly, 33 (1969) 197–209.

WALKER, J. L., "Setting the agenda in the U.S. Senate," British Journal of Political Science, 7 (1977), 423–445.

WEIR, E. Austin, The Struggle for National Broadcasting in Canada, Toronto: McClelland & Stewart, 1965.

WILSON, C. Edward, ed., Mind over Message, London, Ont.: University of Western Ontario, 1974.

WHALE, John, The Half–Shut Eye, London: Macmillan, 1971.

WHALE, John, Journalism and Government, London: Macmillan, 1972.

WHALE, John, The Politics of the Media, Manchester: Manchester University Press, 1977.

WILLIAMS, Francis, The Right to Know: the Rise of the World Press, London: Longmans, 1969.

WILLIAMS, Francis, Dangerous Estate: the Anatomy of Newspapers, London: Longmans, 1957.

WILLIAMS, Raymond, Television: Technology and Cultural Form, Glasgow: Fontana, 1974.

WINHAM, G. R. and R.B. CUNNINGHAM, "Party Leader Images in the 1968 Federal Election," Canadian Journal of Political Science, 3 (1970), 376–399.

YOUNG, Christopher, "What Happened at Accra: Mr. Fleming vs. The Press," The Ottawa Citizen, January 27, 1962, 7.

Index